MISSISSIPPI

OFF THE BEATEN PATH®

OFF THE BEATEN PATH® SERIES

NINTH EDITION

MISSISSIPPI

OFF THE BEATEN PATH®

DISCOVER YOUR FUN

MARLO CARTER KIRKPATRICK

Globe
Pequot
Guilford, Connecticut

All the information in this guidebook is subject to change. We recommend that you call ahead to obtain current information before traveling.

Globe Pequot

An imprint of The Rowman & Littlefield Publishing Group, Inc.
4501 Forbes Blvd., Ste. 200
Lanham, MD 20706
www.rowman.com

Distributed by NATIONAL BOOK NETWORK

Copyright © 2015 The Rowman & Littlefield Publishing Group, Inc.
This Globe Pequot edition 2020
Maps by The Rowman & LIttlefield Publishing Group, Inc.

British Library Cataloguing in Publication Information available

Library of Congress Cataloging-in-Publication Data available

ISBN 978-1-4930-4408-5 (paper : alk. paper)
ISBN 978-1-4930-4409-2 (electronic)

∞™ The paper used in this publication meets the minimum requirements of American National Standard for Information Sciences—Permanence of Paper for Printed Library Materials, ANSI/NISO Z39.48-1992.

About the Author

Marlo Carter Kirkpatrick is a freelance writer and the owner of Mississippi-based advertising agency Marlo Kirkpatrick Creative. She lives in Madison, Mississippi, with her husband, wildlife photographer Stephen Kirkpatrick, and their four dogs.

Marlo is also the author of *It Happened in Mississippi*. She and her husband collaborated on the books *Among the Animals: Mississippi*; *Images of Madison County*; *Mississippi Impressions*; *Lost in the Amazon*; *Romancing the Rain*; *Wilder Mississippi*; and *To Catch the Wind*. The Kirkpatricks' books have captured several awards, including the National Outdoor Book Award, a Benjamin Franklin Award, and three Southeastern Outdoor Press Association Book of the Year Awards. Marlo has received more than 300 awards for creative excellence and has been named the Jackson Advertising Federation's Writer of the Year five times.

Marlo's work has taken her to destinations throughout North, Central, and South America, Africa, Europe, and the Middle East, but Mississippi remains one of her favorite off-the-beaten-path destinations.

Acknowledgments

Mississippi Off the Beaten Path couldn't have been written without the insights, contributions, and cooperation of friends and colleagues statewide.

As usual, I owe the knowledgeable staff at the Mississippi Division of Tourism Development a huge and heartfelt "thank you." I'm also deeply grateful to the many chamber of commerce and convention and visitors' bureau directors and their personnel, who responded to my inquiries and, in many cases, personally guided me around their cities and towns. Thanks are also due to scores of bed-and-breakfast and restaurant proprietors who were so accommodating, to countless local residents who petted my dogs and pointed me in the right direction, and to my hardworking and immensely talented research assistant, Sissy Lynn.

And finally, my heartfelt thanks—and my heart itself—go to Stephen Kirkpatrick, my favorite traveling companion.

MISSISSIPPI

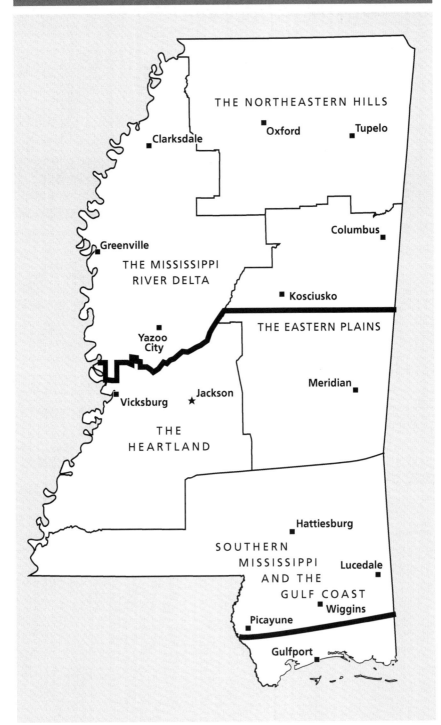

Contents

Introduction

The geography that makes up the state of Mississippi is easily defined. Rolling northern hills and sweeping eastern plains. A pastoral heartland hugged by the Father of Waters. The fertile river delta and sun-drenched southern beaches.

But the real essence of the state is harder to put into words, for Mississippi is not merely a landscape but a state of mind.

Mississippi is nicknamed the "Hospitality State," and it's true that most of the people you'll meet here don't have to know your name to lend you a hand or stop and chat for a while. In fact, Mississippians seem to feel compelled to explain themselves, to make sure you leave with an enlightened view of this place they call home. After all, perceptions of Mississippi are often based on outdated stereotypes. Native Mississippians tend to view every out-of-state visitor as a personal crusade—they may not be able to change the whole world's opinion, but give them half a chance and, by golly, they'll change yours.

Even left to your own devices, you'll soon discover the stereotypes are just that. The real Mississippi is made up of bustling cities and quaint town squares, breathtaking natural wonders, and a rich heritage and distinctive culture like no other.

Sacred Indian mounds and a thriving reservation showcase the past, present, and future of the Choctaw Indians, the first Mississippians. The state is home to graceful antebellum mansions that whisper of a bygone era, Civil War battlefields where the fate of the nation was determined, and civil rights memorials that commemorate a turning point in American history.

Mississippi is the birthplace of the blues, country music, and of Elvis Presley, the King of Rock 'n' Roll. Virtually every song heard on the radio today has its roots in Mississippi. The state's equally rich literary heritage is reflected in the masterpieces of William Faulkner, Willie Morris, Eudora Welty, and William Wright, and in the best-selling novels of Nevada Barr, John Grisham, Greg Iles, Kathryn Stockett, and Angie Thomas.

Artists' colonies statewide nurture the next generation of painters, sculptors, potters, and photographers. Something about Mississippi also seems to inspire the performing arts. Internationally renowned entertainers including Morgan Freeman, Faith Hill, Sela Ward, and Oprah Winfrey are just a few of

Accommodations

Lincoln Ltd. is a full-time reservation service for bed-and-breakfast inns statewide. For reservations in any area of Mississippi, call (601) 482-5483 or visit bandbmississippi.com.

Fast Facts about Mississippi

- **Flower and Tree:** Magnolia

- **Bird:** Mockingbird

- **Fish:** Largemouth bass

- **Wildflower:** Coreopsis

- **Land mammal:** White-tailed deer

- **Water mammal:** Bottlenosed dolphin

- **Water fowl:** Wood duck

- **Stone:** Petrified wood

- **Beverage:** Milk

- **Toy:** Teddy bear

- **Motto:** *Virtute et armis* (By valor and arms)

- **Nicknames:** Magnolia State, Hospitality State

- **Climate:** Mississippi experiences a mild yet noticeable change of seasons. Temperatures are moderate in the spring, fall, and winter; summer highs may be uncomfortable for travelers unaccustomed to the southern heat. January's average low is forty-five to fifty degrees. Spring and autumn temperatures fall anywhere from the low sixties to mid-eighties. From June through Sept, temperatures reach the upper nineties with very high humidity. Accepted dress year-round is casual and comfortable.

- **Time Zone:** Central Standard

the talented performers from Mississippi. Acclaimed chefs like Cat Cora and Nick Wallace are introducing the world to another Mississippi art form, food.

Mississippi is also recognized for its scientific breakthroughs. Leading-edge research centers and universities conduct groundbreaking work in acoustics, medicine, microelectronics, oceanography, polymer science, and telecommunications.

And when Hurricane Katrina roared ashore on August 29, 2005, Mississippi earned yet another reputation—as a state of resilient, hardworking, self-sufficient people who would band together in the face of disaster and would not be beaten by a mere hurricane.

Yet, Mississippi remains outside the limelight. Other than the casinos that line the Mississippi River and the Mississippi Gulf Coast, the state really doesn't have any "manufactured" attractions. Things here are genuine and authentic, preserved rather than re-created. Turnstiles and ticket-takers are replaced by welcome mats and warmhearted people. And once you've had your fill of the amusement parks and souvenir stands that make one place seem just like the last place or the next place, you'll find Mississippi a welcome change.

Mississippi Off the Beaten Path will guide you through the state's diverse geography and its uncommon culture. You'll explore towns tucked away in the rolling hills and standing watch over the plains, and travel alongside the mighty Mississippi River that gave the state its name. You'll experience the timeless charm of life in the historic heartland and the vibrant energy of life along the Gulf Coast.

You'll stop in odd little towns with odd little names like So-So, Why Not, Hot Coffee, Panther Burn, and D'Lo—short for a town once deemed "too damn low." There's even a microscopic community named "It" (there's not much there, but you'll know It when you see It). You'll develop an appreciation for natural phenomena like kudzu and Spanish moss, and an appetite for grits and catfish. Who knows, you may even hear yourself saying "y'all."

Care has been taken to ensure this book is as accurate as possible. Part of their quirky nature, however, is that off-the-beaten-path attractions are frequently subject to change. Ticket prices, days and hours of operation, and telephone numbers may change without notice; establishments may close; and people may move on. If you find discrepancies in *Mississippi Off the Beaten Path,* please accept my apologies for any inconvenience or disappointment. Then, please write or e-mail me or the publisher and tell us what you have learned. Please do the same if you discover an off-the-beaten-path gem that's not included in these pages. Who knows, you may discover Mississippi's next great hidden attraction.

No matter where your Mississippi adventures take you, one thing is certain: You'll experience a land, a people, and a culture like no other.

And perhaps best of all, you won't have to wait in line, make reservations, or know the right people. In many cases, you won't even have to buy a ticket.

All you have to do is find it.

Transportation

Major Interstates in Mississippi

I-20 (east/west)

I-55 (north/south)

I-59 (southwest/northwest)

I-10 (east/west)

Primary Highways in Mississippi

US 80 US 78

US 49 US 82

US 45 US 61

US 98 US 90

Rules of the Road

Speed Limit: The speed limit on Mississippi interstate highways is 70 miles per hour. The state highway speed limit is 65 miles per hour on four-lane highways and 55 miles per hour on two-lane highways unless otherwise posted.

Mandatory Seat Belt Law: Operators and front-seat passengers in any motor vehicle designed to carry ten or fewer passengers are required to wear seat belts. People traveling with children under the age of two are required to restrain the child in an approved child-passenger restraint device or system. Violation of this law will result in a fine of not more than $25.

Emergency Assistance: Contact the Mississippi Highway Patrol at (601) 987-1212 or dial *47 (*HP) on your mobile phone.

Natchez Trace Parkway: The speed limit on the Natchez Trace Parkway is 50 miles per hour and is strictly enforced. Hauling and commercial trucking are not allowed. Charter buses may receive special permits by contacting the Natchez Trace Parkway headquarters at (662) 680-4025 or (800) 305-7417.

The *only* gas station on the parkway is located at Jeff Busby Park, milepost 193.1.

Keep an eye out for deer and other wildlife wandering onto the parkway.

Commercial Airline Service

Delta, United, US Airways, and American Airlines, as well as a number of air-link carriers, provide service into and within Mississippi. Commercial airports are located in Columbus, Greenville, Gulfport, Hattiesburg, Jackson, Meridian, and Tupelo.

Additional gateways in adjacent states include Memphis International Airport (Tennessee), New Orleans/Moisant International Airport (Louisiana), and Mobile/Bates Field Airport (Alabama).

FOR MORE INFORMATION

For more information on Mississippi attractions and events statewide, contact the **Mississippi Division of Tourism Development** at (866) SEE-MISS or visit the website at visitmississippi.org. Also, conveniently located on major interstates and highways entering the state, Mississippi's welcome centers offer free maps, reservations for in-state accommodations, brochures, and other travel information.

Most cities, towns, and convention and visitors bureaus also maintain Web sites, although sites come and go and site names change frequently. If the community you're interested in does not have a website listed here or if the website listed is no longer operational, try entering the name of the community in any search engine.

Train Service

Amtrak services the Mississippi cities below. For more information call (800) 872-7245.

Bay St. Louis	Hazlehurst	Picayune	Gulfport
Hattiesburg	Pascagoula	Greenwood	McComb
Meridian	Brookhaven	Laurel	
Biloxi	Jackson	Yazoo City	

Recreation

State Parks

Located throughout the state, Mississippi's twenty-eight state parks are ideal for a weekend getaway or an extended outdoor adventure. Each park offers its own amenities, from nature trails to float trips, fishin' holes to golf courses. The parks also feature a variety of accommodations, including primitive and developed campsites, rustic cabin rentals, and full-service hotels.

For more information on Mississippi's state parks, call (800) GO-PARKS or visit mdwfp.com.

Golf

Mississippi's diversity of courses and mild year-round climate make the state a favorite among golfers. Opportunities range from simple nine-hole courses to spectacular resort courses created by Tom Fazio, Jack Nicklaus, Arnold Palmer, Davis Love III, Jerry Pate, and other renowned designers.

Mississippi has a golf course to meet every level of challenge—and every budget. For a complete list and detailed descriptions of golf courses in Mississippi, contact the Mississippi Division of Tourism Development at (866) SEE-MISS or visitmississippi.org.

Hunting and Fishing

Mississippi is a sportsman's dream. Hunters from around the nation come to the state in pursuit of turkey, quail, dove, waterfowl, and Mississippi's most popular game animal, the prolific white-tailed deer. Fishing enthusiasts find lakes and streams brimming with bass, bluegill, crappie, and catfish, or can head to the Gulf Coast for the deep-sea challenge posed by mackerel, cobia, sea trout, and red snapper.

For a comprehensive list of hunting and fishing lodges, outfitters and guides, and detailed information on hunting seasons, license fees, and requirements, contact the Mississippi Department of Wildlife, Fisheries, and Parks at (601) 432-2400 or (800) GO-PARKS or visit mdwfp.com.

The Northeastern Hills

The Northeastern Hill country stretches from the edge of the Mississippi Delta to the foothills of the Appalachian Mountains. Traveling west to east, the land gradually becomes more and more hilly, more and more remote, until civilization becomes nothing more than a distant memory. Rich in history, heritage, and scenic beauty, this is the land that inspired both the complex genius of William Faulkner and the raw emotion that permeates the music of Elvis Presley.

This region includes portions of both I-55 and the Natchez Trace Parkway. Both routes take visitors on a north-to-south journey through the area, but the adventures encountered along each path couldn't be more different. From the modern cities that line I-55 to time-capsule towns along the Tennessee and Tombigbee Rivers, the Northeastern Hills offer a new and different adventure just over the next crest.

The I-55 Corridor

The towns and cities that line I-55 share the fast-paced, modern personality of Memphis, Tennessee, just over the border and often referred to as "the largest city in north Mississippi."

THE NORTHEASTERN HILLS

TENNESSEE
MISSISSIPPI

Corinth
72
25
30
Tishomingo
Booneville
45
New Albany
15
78
4
72
Tallahatchie R.
Oxford
7
Holly Springs
Coldwater R.
78
7
Sardis Lake
Batesville
Hernando
Olive Branch
Southaven
Horn Lake
51
55
Senatobia
Arkabutla Lake
278
6
Enid Lake
51
6
MISS.
ARK.

ALABAMA
MISSISSIPPI

Tennessee-Tombigbee Waterway
78
Amory
278
Aberdeen
45
8
Tupelo
ALT 45
NATCHEZ TRACE PKWY
6
15
Houston
278
9W
9
Grenada Lake
8
Grenada
55
7

N

0   25 mi
0   25 km

Even the smaller cities along I-55 boast a sophistication that comes from living just barely off a very well-beaten path. Of course, whizzing past the exits at 70 miles per hour is not the best way to soak up the local ambience. Take a short detour from the impersonal asphalt, and you'll find a wealth of unsung treasures mere minutes from the fast lane.

Begin by following I-55 South out of Memphis into **DeSoto County**, named for Hernando de Soto, the Spanish conquistador who became Mississippi's first "tourist" in 1541 and discovered the mighty river for which the state is named. As you travel DeSoto County, you'll spot frequent markers along a route dubbed the **Hernando de Soto Memorial Trail**. As de Soto's exact path has long been lost to history, this scenic route is designed to showcase the area's attractions and doesn't attempt to follow in the famous explorer's footsteps. Pick up the de Soto Trail just south of Memphis near the communities of **Horn Lake** and **Walls**. Most historians believe it was somewhere near the sites of these towns that Hernando de Soto first gazed upon the Mississippi River.

At 5921 Goodman Rd. West, just west of the intersection of Goodman Road and MS 301, you'll spot **Elvis and Priscilla Presley's Honeymoon Cottage.** This unassuming structure was the spot where Elvis Presley brought his young bride, Priscilla, for their 1967 honeymoon. The cottage was once a part of Elvis's sprawling Circle G Ranch. Elvis and Priscilla went horseback riding on the property, and the King of Rock 'n' Roll was often spotted riding his motorcycle up and down Goodman Road. The cottage is not open for tours, so fans of the King will have to be content with a look from the road.

Just east of Horn Lake on MS 302, the bustling community of **Olive Branch** is one of the fastest-growing cities in the United States. In the 1990s there was talk of bulldozing Olive Branch's old downtown area. Saved from demolition by visionary developer Bill Cruthirds, the old downtown was instead renovated and reopened as **Olive Branch Old Towne.** Today, Old Towne is a quaint area of antiques and gift shops surrounding the open-air

AUTHOR'S FAVORITES IN THE NORTHEASTERN HILLS

Antebellum home tours, Holly Springs

Brussel's Bonsai Nursery, Olive Branch

The Grove at Ole Miss on Football **Saturdays,** Oxford

The Square, Oxford

The writing on the wall at **Taylor Grocery,** Taylor

The University of Mississippi, Oxford

Pigeon Roost Plaza. Visitors can easily spend an afternoon browsing among the china, furniture, clothing, home accessories, and other unique merchandise in Old Towne's boutiques.

Gulliver would feel right at home at **Brussel's Bonsai Nursery.** Brussel's showcases the Japanese art form of bonsai, the cultivation of miniature trees. Founded by Brussel Martin in 1972, the nursery is the largest importer and grower of fine bonsai in the United States. Several members of the staff at Brussel's have studied this ancient art form under Japanese masters and are happy to provide visitors a glimpse into the painstaking world of bonsai. The nursery offers hundreds of specimens, accessories, and tools for sale, and features elaborate display gardens filled with tiny trees decades—and sometimes more than a century—old. You'll find Brussel's at 8125 Center Hill Rd., just east of Olive Branch off Goodman Road (MS 302). For more information or a mail-order catalog, call (662) 895-4526 or (800) 582-2593 or visit brusselsbonsai.com.

North Mississippi is best known for Elvis Presley lore, but the area is also home to another rock 'n' roll legend. The **Jerry Lee Lewis Ranch**—sometimes referred to as "DisGraceland"—is just south of Horn Lake in Nesbit. Lewis was as famous for his multiple marriages (including a marriage to his own cousin) and tumultuous personal life as for hit songs like "Great Balls of Fire." The ranch's most famous features are its distinctive security gates, emblazoned with pianos and the words "The Killer," and its piano-shaped swimming pool, complete with black and white "keys."

The ranch is open for tours, which are limited to 15 people at a time and cost $45 per person. The Jerry Lee Lewis Ranch is located at 1595 Malone Rd. From I-55, take exit 284 (Pleasant Hill Road). Head east to Malone Road, and turn right. Three houses down on the right, the Ranch is easily recognized by its graffiti-plastered fence, which bears hundreds of messages from The Killer's loyal fans. For more information, call (901) 488-1823.

Next, head south of Nesbit and follow the signs to downtown Hernando, where the focal point is the **DeSoto County Courthouse.** Inside, the story of Hernando de Soto, from his voyage to America through his death and burial in the Mississippi River, is depicted in sweeping oil murals hanging in the courthouse gallery. Painted on canvas by American muralist Newton Alonzo Wells, the murals were completed in 1902 and hung for decades in the old Gayoso Hotel in downtown Memphis. Donated to DeSoto County and installed in the courthouse in 1953, they carry an estimated value of $700,000. Visitors are invited to view the paintings Mon through Fri during normal business hours.

The courthouse was once a hot spot for "quickie" marriages, earning quaint little Hernando the nickname "Las Vegas of the Mid-South." Marriage laws were once much more relaxed in Mississippi, and Hernando became a

Mississippi's Playing Your Song

Mention Mississippi music, and most people think of the blues or Elvis Presley. But the songs don't stop there. Whether you tune in to a country, pop, rhythm and blues, or classical station, you're virtually guaranteed to hear a voice from Mississippi.

Mississippians who've made their voices heard include Steve Azar, Brandy, Jimmy Buffett, Bo Diddley, Pete Fountain, Mickey Gilley, W. C. Handy, Faith Hill, Robert Johnson, B. B. King, Elvis Presley, Leontyne Price, Charlie Pride, LeAnn Rimes, Jimmie Rodgers, Fingers Taylor, Son Thomas, Paul Thorn, Ike Turner, Conway Twitty, Muddy Waters, Tammy Wynette, and the members of the group 3 Doors Down.

Another famous Mississippian doesn't sing himself, but came up with a groundbreaking idea that forever changed the world of music. He's Bob Pittman, the founder of MTV.

magnet for lovebirds from Memphis who just couldn't stand the three-day waiting period required in Tennessee. In more recent years the courthouse served as the setting for real-life dramas for lawyer-turned-blockbuster-novelist John Grisham. Before his phenomenally successful legal thrillers allowed him to quit his day job, Grisham kept law offices in nearby Southaven and sometimes met with clients and legal associates in the marbled corridors of the courthouse.

Learn more about Grisham, Jerry Lee Lewis, Elvis, and Hernando de Soto's ties to the area during a visit to the *Historic DeSoto Museum.* The museum brings the colorful histories of all of DeSoto County's towns together in one facility. Along with exhibits on notable residents and events, the museum features an antebellum log cabin used as a field hospital during the Civil War. The Historic DeSoto Museum is located at 111 E. Commerce St. The free museum is open Tues through Sat from 10 a.m. to 5 p.m. For more information call (662) 429-8852 or visit desotomuseum.org.

Continue your exploration of the past with a visit to one of DeSoto County's many antiques shops. Shops are scattered around Southaven, Olive Branch, Nesbit, and Hernando, offering treasure hunters a wide selection of furniture, glass, collectibles, and accessories. For a complete list of antiques shops, visit desotocountytourism.com. A favorite stop for shoppers and art lovers is *Joseph Eckles Stoneware* (2650 Scott Rd., Hernando; 662-429-1621), where the handmade pottery includes dinnerware, vases, bird feeders, and decorative pieces. For a sneak peek, visit josephecklessstoneware.com.

Overnight visitors to DeSoto County should plan a stay at Nesbit's *Bonne Terre Country Inn,* a charming bed-and-breakfast inn situated on 120 scenic, secluded acres just twenty-five minutes from Memphis. *Southern Living* magazine describes Bonne Terre as, "not just a place you stay for the night. . . . It's a destination, a place to go and stay and savor." After a visit there, you're sure to agree. Each of the fifteen rooms at Bonne Terre (French for "good earth") features a balcony or patio overlooking the five-acre lake, swimming pool, pecan tree grove, or wildflower garden. Enchanting individual decor, French and English antiques, in-room fireplaces, whirlpool tubs, and fresh flowers contribute to each room's welcoming ambience. Favorite pastimes at Bonne Terre include fishing in three lakes, strolling in the herb and flower gardens, picnicking in the pecan grove, or simply relaxing poolside. For room reservations and rates at the Bonne Terre Country Inn, call (662) 781- 5100 or visit bonneterre inn.com.

For a bed-and-breakfast with a more rustic touch, visit **Brigadoon Farms,** a sprawling country retreat in Olive Branch. Proprietor Jeanette Martin began developing this rural refuge as a form of grief therapy following the death of her husband. Today, the Brigadoon Farms retreat and conference center encompasses tranquil nature trails, picturesque lakes ideal for fishing and pedal boating, and a relaxing hot tub and swimming pool. Accommodations are available in the farm's Country Goose Inn, a log lodge overlooking the lake; the Honeymoon Cottage, a modern house overlooking the swimming pool; and the Bunk House, a spacious facility ideal for youth or other groups. Brigadoon Farms is located at 350 MS 305 in Olive Branch. For rates or reservations call (662) 895-3098 or visit brigadoonfarms.com.

Continue south on I-55 to the DeSoto/Tate County border, where signs point the way to **Arkabutla Lake.** Some two million outdoor enthusiasts visit Arkabutla each year, drawn to the lake for fishing, swimming, and waterskiing, and to its wooded shores for camping, hiking, and hunting. The 12,700-acre lake is the windiest lake south of Chicago, making Arkabutla a favorite for sailing and windsurfing. A strong wildlife management program has also made Arkabutla a popular area for wildlife watching. Pack your binoculars and keep an eye out for wood ducks, turkeys, quail, rabbits, and white-tailed deer.

Continue down I-55 South to tiny **Como,** population less than 1,300. Como is famous in musical circles as the longtime home of the late "Mississippi" Fred McDowell, the father of the Hill Country Blues; and of the late Otha Turner, a

TOP ANNUAL EVENTS IN THE NORTHEASTERN HILLS

APRIL

Double Decker Arts Festival
Oxford
(662) 232-2477 or
(800) 758-9177
doubledeckerfestival.com

Southern Heritage Spring Pilgrimage
Aberdeen
(662) 369-9440
aberdeenms.org

Spring Pilgrimage
Holly Springs
(662) 252-2515 or
(888) 687-4765
visithollysprings.com

MAY

Blue Suede Cruise
Tupelo
(662) 213-8873
bluesc.com

JUNE

Tupelo Elvis Presley Festival
Tupelo
(662) 841-6598
tupeloelvisfestival.com

JULY

Slugburger Festival
Corinth
(662) 287-8300
corinth.net

AUGUST

Watermelon Carnival
Water Valley
(662) 473-1122

SEPTEMBER-NOVEMBER

Football Season at Ole Miss
(662) 915-7167 or
(888) 732-8587
Olemisssports.com

noted performer of African-rooted fife-and-drum music. McDowell is buried in a nearby cemetery in a silver lamé suit given to him by the Rolling Stones; he rests beneath a marker purchased by longtime friend and protégé Bonnie Raitt.

Make sure your arrival in Como coincides with dinnertime. Next to its musical heritage, the town's biggest claim to fame is the *Como Steakhouse,* a

Success Can't Spoil a Bluesman

Even after his international success as a blues musician and recording star, "Mississippi" Fred McDowell continued to work pumping gas at a Como, Mississippi, Stuckey's store. When his agent asked him why, McDowell replied, "All my friends are here, so you know I'm going to be here."

Because he never got around to installing a telephone in his home, McDowell also used the Stuckey's as a makeshift office. Other employees could be heard calling out to the pumps, "Hey, Fred! We got Paris, France, on the phone for you!"

beef-lover's delight housed in the old town post office at 203 S. Main St. You can watch as the cook prepares your juicy steak over an open charcoal pit in the dining room, or cook your own and take $1 off the tab. Enjoy a predinner drink and appetizers upstairs at **Oyster Bar**, a cozy bar offering seasonal crawfish and oysters on the half shell, as well as a balcony overlooking Main Street. For more information call (662) 526-9529 for the Como Steakhouse or (662) 526-0474 for the Oyster Bar.

After dinner, take a short stroll down Main Street to **The Como Courtyard** (235 Main St.), a New Orleans–style bed-and-breakfast retreat. Housed in a restored 125-year-old mercantile building, The Como Courtyard features tin ceilings, exposed brick walls, and antique furnishings, but the B&B's most memorable feature is its lushly landscaped interior courtyard, complete with fountain and hot tub. Rooms are available in the main townhouse and in a guest cottage; rates begin at $125. For information or reservations call (662) 526-5494 or visit comocourtyard.com.

From Como it's just 5 miles south to **Sardis,** another quiet little town where "action" is for the most part limited to water-skiing and swimming at **Sardis Lake.** There is the **Heflin House Museum** (304 S. Main St.), constructed in

'Til Death Do Us Part

The city now known as **Grenada** was established in 1836 by the union of the towns of Pittsburgh and Tullahoma. While the two communities were actually joined in a marriage ceremony—complete with an officiating minister—it was not a case of love at first sight.

Originally settled in the early 1830s, the towns were separated only by a surveyor's line, known today as Line Street. Neither town would concede one inch to the other. Each operated its own ferry across the Yalobusha River, a mere mile apart. When Pittsburgh established the area's first newspaper, Tullahoma enticed the cash-strapped editor to move it to their city by paying off his mortgage. Pittsburgh, however, still claimed the area's only post office—until, that is, the residents of Tullahoma stole it, actually moving the building and its contents across the city line in the dark of night.

Eventually both sides wearied of the rivalry, and in 1836, agreed to consolidate. The union would take the form of a wedding ceremony, followed by a community barbecue.

The ceremony was performed on July 4, 1836, but before the barbecue got cold, arguments broke out over which name the new town would be known by. A wise wedding guest suggested starting over with a new name. Grenada was chosen in honor of Granada, Spain, the citizens shared a reconciliatory toast, and the town has enjoyed an atmosphere of matrimonial bliss ever since.

1858 and now operated as a historical museum by the Heflin House Heritage Association. The house is open for tours the third Sun of every month from 1 to 4 p.m., and hosts an annual Christmas open house the first Sun of Dec. Rental cabins and camping are available at *John W. Kyle State Park* overlooking Sardis Lake. Call (662) 487-1345 or visit mdwfp.com.

Continue along I-55 South to *Grenada*, where a brochure for a historic Grenada walking and driving tour is available from the Grenada Tourism Commission (662-226-2060). Highlights include the *Confederate Cemetery*, where 180 unknown Civil War soldiers are buried; the *Yellow Fever Cemetery*, created by a dreadful 1878 epidemic that claimed 80 percent of the city's population; and *Golliday House*, an antebellum home that briefly served as headquarters for Confederate president Jefferson Davis during the Civil War and was the scene of a still-unsolved murder in the 1930s.

No trip to Grenada is complete without a stop at the *Grenada Lake Visitor Center* (2151 Scenic Loop 333), which features a large observation deck overlooking the 36,000-acre reservoir, the largest lake in Mississippi. For more information, call (662) 226-1679 or visit visitgrenadams.com.

From Grenada, head back north on I-55 a short distance until you reach MS 7, then travel northeast toward the Central Crests.

The Central Crests

The gently rolling hills to the east of the interstate seem far removed from the hustle and bustle of urban life. This is Faulkner country, a timeless realm of Civil War battlefields, well-tended historic homes, and picturesque town squares. Most of the more than 500 Civil War battles waged on Mississippi soil were fought in this area, making the few antebellum towns that survived the Union torch all the more impressive. With a rich legacy of history, heritage, and literature, this peaceful area of gently rolling hills is widely regarded as a center for American southern culture.

Mississippi Writers

Mississippians are fond of saying, "We may not be able to read, but we sure can write." Works by Mississippians Margaret Walker Alexander, Nevada Barr, Larry Brown, Ellen Douglas, William Faulkner, Shelby Foote, John Grisham, Carolyn Haines, Thomas Harris, Beth Henley, Greg Iles, Kathryn Stockett, Willie Morris, Angie Thomas, Eudora Welty, and Tennessee Williams would certainly seem to justify that claim.

Railroad buffs and hobos at heart can pay tribute to one of the South's cultural icons in **Water Valley.** Located on MS 7, the town is home to the **Water Valley Casey Jones Railroad Museum,** a heartfelt tribute to the legendary engineer and folk hero killed in the crash of engine No. 382. Housed in the restored Water Valley Depot, the museum showcases the extensive railroad memorabilia and photography collection of the late Bruce Gurner of Water Valley, a retired railroader and schoolteacher who spent almost fifty years researching the legend of Casey Jones and the history of the Mississippi Division of the Illinois Central Railroad. Gurner began collecting Casey Jones memorabilia in 1955 and continued until his death in 2002. In his later years Gurner spoke of the day when he could "ask Casey in person why he didn't jump." The Water Valley Casey Jones Railroad Museum is open Thurs, Fri, and Sat from 2 to 4 p.m. and by appointment. Climb aboard at 105 Railroad Ave. Call (662) 473-3828 or visit caseyjonesmuseum.weebly.com.

The dog days of August may not seem like the best time to visit Mississippi—unless you happen to be visiting Water Valley during the annual **Watermelon Carnival.** The juicy festivities here date back to the early 1930s. When the town's economy suffered from a dramatic drop in cotton prices, local farmers chose watermelons as their new cash crop. The chamber of commerce organized a carnival to introduce the world to Water Valley watermelons, and a tradition was born. Today the three-day "melonbration" includes a music festival, motorcycle parade, arts and crafts show, the crowning of the Watermelon Queen, and, of course, all the chilled, juicy watermelon you can slurp up. For this year's dates, call (662) 473-1122.

Continue on MS 7 North from Water Valley into **Oxford,** a postcard-pretty college town and literary center listed in the books *The 100 Best Small Towns in America* and *The 100 Best Small Art Towns in America* and called a "thriving New South arts mecca" by *USA Today* and "the best place in the South to retire" by *Money* magazine. Oxford's folksy town square, graceful antebellum homes, tree-shaded boulevards, and quintessential southern college campus have been immortalized in more pages than the city has residents.

Begin a literary tour of Oxford with a trip down MS 6 West and a look at the big yellow Victorian on the left. It's the part-time **home of John Grisham,** former Mississippi state legislator and best-selling author of *The Firm, The Client, A Time to Kill, The Chamber, The Testament, The Brethren, The Summons, The King of Torts, The Associate,* and other legal thrillers. The estate includes a full-size baseball diamond where Grisham once coached a local Little League team.

Of course, Oxford's dust jackets don't stop with Grisham. Willie Morris, Barry Hannah, and Larry Brown all felt their genius stirred by Oxford's landmarks and landscapes, but it was Nobel Prize–winner William Faulkner who first put Oxford on the literary map.

Even if you haven't thought of Faulkner since high school English class, a trip to Oxford will have you searching for your old paperbacks. Faulkner modeled the mythical Yoknapatawpha County, the setting for his tales of glory and decadence in the South, after Oxford and Lafayette County. As a child, Faulkner lived in a small cottage at the corner of South Eleventh and Buchanan Streets, but **Rowan Oak,** Faulkner's antebellum home at the bend of Old Taylor Road, is the place where his genius came to life. The house remains much as Faulkner left it, with his black manual typewriter on display in the study and the outline of his Pulitzer Prize–winning novel, *A Fable,* scrawled on the wall.

Rowan Oak is open for tours. Non-summer hours: 10 a.m. to 4 p.m. Tues through Sat, and 1 to 4 p.m. on Sun. Closed every Mon. Summer hours: June 1 through Aug 1, Mon through Sat, 10 a.m. to 6 p.m., and Sun 1 to 6 p.m. Holiday schedules are as follows: Closed on July 4, Thanksgiving, December 24, 25, 31, and January 1.

Guided tours are available by appointment; call (662) 234-3284 for more information. Even when the house isn't open, the tree-shaded grounds and adjacent Bailey's Woods are the perfect place to enjoy a quiet afternoon stroll.

During his lifetime, Faulkner was regarded as a bit of a character around town. He served briefly as the University of Mississippi's postmaster and was reportedly the worst postmaster in the school's history. Faulkner himself generally agreed with this assessment, explaining that he "didn't care to be at the beck and call of any fool who could afford a postage stamp." Rowan Oak is owned by the **University of Mississippi,** where Faulkner was briefly enrolled as a lackluster student. The university's **J. D. Williams Library** displays Faulkner's 1949 Nobel Prize, first-edition prints of his books, and early handwritten manuscripts. The inscription on the library's wall, "I decline to accept the end of man. I believe that man will not merely endure, he will prevail,"

The Blind Side

The blockbuster film *The Blind Side* recounts the inspirational story of **Michael Oher**, former NFL star offensive tackle. *The Blind Side* tells the story of Oher's difficult childhood on the mean streets of Memphis, his life with adoptive parents Sean and Leigh Anne Tuohy, and the incredible athletic talent that won Oher a football scholarship to the University of Mississippi and his career as an NFL pro. The film stars Sandra Bullock as Leigh Anne Tuohy, Tim McGraw as Sean Tuohy, and Quinton Aaron as Michael Oher.

was pulled from Faulkner's Nobel Prize acceptance speech. Faulkner is buried in nearby *St. Peter's Cemetery* at the corner of Jefferson Avenue and North Sixteenth Street. Faithful readers and aspiring writers leave dog-eared paperbacks—and the occasional bottle of bourbon—on the author's grave.

Oxford's rich literary heritage is showcased in the annual *Oxford Conference for the Book,* which attracts aspiring writers and renowned authors from around the world; past speakers have included John Grisham and Stephen King. For a list of conference speakers and dates, visit oxfordconferenceforthe book.com.

Much of the activity in Oxford is focused on the town square (known simply as *"The Square"*), where the focal point is the imposing *Lafayette County Courthouse,* which played a starring role in Faulkner's *The Sound and the Fury.* Faulkner fans will also want to visit *City Hall,* where a bronze statue of the literary genius gazes out over the courtyard.

The Square is also home to a number of restaurants and specialty and antiques shops. Excellent dining choices located on or near The Square include

A (Religious) Conversion on the 10-Yard Line

It's been said that in the South, college football is a religion, and Saturday is the day of worship.

Of course, casual spectators may question whether heaven really cares about the outcome of a football game. For these naysayers, devout Mississippians have but one reply—November 19, 1983.

On that fateful day, the University of Mississippi Rebels and the Mississippi State University Bulldogs met for the annual intrastate bloodletting known as the Egg Bowl. State dominated the first half, but Ole Miss rallied in the second, battling to a precarious 24 to 23 lead in the fourth quarter. Not to be denied, the Bulldogs drove to the Rebel 10-yard line, and with seconds remaining, lined up to kick the game-winning field goal.

The kick was up, it had the distance, it split the uprights . . . and then, miraculously, a strong gust of wind *blew the winning kick back outside the goal posts.*

The ball fell harmlessly back to earth. MSU kicker Artie Cosby stared in disbelief. The Ole Miss team began a wild celebration that lasted into the night. Fans on both sides fell to their knees.

Headlines the next day screamed "The Immaculate Deflection!" and the 1983 Egg Bowl—and its supernaturally influenced kick—made history and highlight reels for years to come.

City Grocery (152 Courthouse Sq.), *Saint Leo* (1101 Jackson Ave.), and the
Ajax Diner (118 Courthouse Sq.).

A stroll around The Square isn't complete without a visit to *Square Books*
(160 Courthouse Sq.), a favorite hangout of Oxford's many famous and aspiring
writers and widely regarded as one of the South's premier bookstores. Square
Books packs the calendar with signings and readings from best-selling and
soon-to-be-best-selling authors year-round. Located five doors down from the
main store, *Off Square Books* is a sister store featuring thousands of reduced-
price and remaindered titles, as well as rare, out-of-print, and collectible books.
Fall and spring Thursday evenings 5:30 to 6:30 p.m., Off Square Books hosts a
standing-room-only crowd for the live broadcast of *Thacker Mountain Radio*
(thackermountain.com), a quirky program that showcases two of Oxford's
greatest treasures: literature and music. Described as *Prairie Home Companion*
meets the South, Thacker Mountain Radio features authors reading from their
latest works and live music performed by local and national talent. Tickets
aren't required; you're welcome to walk in and choose a folding chair. If you
can't stop by for the show, tune in locally to Rebel Radio 92.1 FM or Mississippi Public Radio for a distinctive radio program like no other in the country.
For reading recommendations and a calendar of events at Square Books, Off
Square Books, and Thacker Mountain Radio, visit squarebooks.com.

Even for non-bibliophiles, shopping opportunities abound on The Square.
The *Southside Gallery* (150 Courthouse Sq.) brings the international art scene
to Oxford with exhibits by noted painters, photographers, and folk artists.
Mississippi Madness on the Square (141 Courthouse Sq.) offers gourmet
foods and handmade Mississippi pottery, and *University Sporting Goods
Company* (105 Courthouse Sq.) is the place to shop for Ole Miss apparel.
You'll also want to browse in the *J. E. Neilson Company Department Store*
(119 Courthouse Sq.), the oldest continuously operating department store in
the South.

Anywhere you go in Oxford, you're bound to run into a student or two.
The city fathers chose the name "Oxford" in 1837 in hopes of improving their
chances of landing Mississippi's first public university. Their efforts were successful; the *University of Mississippi,* known affectionately as "Ole Miss,"
was founded in Oxford in 1848.

Perhaps the University's most famous feature is the ten-acre, parklike
retreat known simply as *The Grove.* Normally a peaceful spot for strolling,
counting tulips, or relaxing in the shade, The Grove is packed with enthusiastic
tailgaters on Southeastern Conference football weekends when many put out
their best silver and finest table linens—along with a brass candelabra or two—
in honor of the pregame festivities. For really *big* games and homecoming,

waiters, bartenders, and big-screen TVs are the norm. If you attend a football game at Ole Miss, don't come in blue jeans. Football is serious business in Oxford, with an unwritten student dress code that demands blue blazers and ties for gentlemen and skirts and high heels for ladies. Attire has relaxed a little since the 1950s and 1960s, when women often sported full-length furs for ninety-degree September kickoffs.

The university has closed its doors only once—when the entire male faculty and student body marched away to fight in the Civil War. The wounded from the fierce battles of Corinth and Shiloh were treated in the university's buildings, and legend has it that spiteful Union troops rode their horses through the university's most hallowed halls. A handful of the university's original buildings survived the 1864 torching of Oxford, including the **Lyceum,** a white-columned Greek Revival structure that houses the administrative offices and serves as the campus focal point and university logo. Also of interest is 1889 **Ventress Hall,** where stained-glass windows honor the University Greys, a company of faculty and students who were wiped out in the Battle of Gettysburg.

The **Barnard Observatory** was built to house a magnificent telescope ordered with great excitement by the university science department but never delivered due to the outbreak of the war. Today, the observatory houses the **Center for the Study of Southern Culture,** a teaching and research center dedicated to the study of the South. Researchers at the center produced the highly acclaimed *Encyclopedia of Southern Culture,* an eight-and-a-half-pound tribute to everything southern. Bone up on your southern culture with a visit to the center's website at southernstudies.olemiss.edu.

The **University of Mississippi Blues Archive** is the only research facility in the country dedicated to the study of the blues. The archive includes the personal collection of blues legend and Mississippi native B. B. King. View the artifacts and photographs or listen to any of the more than 60,000 soulful recordings Mon through Fri from 8 a.m. until 5 p.m. Call (662) 915-7753 for more information.

University Museums usually promotes its Greek and Roman antiquities, but the average person would probably tell you the real attraction there is the Amazing, Ingenious, and Grotesque Display. Housed in its own "cabinet of curiosity," this Ripleyesque collection includes a wreath made entirely of human hair, an unidentified "critter" fashioned into a purse, and a pair of fleas dressed as a bride and groom posing for wedding photos under a magnifying glass.

University Museums also houses an extensive collection of paintings by former Oxford resident Theora Hamblett. Hamblett launched her artistic career at the age of fifty-five, painting scenes from her childhood, dreams, and religious visions. A growing collection of southern folk art includes works in textiles, wood, clay, paint, and natural materials, and the museums' collection of World War I posters is one of the most complete in existence. You'll find University Museums on the edge of campus at the corner of Fifth Street and University Avenue. Hours are 10 a.m. to 6 p.m. Tues through Sat. Admission is free. Call (662) 915-7073.

If you stay overnight in Oxford, you'll also find comfortable accommodatations on The Square at **The Chancellor's House** hotel (662-371-1400; chancellorshouse.com) or **The Graduate** hotel (662-234-3031; graduatehotels .com). You can also stay with the locals at one of the town's bed-and-breakfast inns. Delightful, moderately priced accommodations are available at **The Z Bed and Breakfast** (281-804-8022; thez-oxford.com), conveniently located near the university and the town square. If you're seeking a little peace and quiet after the hustle and bustle of the Square and the campus, take a short drive into the country and stay the night at **The Nests at Holly Grove Farm**. You'll enjoy private accommodations in cottages just steps away from the home of your congenial and knowledgeable hosts, Holly and Linda Raney. Call (662) 801-9369 or visit thenestsoxford.com.

Seven miles southwest of Oxford, tiny **Taylor** has carved out quite a reputation as an artists' colony. The community is home to writers, sculptors, photographers, and painters, most of whom live and work within walking distance of one another.

"Downtown" Taylor is anchored by a wonderful combination of cholesterol and artwork known as the **Taylor Grocery.** Once a country grocery store that served catfish in the back, Taylor Grocery has removed the old shelves and merchandise and devoted the entire ramshackle building to the art of preparing

Monument to the Movement

When James Meredith became the first African American to enroll at the University of Mississippi in 1962, his arrival on campus was signaled by rioting, tear gas, and the deployment of the National Guard. Forty years later, the university launched a fund-raising campaign to erect a permanent memorial on campus honoring Meredith and other heroes of the civil rights movement in Mississippi.

The $150,000 project was funded through donations from students, businesses, and private citizens, and through state and federal arts grants. The completed memorial stands between the historic Lyceum and the John D. Williams Library at the heart of the Oxford campus—the same spot where James Meredith fought to make history in 1962.

and serving fried catfish and perfectly grilled steaks, operating under the motto "Eat or we both starve." While the steaks are delicious, traditionalists prefer to stick with the catfish that made the place famous—a deep-fried indulgence that actually does your heart good every once in a while.

Both the catfish and the steaks come with a side order of Magic Markers and an invitation to add your own clever maxims to Taylor Grocery's graffiti-plastered walls, floors, furniture, and ceiling. If you're lucky enough to visit this mecca for fish-lovers and aspiring poets, be sure to scribble a witty message for those who come after you. And don't forget to check the walls for words of wisdom from US senator Thad Cochran, actress Lauren Hutton, singer Jimmy Buffett, and aspiring writer Marlo Carter. Call (662) 236-1716 or visit taylorgrocery.com for more information.

From Taylor, take MS 7 North from Oxford to **Holly Springs.** This pretty little town is home to some sixty antebellum homes and churches, spared

mississippi footballgreats

Football greats Brett Favre, Archie Manning, Deuce McAllister, Steve "Air" McNair, Walter Payton, and Jerry Rice all hail from Mississippi. Former New York Giants quarterback Eli Manning hails from New Orleans but played quarterback for the University of Mississippi.

destruction because the ladies of Holly Springs devoted themselves to distracting the Union soldiers sent to torch the town. In this charming setting of white-columned homes and colorful gardens, hoopskirts seem almost mandatory, but the only time they're considered appropriate street attire is during the annual **Spring Pilgrimage.**

The original Holly Springs Pilgrimage allowed visitors to tour twenty-three homes for a quarter. Today, the pilgrimage offers tours of seven homes with two open each year on a rotating basis, guaranteeing repeat visitors new tours each spring. Approximately 5,000 pilgrims visit Holly Springs during the three-day event, usually held the second weekend in Apr. For next spring's dates and ticket prices, call the Holly Springs Tourism Bureau at (662) 252-2515 or (888) 687-4765 or visit visithollysprings.com.

Located at 148 East College Ave., the Tourism Bureau offers self-guided walking and driving tour maps, and brochures featuring historic homes, churches, and landmarks. One of the homes is **Hamilton Place,** where the mistress of the house hosted parties, teas, and concerts for the Union troops, hoping to take their minds off their torches. One Union general particularly enthralled with her musical gifts told her, "You and your piano can take credit for saving Holly Springs." You'll also want to drive by **Airliewood,** where General Grant established headquarters and his restless troops shot every picket off the iron fence. ***Montrose,*** the lushly landscaped home of the Holly Springs Garden Club, is open for tours during limited hours and by appointment. The ***Montrose Arboretum*** on the grounds showcases native trees labeled with common and botanical names. For tour hours or to arrange an appointment, call (662) 252-2515.

History buffs will also want to stop by the ***Marshall County Historical Museum,*** three floors and 22 viewing rooms filled to the rafters with artifacts and displays. The building itself was constructed in 1903 as a dormitory for the old Mississippi Synodical College, the first junior college for women in the state. A $5 admission fee for adults, $3 for children buys a look at Chickasaw Indian artifacts, vintage clothing, Civil War relics, antique toys, and a display detailing events from the 1878 yellow fever epidemic, which claimed more lives in Holly Springs than the Civil War. Notable artifacts include a condolence card from Mrs. Jefferson Davis to a Mississippi war widow, and an 1869 income tax return listing a total tax liability of $27.95. The museum is located at 220 E. College Ave., and is open all year except Christmas, New Year's Day, and Thanksgiving. Normal operating hours are from 10 a.m. to 4 p.m. Tues through Fri, and 10 a.m. to 2 p.m. on Sat. Admission is $5 for adults and $3 for children. For more information or to arrange for a group tour, call (662) 252-3669.

Nearby ***Hillcrest Cemetery*** (Elder St. and S. Market St.) is the final resting place of hundreds of yellow fever victims and of Hiram Revels, the country's first black United States senator. Five Confederate generals and a number of Civil War soldiers are also buried at Hillcrest.

A Holly Springs attraction of a different sort is the ***Kate Freeman Clark Art Gallery*** (300 E. College Ave.), a collection of more than 1,200 paintings by a single Holly Springs native. The collection is believed to be one of the world's largest single collections of paintings by a single artist. Clark's paintings were shown in Chicago, Boston, Philadelphia, and New York, but she refused to sell even one, perhaps because her mother told her it would be "like selling a child." Instead, Clark willed the entire collection to the town of Holly Springs, including sketches, still lifes, landscapes, even a colorful bird painted on a real leaf. Clark is buried in Hillcrest Cemetery. Hours are 10 a.m. to 3 p.m. Tues through Fri. Tours are arranged by appointment by calling (662) 252-5300 or (662) 252-9745 after hours. Visit katefreemanclark.org.

The ***Ida B. Wells Art Gallery*** (220 N. Randolph Ave.) showcases work by African and African-American artists. The collection is housed in the historic Spires-Boles home, the birthplace of journalist and activist Ida B. Wells. The gallery is open Mon through Fri from 10 a.m. until 5 p.m., and on Sat from noon to 5 p.m. Call (662) 252-3232.

Holly Springs's **Rust College** (150 Rust Ave.) is the second-oldest private college in Mississippi and the oldest African-American college in the state. Founded in 1866, the institution represented one of the first post–Civil War efforts made by the national Freedmen's Bureau to educate African-American children and adults and to train African-American teachers. The college is located on the site of the former slave auction grounds of Holly Springs. Each year, the Rust College graduating class holds a candlelight ceremony at a gazebo where the auction block once rested.

If sightseeing leaves you hungry, stop by **Phillips Grocery** (541 E. Van Dorn Ave.; 662-252-4671), where the burgers were named among the nation's best by *USA Today*. Located next door to the old railroad depot, Phillips was originally opened as a saloon in 1882 by Oliver Quiggins, a former Confederate soldier. The establishment did a thriving business serving the constant flow of train passengers, many of whom arrived in Holly Springs from the North. The colorful Quiggins delighted in ordering his "Yankee" customers to take off their hats, explaining in no uncertain terms, "I've always been a Southern gentleman and I used to shoot you during the war, so you'll take off your hat if you expect service in my place."

Gardening enthusiasts and bird-watchers will enjoy a side trip to the lovely **Strawberry Plains Audubon Center.** Located 3 miles north of Holly Springs on MS 311 (285 Plains Rd.), Strawberry Plains is a 2,500-acre preserve and nature center bursting with native plants, flowers, birds, and butterflies. A winding country road leads visitors through the lushly landscaped grounds to **Davis House,** a stately antebellum mansion that's open for tours by calling (662) 252-2515. The headquarters for the Mississippi Audubon Society, the center offers birding hikes, nature walks, and educational programs year-round. The first Sat in Sept, more than 1,000 visitors descend on Strawberry Plains to celebrate the spectacular migration of thousands of hummingbirds. Strawberry Plains welcomes visitors Tues through Sat from 8 a.m. to 4 p.m. For more information about programs and events at Strawberry Plains, call (662) 252-1155, (888) 687-4765 or visit strawberry.audubon.org.

Walnut's Original Keg Party

The tiny north Mississippi town of *Walnut* was originally known as Hopkins, but was rechristened in 1872 when a keg of whiskey was mistakenly delivered to nearby Hopkinstown. The train was forced to backtrack an hour to correct the error. The townspeople changed the name on the spot to avoid further mix-ups, celebrating the new name with toasts from the recovered keg.

Make your next stop the history-rich town of **Corinth.** The city's location at the junction of two railroads made Corinth a strategic prize in the Civil War. More than 300,000 soldiers and 200 generals occupied the city between 1861 and 1865. Generals William T. Sherman and Ulysses S. Grant both spent time in the Corinth area, and the 1862 siege of Corinth broke the record for the largest concentration of troops in the Western Hemisphere. Julia Grant, the general's wife, was also a wartime visitor. According to local historians, Mrs. Grant, accompanied by her own slave, set up quarters in a local plantation house. When she left she stripped the place clean, taking even the doors and window glass with her.

By the spring of 1862, Union troops were entrenched so close to Corinth they could hear the rattle of supply trains and the beat of Confederate drums inside the fortified city. Vastly outnumbered, Confederate general Pierre Gustave Toutant Beauregard decided to retreat to nearby Tupelo. The evacuation was conducted with the utmost secrecy. Dummy cannons guarded the line, campfires burned, and buglers serenaded the deserted works. When Union troops cautiously entered the city at daybreak, they discovered only a deserted town.

The Battle of Corinth took place in Oct 1862, when the Confederates attempted to retake the town in what was to become the bloodiest battle in Mississippi history. Hand-to-hand fighting engulfed the city, and the Confederates were driven out of Corinth. The site of the Battle of Corinth includes the **Corinth National Cemetery,** the final resting place for Union soldiers killed in some twenty battles in Mississippi and Tennessee.

Battery Robinett, the scene of fierce fighting in the fall of 1862, is the site of the National Park Service's $9.5 million **Civil War Interpretive Center.** The Corinth Unit of Shiloh National Military Park, the 15,000-square-foot center is home to an auditorium, museum, research room, and interpretive courtyard. Interactive exhibits tell the compelling story not only of the 1862 battle but also of the plight of citizens left to forage for themselves in an occupied city. The center runs a fifteen-minute video on Corinth and the war, offers a self-guided-historic-tour brochure and map to important historic sites, and sells Civil War prints and other memorabilia. Located at 501 W. Linden St., the center is open daily 8 a.m. to 5 p.m. Call (662) 287-9273.

It's difficult to take a drive through any part of Corinth without crossing the ring of **earthworks** that encircled the city during the war. These hastily constructed ridges of earth formed a protective buffer for the weary soldiers to sleep behind. While the earthworks are found all over town—even running through the occasional front lawn—the larger, more intact sites require a short hike through the woods off Shiloh Road. The 4-foot-high mounds don't look

Roscoe Turner and Gilmore

One of Corinth's most colorful residents was the high-flying **Roscoe Turner**, an early stunt pilot famous not only for his daring aerial maneuvers but for his copilot—a pet lion dubbed Gilmore. Both Turner and Gilmore received national recognition—Turner was the first (and so far, the only) Corinth native to appear on the cover of *Time* magazine, and Gilmore, now handsomely stuffed, occupies a spot in the Air and Space Museum in Washington, D.C.

especially impressive until you consider they were constructed by hungry, tired soldiers working in the dark with handheld shovels the size of garden trowels. Many of the more remote sites haven't changed in the 140-plus years since the war. If a soldier from 1862 woke up today in the wooded area off Shiloh Road, he'd still know exactly where he was.

Built in 1857, the **Historic Verandah Curlee House** (705 Jackson St.) served as headquarters for Confederate generals Braxton Bragg and Earl Van Dorn and for Union general Henry Halleck. Today the house is owned by the city and is open for tours Thurs through Sat 9:30 a.m. to 4 p.m., and Sun from 1 to 4 p.m. Call (662) 287-9501 or visit verandahcurleehouse.com for more information.

If you have any questions about Corinth history, the volunteers at the **Crossroads Museum** at 221 N. Fillmore St. in Corinth's historic Depot building are sure to have the answers. The museum displays Civil War relics, Indian artifacts, and local memorabilia, but its biggest asset is a friendly staff of volunteers who delight in spinning tales for out-of-town guests. Visit the museum Mon through Sat from 10 a.m. to 4 p.m., or on Sun from 1 to 4 p.m. Admission is $5 for adults, $3 for seniors over the age of 50. Children 16 and under are admitted free. Call (662) 287-3120 or visit crossroadsmuseum.com.

Downtown Corinth is a handsome commercial district of Italianate, Colonial Revival, and art deco architecture. You'll discover a number of interesting shops in the area, including **Borroum's Drug Store** (604 Waldron St.), the oldest continually operated drugstore in Mississippi. Founded in 1869, Borroum's still serves up thick grilled-cheese sandwiches and frosty Coke floats from a gleaming soda fountain. Locals gather beneath the deer heads at Borroum's to watch Ole Miss football games and exchange gossip. Visitors may even hear a tale or two about Sheriff Buford Pusser, whose life was chronicled in the *Walking Tall* movie series. Pusser was sheriff of McNairy County, Tennessee (just across the state line), and was a frequent visitor to Corinth. Call (662) 286-3361.

With so much Civil War history in the area, it's no wonder that **C&D Jarnagin**, the nation's largest supplier of uniforms and accessories to Civil War reenactors, is also located in downtown Corinth. The retail shop at 518 Wick St. is open Mon through Fri from 9 a.m. to 4:30 p.m. In addition to detailed reproductions of Confederate and Union uniforms, C&D Jarnagin carries authentic reproductions of Civil War–era money, toys, civilian clothing, jewelry, accessories, and even toiletry items. Merchandise is also available through the company's website, jarnaginco.com. Call (662) 287-4977.

No stroll around downtown would be complete without a snack from **Dilworth's Tamales** (111 Taylor St.), a Corinth tradition since 1890. Call (662) 223-3296.

Corinth hosts several colorful festivals, the most notable of which is the **Slugburger Festival**, which celebrates that unique southern delicacy, the slugburger. Not to be confused with the garden pest of the same name, the slugburger is a part-beef, part-breading concoction made popular during the Depression when families were hungry and meat was scarce. The origin of the name is subject to some local debate, with theories ranging from "slug" as slang for a nickel, the burger's original cost, or another word for "fake," as in fake meat. In spite of its less-than-appetizing name, the slugburger attracts some 15,000 hungry fans to the July festival held in its honor. For this year's dates, call the Corinth Area Convention and Visitor's Bureau at (662) 287-8300 or visit corinth.net.

mississippitrivia

There's literally "something in the water" in northeast Mississippi. The state's record striped bass, flathead catfish, and walleye were all pulled from local lakes and rivers.

Overnight guests in Corinth can make themselves at home in luxury hotel suites in the **Franklin Cruise** building. A completely restored circa-1886 building located in the heart of downtown, Franklin Cruise houses an antique- and Oriental-rug showroom downstairs and two luxury hotel suites upstairs. Amenities in these handsome, well-appointed suites include antique furnishings, spacious sitting areas, a gas log fireplace, stainless-steel kitchen appliances, and high-speed Internet access. The Franklin Cruise is located at 515 Cruise St., across the street from the tourism office and within walking distance of major attractions and restaurants. For rates and reservations, contact host/owner John Frame at (662) 287-8069.

Take US 45 south of Corinth and then go 9 miles east on MS 356 to the **Jacinto Courthouse**. Once the political and cultural center of northeast Mississippi, Jacinto was founded in 1836 as the county seat of Old Tishomingo

County. In its heyday, Jacinto was home to a boys' boarding school, a busy stagecoach stop, numerous churches, and even more plentiful bars and taverns.

Jacinto was home to two classes of people—those who drank, fought, and committed adultery, and those who went to church, to temperance meetings, and to bed early. Court was the main source of entertainment for both groups, and the two-story brick courthouse—built in 1854 at a whopping cost of $7,199.72—was the town's focal point.

But just as construction on the courthouse was completed, Jacinto's population began to decline. People moved to cities where the railroad created jobs and business opportunities, and the Civil War claimed many of the residents who stayed behind. The final bell tolled for Jacinto in 1870, when one-million-acre Tishomingo County was divided into the present Alcorn, Prentiss, and Tishomingo Counties. No longer a seat of government, Jacinto faded into a ghost town.

Today the town is maintained and operated by the Jacinto Foundation. Tour buildings include the courthouse museum, an 1850s doctor's office, and a country store. For information on tour times and availablity, call (662) 286-8662.

The Appalachian Foothills

The Appalachian Mountains begin in the extreme northeastern corner of the state, creating a rugged terrain of rocky outcroppings, thick woodlands, and bubbling streams that run cool and clear even in the heat of a Mississippi summer.

The most remarkable feature of the Appalachian Foothills is the complete solitude, deafening quiet, and total lack of urbanization. In this tranquil, unspoiled section of Mississippi, Mother Nature is the main attraction.

From Corinth, take US 72 East to MS 25 North and then follow MS 25 to **J. P. Coleman State Park**. Bordered by the **Tennessee River** and beautiful **Pickwick Lake**, J. P. Coleman is a popular resort attracting outdoor enthusiasts from northeast Mississippi and nearby Memphis, Tennessee. The area is home to the largest inland marina in the United States and a scenic waterfall frequented by boaters. Call (662) 423-6515 for more information or cabin rental reservations.

From J. P. Coleman it's just a short drive south along MS 25 to **Iuka**. The land around Iuka is woodsy, hilly, and completely unspoiled, characterized by a peace and quiet so complete that urban dwellers may find it a bit unnerving. Named for a Chickasaw Indian chief drawn to the area by its healthful mineral springs, Iuka was a popular spa of the 1880s. The water was bottled in the early 1900s and won first place in the 1904 World's Fair. The **Iuka Mineral Springs**

Park on MS 172 East offers travelers a taste of the same sparkling water Chief Iuka discovered centuries ago.

The ***Old Tishomingo County Courthouse*** (circa 1889) at the corner of Fulton and Quitman Streets houses a collection of Indian relics, Civil War artifacts from the 1862 Battle of Iuka, and other collections related to local history. The museum is open Wed through Fri from 9:30 a.m. to 4:30 p.m., and Sat 9 a.m. to noon. Lunch is the best time to check out ***Ellie's Snack Bar***, which specializes in slugburgers. Ellie's has been in operation in the one-room building at 108 W. Front St. since the early 1940s. Call (662) 423-2494.

Avid cooks may want to schedule a visit to the Iuka ***Apron Museum***. Owner Carolyn Terry has collected thousands of vintage aprons to admire and

mississippitrivia

Whether they're headed for the river, the lake, or the beach, Mississippians love the water. The state averages one boat for every ten people.

to purchase, some once worn by cooks more than a century ago. The Apron Museum gift shop offers new and vintage quilts, linens, and local crafts, including unique birdhouses. Located at 110 W. Eastport Street in Iuka, the shop is open by appointment only. To arrange a visit, contact Carolyn at (662) 279-2390.

Head south on MS 25 about 1 mile outside the Iuka city limit, turn right on CR 187, and follow the signs to ***Woodall Mountain***, the highest point in Mississippi. At an elevation of 807 feet, Woodall Mountain doesn't require crampons or bottled oxygen, but the view is scenic, the landscape is unspoiled, and the tranquil atmosphere is perfect for a quiet picnic.

Return to MS 25 and head south to ***Tishomingo*** and ***Tishomingo State Park***. The park offers a unique landscape of imposing rock formations and fern-filled crevices found nowhere else in Mississippi. Massive boulders blanketed in moss jut out from the steep hillsides, and colorful wildflowers border winding trails once walked by the Chickasaw Indians. The historic ***Natchez Trace Parkway*** runs directly through the park.

Visitors may stay overnight in the rustic cabins clinging to the boulder-studded hillsides, then explore a 13-mile nature trail that winds along rocky ridges with spectacular views, through shallow canyons, and beside the rushing waters of ***Bear Creek***. Hikers beware—a walk on the swinging bridge high above the creek is not for the faint of heart. A float trip about 6 miles down Bear Creek is offered mid-Apr through mid-Oct. Rappelling and disc golf are also popular park attractions. For information and cabin rental reservations, call (662) 438-6914 or (800) 467-2757.

From Tishomingo, take MS 30 West to **Booneville**, Like most Mississippi towns, Booneville boasts a Civil War "So-and-So slept here" landmark. The white frame **Cunningham House** (located behind the restored depot that houses the Booneville Chamber of Commerce) played host to General Nathan Bedford Forrest the night before the 1864 Battle of Brice's Cross Roads.

From Booneville it's just a short drive south on US 45 to **Baldwyn** and the **Brice's Cross Roads Battlefield**. Located 6 miles west of Baldwyn on MS 370, the former Civil War battlefield is a National Park Service site.

The Battle of Brice's Cross Roads took place in June 1864, when Confederate general Nathan Bedford Forrest organized his cavalry for an attack on Union general William T. Sherman's supply line. Union forces moved out of Memphis to stop him, and the opposing units met at Brice's Cross Roads. The outnumbered Confederates attacked vigorously and forced the Union troops back. Union forces began a careful withdrawal, but as the troops crossed Tishomingo Creek a supply wagon overturned, panicking the soldiers and turning their orderly retreat into a full-blown rout. More than 1,500 Union soldiers were captured and nearly as many were killed during the wild flight back to Memphis. A soldier described the scene as a horrible melee in which "live and dead mules were mixed up with live and dead men in the mud and water." The remains of a Federal soldier trampled in the retreat were discovered impacted in the creek bed nearly one hundred years later. The Confederate victory was a brilliant success for Forrest, a colorful military genius who based his strategies on the maxims "Get there first with the most men" and "Shoot at everything blue and keep up the scare."

Today, well-marked trails and interpretive markers guide visitors through the park, which includes Civil War cannons, a monument, and the Bethany Confederate Cemetery. Audiotapes of a driving tour are available at the visitor center, which houses a battlefield diorama and interactive exhibits and screens a video program narrated by late Civil War historian and author Shelby Foote. The visitors' center at 607 Grisham St. is open Tues through Sat from 9 a.m. to 5 p.m., and on Sun from 12:30 to 5 p.m. Admission to the visitors' center is $5 for adults and free for children under 7. For more information or to find out about group discounts, call (662) 365-3969.

From Baldwyn, follow MS 30 West into **New Albany**. More often associated with nearby Oxford, Nobel Prize–winner William Faulkner was born in New Albany. The house is no longer standing, but a historic marker designates the site. Learn more about Faulkner and other people and events important to New Albany's history at the **Union County Heritage Museum** (114 Cleveland St.). The museum grounds are home to the **William Faulkner Literary Garden**, which features plants Faulkner referenced in his novels. The small but interesting museum is open Tues through Fri from 9 a.m. to 4 p.m., and on Sat from 10 a.m. to 3 p.m. Call (662) 538-0014 or visit ucheritagemuseum.com.

New Albany also offers some interesting sights outside the main part of town. As you approach the intersection of MS 15 North and CR 82, look for the small white picket fence next to the railroad tracks. The fence marks the **Grave of the Unknown Frenchman**. In the 1880s, convict labor was used to build the railroads. According to legend, a wrongly accused Frenchman working on the chain gang received word his wife was dying. Desperate to reach her side before it was too late, he made a break for freedom, was shot and killed by a guard, and was buried where he fell.

Rivers and Rails

The cities and towns in the Rivers and Rails section of Mississippi sprang up as shipping hubs along the railroads and the Tennessee and Tombigbee Rivers, a heritage still celebrated there today.

This is an area where festivals revolve around "railroad days" and bands play on the rivers' banks, where museums display old train whistles and elegant old neighborhoods have their roots in the cotton-shipping trade.

Today the focus of commercial shipping is the **Tennessee-Tombigbee Waterway**, a 234-mile transportation route, scenic passage, and recreational area connecting the inland South with the Gulf of Mexico. The Tenn-Tom is a haven for sportsmen, boaters, campers, and other outdoor enthusiasts; the communities along its banks are dotted with boat ramps and campgrounds offering direct access to the water.

But perhaps first and foremost, this area is Elvis Presley's homeland. From New Albany, take I-22 East to **Tupelo**. A modern industrial center listed in Hugh Bayless's *The Best Towns in America*, Tupelo is best known as the birthplace of Elvis Presley, the King of Rock 'n' Roll. No matter which route you follow into the city, it's impossible to miss the many directional signs that point visitors toward the Elvis Presley Birthplace. Vernon Presley, Elvis's daddy, borrowed $180 to construct the two-room, shotgun-style house where the King of Rock 'n' Roll was born.

mississippitrivia

Built in 1937, Tupelo's **Church Street School** was hailed as one of the most outstanding designs of its time. A scale model of this Art Moderne structure was displayed at the 1939 New York World's Fair as "the ideal elementary school."

Two years later, the Presleys were evicted when they couldn't scrape together enough money to repay that modest loan.

The worn furnishings and sepia-toned family portrait are a sharp contrast to the flashy cars, sequined jumpsuits, and extravagant lifestyle more often associated with Elvis. The entire structure is only 450 square feet, and the guide at the door is quick to mention that Graceland, Elvis's estate in Memphis, holds a sofa longer than this entire house.

When the property went up for sale in 1957, Elvis gave the city the money to purchase the home; he also donated funds to purchase the fifteen acres surrounding the property and convert it into a park so that local children would have a place to play. Today more than 75,000 tourists and fans take the exit off I-22 to Elvis Presley Drive each year, headed for the tiny shotgun shack at the end of the road.

Worshipping the King

In the summer of 1982, I entered the workforce as a tour guide at Jimmy Velvet's Elvis Presley Museum in Memphis. A personal friend of the King of Rock 'n' Roll, Velvet remodeled an old gas station across the street from Graceland and filled it with a hodgepodge of photos, costumes, jewelry, and furniture, all of which once belonged to Elvis. Fans from around the world paid $3 for me to lead them through the "exhibit hall" and snap their photos in front of Elvis's baby-blue Lincoln Continental or perched on the edge of his king-size bed.

The following summer, I graduated to working at Graceland itself, where my job duties included calming guests who claimed to have seen Elvis's ghost lurking on the staircase, providing tissues for fans who still "can't believe he's gone," and shaking hands with Priscilla Presley, who donned dark glasses and hid in the crowd during a top-secret, undercover inspection tour. The hottest-selling item in the gift shop? Bags of dirt from Graceland, each accompanied by a "certificate of authenticity."

But even two summers immersed in Elvis doesn't qualify me as a true fan of the King. "Fan," after all, is short for "fanatic," which is really the only way to describe the hordes of people who travel from around the world to see where Elvis lived and died.

Even today, nearly forty years after his death, fans wait in line for hours to tour the house, the cars, and the airplanes. They invest their hard-earned cash in T-shirts bearing his likeness and dirt from his flower beds. They tattoo his name on their bodies and name their children "Elvis Aaron Presley Jones." They are obsessed.

So what was it about the boy from Tupelo that changed people's lives and continues to touch them today? Was it his unforgettable voice? His smoldering eyes? His undulating pelvis? His tragic, early death? Or was it purely and simply charisma?

No one has ever been able to pinpoint the quality that made a poor country boy a King, but one thing is certain: If you could bag that with a certificate of authenticity, it'd be a bargain at any price.

The guest book bears signatures from visitors from all over the world. Most of their comments echo the sentiments of a visitor from England who wrote, "You were my idol. Rest in peace."

A museum behind the birthplace houses clothing, costumes, photographs, records, and other Elvis memorabilia. Dozens of photos depict Elvis as a schoolboy and young adult. Some of the earlier shots reveal a little-known secret: Elvis was actually a dark blond who dyed his hair black. Among the quirkier artifacts are "souvenirs" recovered from Elvis's hotel room by an enterprising pair of fans who paid hotel security $40 for admittance to the room after the King checked out. Their spoils included two used coffee cups (still stained) and a damp bath towel that was sealed in plastic and stored in a deep freezer to preserve its moisture.

Perhaps most poignant is a quotation from the King himself. Stenciled on a wall are Elvis's own words, "I could never become so rich that I would forget what it's like to be poor." Elvis lived up to those words; many of his concerts were benefits.

As he strolled the grounds of his birthplace with his friend Janelle McComb shortly before his death, Elvis mentioned that he would like to see a small chapel erected somewhere on the grounds. After Elvis's passing, McComb launched a personal crusade, raising donations from friends and fans to construct the intimate Memorial Chapel that now graces the grounds. Though many weddings have been held beneath the stained-glass windows, the birthplace guide is quick to mention that contrary to rumor, there is not and will never be an Elvis impersonator on-site to perform marriages. Like the rest of the park, the chapel is marked by an aura of dignity and peace.

In 2002 the Elvis Presley Birthplace unveiled a bronze statue of "Elvis at 13." Sculpted by North Carolina artist Michiel Van der Sommen, the statue depicts Elvis in overalls carrying his guitar, much as he would have looked when the family relocated from Tupelo to Memphis in 1948. The grounds also feature a "story wall" showcasing quotations and quips from friends of the King.

Grand Tour admission prices to the birthplace are $19 for adults, $15 for seniors 60 and older, $9 for children 6 to 12, and free for children under age 6. Admission prices for the house only tour are $9 for adults, $9 seniors, and $3 for children 6 to 12. The Elvis Presley Birthplace is open Mon through Sat from 9 a.m. to 5:30 p.m., and Sun from 1 to 5 p.m. (May 1 through Sept 30) and Mon through Sat from 9 a.m. to 5 p.m., and Sun from 1 to 5 p.m. (Oct. 1 through Apr 30). Call (662) 841-1245 or visit elvispresleybirthplace.com.

Die-hard fans of the King should stop by the ***Tupelo Convention and Visitors Bureau*** (399 E. Main St.; 662-841-6521) and pick up information on

Elvis' Tupelo Driving Tour or Elvis' Tupelo Self-Guided Bicycle Tour.
The tours take you to 14 stops that were influential in Elvis's life as he lived in Tupelo until he was 13 years old. Stops include Lawhon Elementary and Milam Junior High Schools, where Elvis was a student; Johnnie's Drive-In, where Elvis often stopped for a cheeseburger and an RC Cola; and the site of the old Mayhorn Grocery, where the future King of Rock 'n' Roll was inspired by the blues.

Perhaps the most popular stop along the route is ***Tupelo Hardware*** (114 W. Main St.), where Elvis purchased his first guitar. As the story goes, Elvis's mother, Gladys, brought him to the store in 1946 to buy a bicycle, but a rifle caught young Elvis's eye. Mother and son compromised on a guitar, and the rest is rock 'n' roll history. Today, Tupelo Hardware is a major stop for the Elvis faithful, with busloads of fans pouring into the store at all hours. Radio shows have been broadcast live from the very counter where the young Elvis forked over his $7.75, and the staff has long since learned that a typical day at work involves as much rock 'n' roll as hammer and nails. Souvenir T-shirts, postcards, and guitar-shaped key chains are emblazoned with the message "Where Gladys bought her son his first guitar." Call (662) 842-4637 or visit tupelohardware.com.

Tupelo's year-round Elvis frenzy reaches its peak each June, when Elvis fans, music lovers, locals, and folks who just enjoy a good party descend on the town for the annual ***Tupelo Elvis Presley Festival.*** For a schedule of festival events and a list of this year's headliners, call (662) 841-6598 or visit tupeloelvisfestival.com.

Believe it or not, there is more to Tupelo than Elvis. Children and adults alike will enjoy a visit to the ***Tupelo Buffalo Park and Zoo*** (2272 N. Coley Rd.), where the residents include just about everything but a hound dog. This mini-zoo is home to more than 260 animals, including a Bengal tiger, a giraffe, monkeys, snakes, goats, rabbits, horses, iguanas, and a pair of hedgehogs. The real attractions, however, are the massive, shaggy bison grazing on the park's 145 acres. The largest bull tips the scale at 2,500 pounds; at more than 250 head, the herd itself is the largest east of the Mississippi River. Visitors board a Monster Bison Bus—a school bus equipped with a monster truck kit—and ride through the herd, which shares its range with a handful of water buffalo, a few Texas longhorns, and a pair of yaks. The bus stops at a feeding station, where visitors have the opportunity to stand inside a safely enclosed pen and hand-feed the bison. The bus tour lasts about 45 minutes, leaving plenty of time for kids to explore the park's playground and petting zoo. Along with T-shirts and caps, the Buffalo Park gift shop sells bison meat and hides (sorry, no blue suede shoes).

Park hours are Mon through Thurs from 9 a.m. to 4 p.m., Fri and Sat from 9 a.m. to 5 p.m., and on Sun from 11 a.m. to 4 p.m. For more information, including admission and rates for various tour packages, call (662) 844-8709 or visit tupelobuffalopark.com.

Like most of north Mississippi, Tupelo was the site of a fierce Civil War battle. The Battle of Tupelo is remembered in a small park on West Main Street. After the disastrous Union rout at Brice's Cross Roads, General Sherman ordered General A. J. Smith to "Go out and follow (Nathan Bedford) Forrest to the death, if it costs 10,000 lives and breaks the Treasury." Smith drew the Confederate forces under Forrest and General Stephen D. Lee into battle at Tupelo. A misunderstood direction cost the Confederates the battle—an incident that one of Forrest's men described as "making the General so mad he stunk." Smith, however, was short of supplies, and many of his troops were suffering from heat exhaustion. The Union troops hastily retreated, leaving their own wounded behind.

As Generals Lee and Forrest discussed the day's events around the campfire, Lee wondered aloud why the other Confederate generals couldn't match Forrest's success in battle. "Well General," Forrest is said to have replied, "I suppose it's because I'm not handicapped by a West Point education."

The one-acre **Tupelo National Battlefield** features a large memorial honoring both armies, cannons, and an interpretive marker and map. The **Oren Dunn City Museum**, located at 689 Rutherford Rd. just south of West Main Street, displays relics from the battle, as well as Indian artifacts and a collection of historic buildings. The museum is open Mon through Fri from 8 a.m. to 5 p.m. Admission is $4 for adults, $3 for senior citizens 60 and older, $2 for children 4 to 12, free for veterans and children 3 and under. The museum also provides group tours for 10 or more persons. Call (662) 841-6438 or tupeloms .gov/oren-dunn-city-museum.

History and nature are the focal points at the **Natchez Trace Parkway Visitor Center.** A scenic route more than 8,000 years old maintained by the US Department of the Interior, the fabled **Natchez Trace Parkway** is headquartered in Tupelo. The visitor center offers information to Natchez Trace Parkway travelers and houses exhibits related to the route's history. Three miles north of the visitors' center is a preserved segment of the original trail, which leads to the graves of thirteen unknown Confederate soldiers. Local legend has it the men were executed by their own commander, the ill-tempered Braxton Bragg. You'll find the visitors' center at the intersection of West Main Street and the Natchez Trace Parkway just north of town.

For a unique shopping experience and one-of-a-kind gifts, visit **The Main Attraction and Coffee Bar** (214 W. Main St.; 662-842-9617). Grab a cappuccino from the Elvis Coffee Bar; then browse shelves, walls, and racks packed with vintage clothing, funky furniture, lava lamps, beaded curtains, Moroccan hand drums, and off-the-wall refrigerator magnets. The Main Attraction also offers a spectacular assortment of jewelry, from very inexpensive to high-dollar pieces made with exotic stones.

Tupelo is home to several wonderful restaurants, but only one can make the claim "Elvis ate here." As noted in an affidavit on the wall, *Johnnie's Drive-In* (908 E. Main St.) was a teenaged Elvis's favorite source of cheeseburgers. The oldest restaurant in Tupelo, Johnnie's has won almost as many fans as the King himself. Revered for its burgers and barbecue, the restaurant has been owned by only two families since opening in 1945. The decor is still vintage 1950s, and Johnnie's still offers curb service. Drive in from 6 to 9 p.m. Mon through Sat. Call (662) 842-6748.

From Tupelo, take US 278 west to *Pontotoc.* This gracious community features a number of lovely old homes and historic sites. The homes aren't open for tours, but driving-tour maps and audio guides are available at the *Town Square Post Office and Museum.* Sites on the tour include antebellum homes, Civil War battlegrounds, and sites related to the Chickasaw Indians. The Town Square Post Office and Museum also features a Chickasaw Indian display and blacksmithing display, and showcases work by local artists. Located at 59 S. Main St., the museum is open Mon through Fri from 10 a.m. to 4:30 p.m. and other hours by appointment. Call (662) 488-0388 or visit townsquaremuseum.org.

mississippitrivia

In 1959, Mary Ann Mobley became the first Miss Mississippi to win the Miss America crown. Mary Ann was followed by three more Miss Americas from the state—Lynda Lee Meade (1960), Cheryl Prewitt (1980), and Susan Akin (1986).

From Pontotoc, take MS 41 South to US 278 and the railroad town of *Amory.* Named after Harcourt Amory, a shareholder in the railroad company, the town was founded as a train service stop between Memphis and Birmingham. Nearby Aberdeen was first considered as the stopping point, but the residents of that town, concerned about the noisy train whistles and the "riffraff" associated with the railroad, voted against it.

Follow the signs to the *Amory Regional Museum,* located in an old hospital building at 801 Third St. South. Admission is free, and a friendly tour guide will be happy to walk you through the many exhibits related to local history. Displays include Indian artifacts, a military room, and railroad memorabilia housed in an old train car. The most fascinating exhibits, however, are those related to the old hospital itself. Formerly the Gilmore Sanitarium, the museum displays medical equipment from the 1800s through the 1960s. A rate card describes the services of Dr. B. C. Tubb, a prominent local physician of the early 1900s who charged $1 for an office visit and $2 for house calls. An infant-size iron lung, original scrub room, and instrument sterilizer that still smells of disinfectant may look primitive to the modern visitor, but once represented state-of-the-art medical equipment.

A log cabin restored and moved to the museum grounds offers a glimpse of small-town life in the 1840s. The cabin is furnished in the style of the period and includes a children's sleeping loft reminiscent of the *Little House on the Prairie* TV series. The Amory Regional Museum is open Tues through Fri from 9 a.m. to 5 p.m., and Sat from 10 a.m. to 4 p.m. Call (662) 256-2761.

From the museum, go 1 block over to Main Street and head toward downtown Amory and **Bill's Hamburgers.** The menu at Bill's includes hamburgers, hamburgers, and, just for variety, hamburgers. It's hard to get confused at Bill's—your only choice is with or without mustard and onions. The restaurant has changed hands several times, but the menu has remained the same since 1929. You'll find Bill's at 310 N. Main St. at Vinegar Bend. Call (662) 256-2085.

The charming river town of **Aberdeen** is less than 20 miles south of Amory off MS 25. Located on the banks of the **Tombigbee River,** Aberdeen was one of the busiest ports of the nineteenth century. Huge shipments of cotton crowded the city's docks, and for a time Aberdeen was the second-largest city in Mississippi. Wealthy merchants and planters competed in the building of elaborate mansions, purchasing their furnishings in Europe and shipping them up the Tombigbee by steamboat.

Today Aberdeen's main attraction is a collection of elegant old homes showcasing architectural styles from Greek Revival to Victorian to neoclassical. All told, Aberdeen boasts more than 200 homes and buildings listed on the National Register of Historic Places.

Several of the homes are open every April during the **Aberdeen Spring Pilgrimage. The Magnolias,** a palatial 1850 Greek Revival mansion donated to the city by a local resident, is open for tours by appointment. Call (949) 813-1743 to reach the attendant, or contact the Aberdeen Visitors Bureau at (662) 369-9440. Admission is $10.

Located at 204 E. Commerce St., the visitors' bureau also offers a self-guided driving tour brochure. The tour takes visitors past several beautiful homes, including an area of magnificent Victorians known as **Silk Stocking Row.**

The **Old Aberdeen Cemetery** is the site of a tale worthy of Ripley's Believe It or Not. It seems Ms. Alice Whitfield was knitting—a popular pastime in 1854—when she died in her rocking chair. According to local legend, Ms.

mississippitrivia

Mississippi is Choctaw for "Father of Waters," referring to the mighty river for which the state is named. The earliest known written version of the name was the French *Michi Sepe*.

Whitfield was then buried in the rocking chair, knitting and all. The cemetery, located at the corner of Whitfield and Poplar Streets, also includes a number of Civil War–era gravesites. The cemetery and its residents come alive during the Pilgrimage, when local high school students host a candlelight tour called "Lies and Legends of Old Aberdeen Cemetery."

From Aberdeen, take MS 8 West to *Vardaman*, the self-proclaimed Sweet Potato Capital of the World. Mississippi ranks third nationwide in production of sweet potatoes, with 85 percent of those sweet potatoes grown within a 30-mile radius of Vardaman. The town celebrates its venerated vegetable the first week of every November with a *Sweet Potato Festival* that includes recipe competitions, a sweet-potato pie-eating contest, and the crowning of the Sweet Potato King and Queen. The festival attracts as many as 20,000 fans of the fluffy orange veggie—more than 15 times the town's number of residents. For this year's Sweet Potato Festival dates, call (662) 682-7559.

Even if you can't make the festival, you can share in Vardaman's sweet-potato worship year-round with a visit to *Sweet Potato Sweets*. Founded by a trio of sweet potato farmers' wives, the shop sells sweet-potato pies, sweet-potato fudge, sweet-potato cookies, sweet-potato bread, sweet-potato sausage, and . . . well, you get the sweet-potato picture. Follow the sweet smell to Sweet Potato Sweets, located at—you guessed it—117 E. Sweet Potato St. The shop also takes phone and online orders; call (800) 770-5035 or visit sweetpotatosweets.com.

The Natchez Trace Parkway

The *Natchez Trace Parkway* stretches diagonally across Mississippi, cuts a corner through Alabama, then winds to an end in Nashville, Tennessee, following an unspoiled route through lush forests, beside sparkling streams, and into the heart of America's frontier past.

This timeworn scenic path, more than 400 miles long and 8,000 years old, was originally "traced out" by buffalo, then trekked by Indians, and finally trampled into a rough road by trappers, traders, and missionaries. French maps dated as early as 1733 include the Natchez Trace; British maps of the same period refer to it as the "Path to the Choctaw Nation." From 1800 to 1820, the frontier brimmed with trade and new settlements, and the Natchez Trace was the busiest highway in the southwest.

But by the late 1820s, the speed of steamboats made travel along the Natchez Trace impractical, and the once-busy road dissolved into the brush. In 1909 the Daughters of the American Revolution spearheaded a campaign to mark the Old Trace, and their work culminated in the Natchez Trace Parkway, a national highway maintained by the National Park Service.

Today's highway closely follows the original trail. The uniquely southern penchant for sharing good tales preserved the colorful legends surrounding the Trace, and historic markers along the way detail the path's romantic history. Indian mounds, ghost towns, and nature trails beckon from just off the paved road.

Visitors exploring northeast Mississippi via the Natchez Trace will encounter wildlife, enjoy natural beauty free of commercial traffic, and pass historic sites too numerous to list. A few words of caution for first-time Trace travelers—stick to the 50-mile-per-hour speed limit, which is constantly monitored and always enforced. And while the Trace is tranquil and uncrowded by day,

mississippitrivia

The Natchez Trace Parkway is one of only fourteen National Scenic Byways and one of only six All-American Roads in the country. Both designations were awarded by the Federal Highway Administration in recognition of the Trace's historic value and scenic beauty.

Little-Known Facts about the Northeastern Hills

The oldest book in the United States, an ancient Biblical manuscript, is housed at the University of Mississippi.

On December 7, 1874, the Jesse James Gang held up Corinth's Tishomingo Savings Bank, escaping with $15,000.

Elvis Presley was scheduled to play in Corinth in 1954, but had to cancel due to low ticket sales.

Tupelo was one of only four cities in the United States that celebrated the first official Mother's Day in 1908.

The state of Mississippi has produced 36 Rhodes Scholars—27 from the University of Mississippi, seven from Millsaps College, and two from Mississippi State University.

In April 2000, Corinth native Gus McLeod became the first pilot to fly over the North Pole in an open-cockpit airplane. His feat was documented by National Geographic Television. McLeod attributed his lifelong interest in aviation to Roscoe Turner, another famous aviator from Corinth.

ALSO WORTH SEEING

Beale Street, Memphis, TN

Graceland (Elvis Presley home), Memphis, TN

Gumtree Museum of Art, Tupelo

Shiloh National Military Park, Shiloh, TN

Tombigbee State Park, Tupelo

it can seem a little dark and spooky at night. Small towns and cities are located at frequent intervals just off the parkway, but there are no commercial establishments and only one gas station on the Trace itself. Finally, night travelers should keep an alert watch for deer, which are known to bolt into the road unexpectedly.

Traveling north to south on the Trace through northeast Mississippi, visitors pass many of the attractions mentioned previously in this chapter. The parkway runs directly through *Tishomingo State Park,* located in the extreme northeastern corner of the state. Near mile marker 293.4 are wayside exits for the *Tennessee-Tombigbee Waterway,* a 234-mile scenic passage and recreational area connecting the inland South with the Gulf of Mexico.

The Trace is headquartered in Tupelo (see earlier in this chapter), home of the Natchez Trace Parkway Visitor Center. A museum located within the visitor center houses artifacts and displays chronicling the history and development of the Old Natchez Trace and the modern parkway. A scenic nature trail located on the property provides a welcome break from the road.

Places to Stay in the Northeastern Hills

AMORY

The Old Place
60036 County Barn Rd.
(662) 256-4707
theoldplacebandb.com

BELMONT

Belmont Hotel
121 Main St.
(662) 454-7948

CORINTH

The Generals' Quarters
924 Fillmore St.
(662) 286-3325
thegeneralsquarters.com

HERNANDO

Magnolia Grove Bed and Breakfast
140 E. Commerce St.
(662) 429-2626
magnoliagrove.com

Sassafras Inn
785 MS 51 South
(662) 429-5864 or
(800) 882-1897
sassyinn.memphis.to

HOLLY SPRINGS
Court Square Inn
132 E. College Ave.
(800) 926-3686
hollyspringsinn.com

OXFORD
Blue Creek Cabin Bed and Breakfast
535 MS 30 East
(662) 238-2897
bluecreekcabin.com

Castle Hill Resort and Restaurant
120 Castle Hill Dr.
(662) 234-3735
castlehilloxford.com

Oak Hill Stables
670 CR 101
(662) 801-2084 or
(662) 234-8488
oakhillstables.net

Ravine
53 CR 321
(662) 234-4555
oxfordravine.com/inn

SENATOBIA
Spahn House
401 College St.
(662) 288-6851
thespahnhouse.com

Places to Eat in the Northeastern Hills

ABERDEEN
Fountain Grill
303 MS 145
(662) 369-4275
Casual

BYHALIA
Thistledome
118 Hwy. 309 South
(901) 412-4484 or
(901) 383-3887
Antebellum home serving lunch and dinner to groups of six or more by advance reservation

CORINTH
Abe's Grill
803 MS 72 West
(662) 286-6124
Homemade biscuits, hand-cut French fries, and sweet iced tea served in mason jars; breakfast and lunch only

White Trolley Cafe
1215 MS 72 East
(662) 287-4593
Old-fashioned breakfasts, slugburgers

OXFORD
Bouré
110 Courthouse Sq.
(662) 234-1968
boureoxford.com
Casual

Ravine
53 CR 321
(662) 234-4555
oxfordravine.com
New contemporary Southern

Snackbar
721 N. Lamar
(662) 236-6363
citygroceryonline.com/snackbar
Upscale, changing menu from a James Beard Award–winning chef

SENATOBIA
Penny's Pantry
136 N. Front St.
(662) 562-5570
Light lunches, desserts

TUPELO
Clay's House of Pig
205 S. Veterans Memorial Blvd.
(662) 841-6521
Barbecue housed in a bait-and-tackle shop

Finney's Sandwich Shop
1009 W. Main St.
(662) 842-1746
Sandwiches, soda fountain; don't miss the signature potato salad

King's Chicken
3897 McCullough Blvd.
Kingchickentupelo.com
Fried chicken

Woody's
619 N. Gloster St.
(662) 840-0460
woodyssteak.com
Seafood, wild game, beer

The Eastern Plains

The Eastern Plains span rich black prairies, pastoral cattle farms, sacred Indian homelands, and bustling industrial centers. Tradition runs deep here, whether it's found in a carefully restored antebellum home, a hallowed Indian mound, or a modern company's success story.

The stops here have more in common than just freshly painted front porches, and it's more than just the sights and scenery that make this region special. The Eastern Plains are blessed with a singular culture centuries in the making and a rich history that's mellowed into legend.

The Golden Triangle

The small cities of Columbus, West Point, and Starkville make up the region known locally as the Golden Triangle. The three cities work together to promote themselves, capitalizing on the rich diversity of activities and attractions available in this small geographic area.

A tour of the Golden Triangle begins in *Columbus*, a pretty little town of antebellum homes and antiques shops near the Mississippi–Alabama line. Entering Columbus from

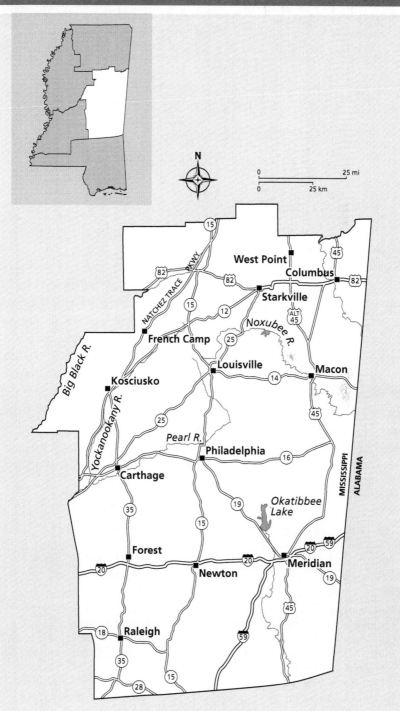

US 82 West, take the Main Street exit and make your first stop the ***Tennessee Williams Home/Mississippi Welcome Center*** (300 Main St.). This cheerful yellow-and-green Victorian built in 1878 was the first home of the famous playwright who introduced the world to Blanche DuBois and penned Marlon Brando's most memorable line—"Stella!" Inside, a friendly staffer will provide you with maps, a walking- and driving-tour brochure, an African-American Heritage driving-tour brochure. The Welcome Center is open Tues through Sat from 8:30 a.m. to 5 p.m., and on Sun from noon to 5 p.m. Call (662) 328-0222.

The city's two historic districts showcase one of the greatest diversities of antebellum architecture in the South. Shaded streets are lined with carefully preserved examples of Greek Revival, Italianate, Federal, and Gothic Revival mansions and cottages. At least two homes are open for tours any day of the week. Pick up the tour schedule and purchase tickets at the Tennessee Williams Birthplace. Tickets range from $10 to $15 per person per home, depending on

The Ghost of Waverley Plantation

When Robert and Donna Snow purchased the old *Waverley Plantation* in the early 1960s, they knew they were buying a piece of history. They didn't know they were also inheriting a former resident.

The Snows had lived in Waverley for about two years when the ghost made her first appearance. Donna Snow heard a child crying, sometimes calling for her "mama." A small indentation began appearing on the upstairs bed, about the size of a child napping. The Snows once sat in the room for an entire afternoon and actually saw the bedclothes straighten themselves when the ghost child "awakened." The little girl has appeared only once, dressed in a ruffled nightgown and standing on the stairway. To this day, her identity remains a mystery.

the home. Homes are generally open from 10 a.m. to 4 p.m. Mon through Sat and from 2 to 4 p.m. on Sun, but hours may vary from home to home. For assistance in scheduling your visit, call Visit Columbus at (662) 329-1191.

Tour homes include **Amzi Love**, built in 1848 and continuously occupied by generations of the Love family ever since; the **Stephen D. Lee Home and Museum**, former residence of Confederate general Stephen D. Lee; and **Temple Heights**, supposedly haunted by an eccentric ghost named Elizabeth. Some of the tour homes double as bed-and-breakfast inns. Call (800) 327-2686 or (662) 329-1191 for rates and reservations, or contact the individual bed-and-breakfasts listed at the end of this chapter.

All of Columbus's tour homes boast their share of history and charm, but the most fascinating home on tour is the magnificent **Waverley Plantation.** Waverley was built in 1852 and served as home to the original builder's family until the last descendant died in 1913. For nearly fifty years Waverley sat vacant. Then, in 1962, Robert and Donna Snow fought their way through the overgrown grounds, stepped into the graffiti-plastered foyer, and fell in love. The Snows bought Waverley and began the painstaking process of restoration.

It was a daunting task. Vines had crept in through the broken windows, birds and bats called the cupola home, and every wall was covered with graffiti. The late Donna Snow once remarked that "you weren't anyone unless you had written your name, the date, and who you loved on the wall. I've been privy to every love affair from 1913 to 1962." Remarkably, the vandals and curiosity seekers left the house largely intact. Of the original 718 staircase spindles, only three were missing. Just two panes were broken in the front door glass, and the only damage to two towering, gilded mirrors was a crack inflicted during a Civil War dance.

Room by room, the Snows restored Waverley to its former glory. Today it's hard to believe the opulent mansion was once an abandoned ruin. From the first-floor foyer (so spacious it doubles as a ballroom), two curved, freestanding staircases rise to join balconies on the second, third, and fourth floors. Sixteen windows surround the mansion's lofty cupola, 65 feet above the entry.

Waverley is located at 1852 Waverley Mansion Rd., 10 miles north of Columbus and 15 miles east of West Point on MS 50 near the Tombigbee River. The house is open for tours 9 a.m. to 5 p.m. Tues through Sat. Admission is $10. Call (662) 494-1399.

Twelve antebellum homes are open during the annual **Columbus Spring Pilgrimage.** In addition to the obligatory hoopskirts and blooming gardens, the Columbus extravaganza offers a look at period crafts, with demonstrations ranging from antique doll restoration to lace making to china painting staged in several of the tour houses. Pilgrimage tickets are $30 per three-home tour

Y'all Come Back Now, Ya Hear?

I've lived in Mississippi for more than thirty years now, and the natives still say they can tell I'm "not from around here." My hometown is Memphis, Tennessee—a city, it seems, that's too far north for me to have a truly southern accent.

The much-maligned, equally celebrated, and often-imitated southern drawl is as indigenous to Mississippi as grits and humidity. Visitors may poke fun at the slow, fluid pace of our speech, but can anyone really find the fast-paced, short-clipped, now-now-now! cadence of a Yankee tongue more pleasing than the soothing, melodic, drippin'-with-molasses rhythm of a genuine, southern-fried voice asking for "moah ahs tae, plase?" ("more iced tea, please?")

In the movies, the southern drawl is used as a kind of unflattering shorthand, a lazy way to characterize ignorance, poverty, or redneckism. But we southerners (even those of us from as far north as Memphis) are actually proud of our melodious, genteel drawl. Down here, slow, sultry, vowel-laden speech is a sign of good breeding, the hallmark that separates the Scarlett O'Haras from the no-count riffraff.

To us, it's the northern tongue that sounds so foreign. But be warned—one of the gravest sins a visiting northerner can commit is attempting to imitate the southern style of speech. Trust me, you aren't fooling anyone.

Of course, most Yankees are able to enjoy a visit to Mississippi without bringing along a translator. Just listen a little more slowly, and you'll be able to communicate with us just fine. But if you learn only one thing about the southern way of speaking during your visit, make it this: The word "y'all" is short for "you all" and is never, ever singular.

package (military, senior and group discounts available). Several antebellum churches that served as Civil War hospitals also open their doors for free tours during pilgrimage week. For complete information on all pilgrimage events and this year's pilgrimage dates, call the Columbus-Lowndes Convention and Visitors Bureau at (662) 329-1191 or (800) 327-2686 or go to visitcolumbusms.org.

Columbus was one of a handful of Mississippi cities never occupied by Union troops during the Civil War. In fact, the most significant war-related event in Columbus occurred on April 25, 1866, a year after the war ended. A group of war widows visiting **Odd Fellows Cemetery** decided to decorate not only the graves of their husbands and fathers but of the Union soldiers buried there as well. A newspaper account of the event read, "We are glad to see that no distinction was made between our own Confederate dead and Federal soldiers who slept their last sleep by them . . . Confederate and Federal—once enemies, now friends receiving their tribute of respect." The gesture was immortalized in a poem titled "The Blue and the Gray," which was carried in newspapers nationwide. News of the good deed of the ladies of Columbus quickly spread, spurring other communities to follow suit and earning Columbus a reputation as the city "where flowers healed a nation." This simple Decoration Day evolved into America's national Memorial Day, and the cemetery was renamed "Friendship."

Twelve Gables, the home where the ladies met to plan their Decoration Day, is sometimes open for tours during the Spring Pilgrimage. The Decoration Day itself is periodically reenacted in Friendship Cemetery. Costumed reenactors from the Stephen D. Lee Chapter of the United Daughters of the Confederacy lay flowers on the graves of soldiers who fell more than a century ago. Today, their gesture honors not only the Blue and the Gray but the four women who replaced the bitterness of war with the grace of reconciliation. For more information on the Columbus *Decoration Day Reenactment,* call (662) 329-1191 or (800) 327-2686.

Friendship Cemetery is located at the end of South Fourth Street in the South Columbus Historic District behind the Tennessee Williams Birthplace. Fourth Street is interrupted by a small warehouse district; to reach the cemetery, go 1 block over to Fifth Street and head south until Fourth Street picks up again. From Fifth Street look to your right until you spot a tall wrought-iron fence surrounding the elaborate 1800s monuments.

A stroll through the oldest section of the cemetery reveals exquisite monuments honoring loved ones of the 1800s. A few of the markers are so old their inscriptions haven't merely faded but have disappeared altogether. Several military graves are marked with swords and Confederate emblems. In the center of the cemetery, the Mississippi state flag, United States flag, and Confederate flag fly over row after row of simple markers honoring the Civil War dead. During Spring Pilgrimage, Friendship Cemetery hosts "Tales from the Crypt," a candlelight tour of the cemetery complete with costumed guides who relate true stories about Friendship's "residents," including the ladies of Decoration Day. For ticket prices and tour schedules, call (662) 329-1191 or (800) 327-2686.

Located at the edge of the South Historic District on College Street, *Mississippi University for Women* was the first state-supported women's college in the country. Organized in 1884 (and coed since 1982), "the W" campus includes twenty-four buildings listed on the National Register of Historic Places.

If you're in the market for an unusual keepsake or exquisite gift, choose a star, cross, or personalized name plaque from *Stained Glassworks, Inc.* (3067 Old West Point Rd.). Each colorful and inspirational piece is truly unique, featuring properties created not only by the studio's talented craftspeople, but by the volatile nature of the glass itself. The Stained Glassworks showroom and gift shop is open to the public Tues through Sat from 10 a.m. to 7 p.m. Tours of the workshop are available with advance notice. To watch the craftspeople at work, call (662) 329-2970 or (800) 605-2970. The studio also takes orders online at stainedglassworks.org.

Columbus is the largest city on the ***Tennessee-Tombigbee Waterway.*** Some $50 million worth of modern recreational facilities were included in the waterway's construction. Parks bordering the 234-mile Tenn-Tom offer nature trails, boat launches, charter excursions, and primitive and developed camping sites. Excellent water quality and a variety of game fish make the Tenn-Tom one of the nation's top fishing spots. Guide service is available, but finding a "honey hole" is usually easy, even for first-time anglers. For more information call the Columbus-Lowndes Convention and Visitors Bureau at or visit visitcolumbusms.org.

From Columbus take US 45 South into the tiny town of ***Brooksville*** and follow the comforting aroma of fresh-baked bread to the ***Ole Country Bakery.*** Tempting cakes, pies, and pastries line the shelves of this old-fashioned bakery operated by the Mennonites, a community similar to the Amish in their dress and lifestyle. A friendly woman clad in a flowered dress and apron and wearing the traditional black cap will take your order for warm baked goods or giant po' boy sandwiches. The bakery is open Mon through Fri from 6 a.m. to 5 p.m., and on Sat from 6 a.m. to 2 p.m., and is closed Sun. Call (662) 738-5795 or visit olecountrybakery.com.

Continue on US 45 South 9 miles to ***Macon***. Take a right onto MS 14 into downtown, turn right on Jefferson Street, and then take the first right past the Noxubee County courthouse. The imposing redbrick building on your left is the ***Noxubee County Library,*** perhaps the only library in the country with bars on the windows and a hanging gallows inside. No, it's not the world's stiffest penalty for an overdue book. The library is housed in the old town jail built in 1907. The original iron doors, window bars, and working gallows all remain; the library books are stored in the old cells. Climb the thirteen steps that lead to the gallows if you dare; the librarian promises to "come find you if you scream." Bring your camera—the librarian will loan you a black-and-white striped uniform to slip on while she snaps your mug shot. Be a convict or a bookworm Mon, Tues, Thurs, or Fri from 8 a.m. to 6 p.m. Use your one phone call to dial (662) 726-5461 for more information.

From Macon, take US 45 Alternate North to ***West Point.*** This point of the Golden Triangle is built around outdoor recreation, with many of its attractions named for nearby Waverley Plantation. You might not expect to find a championship golf course in a community of 11,000 people, but the ***Old Waverly Golf Club*** made *Golf Digest*'s list of the top one hundred courses in America. Designed by Bob Cupp and Jerry Pate, Old Waverly attracts serious players from around the country. Cottages overlooking the course are available for overnight guests. Call (662) 494-6463 or visit oldwaverly.com for rates and reservations.

Avid anglers should plan a stay at ***Waverly Waters.*** This rustic resort offers sportfishing in a seventy-acre lake stocked with largemouth bass, bluegill, and

"The Blue and the Gray"

America's Memorial Day was first celebrated in Columbus in 1866, when a group of war widows decided to decorate not only the graves of their own loved ones, but of the Union soldiers buried in Columbus as well. Their gesture was immortalized in the following poem, originally published in *The Atlantic Monthly* in September 1867.

The Blue and the Gray

By the flow of the inland river,
Where the fleets of iron have fled,
Where the blades of grave grass quiver,
Asleep are the ranks of the dead;
Under the sod and the dew,
Waiting the judgment day—
Under the one, the blue,
Under the other, the gray.
From the silence of sorrowful hours
The desolate mourners go,
Lovingly laden with flowers
Alike for the friend and the foe;
Under the sod and the dew,
Waiting the judgment day—
Under the roses, the blue
Under the lilies, the gray.
Sadly, but not with upbraiding,
The generous deed was done;
In the storm of the years that are fading,
No braver battle was won;
Under the sod and the dew,
Waiting the judgment day—
Under the blossoms, the blue,
Under the garlands, the gray.
No more shall the war-cry sever,
Or the winding rivers be red;
They banish our anger forever
When they laurel the graves of our dead;
Under the sod and the dew,
Waiting the judgment day—
Love and tears for the blue,
Tears and love for the gray.

—*Frances Miles Finch*

bream. The lake is natural, with an underwater structure of treetops, stumps, tires, and other fish habitats designed by Bill Dance. The resort also features a professionally designed sporting clay range and jogging and nature trails.

Guests stay overnight in the rustic cypress lodge or in one of five cabins. Visitors must stay overnight to fish. Call (662) 494-1800 or visit thewaverlywaters .com for lodge, cabin, and boat rental rates or reservations.

With outdoor recreation such a priority, it's only logical that *Mossy Oak,* a national leader in camouflage wear, is based in West Point. Serious hunters nationwide rely on Mossy Oak's "break-up country," "shadow grass blades," and other well-designed camo patterns to keep them out of sight while they're on the hunt. Developed by sportsman Toxey Haas, Mossy Oak camo wear is designed and manufactured in West Point. Although their clothing may blend in perfectly with its surroundings, you'll have no trouble spotting the *Mossy Oak Mall* on US 45 South.

Non-outdoorsy types can while away an hour or two exploring West Point's well-maintained city parks and a pair of museums focusing on local heritage. The *Howlin' Wolf Museum* (57 E. Westbrook St.; 662-295-8361) pays homage to West Point native and blues legend Chester "Howlin' Wolf" Burnett. By appointment only. The *Sam Y. Wilbite Transportation Museum* (5 Depot Dr.; 662-494-8910) traces the history and various modes of transportation from the 1700s to the present and is a must for railroad buffs. It is open Thurs through Sat from 10 a.m. to 5 p.m.; admission is free.

Dinnertime in West Point calls for a trip to *Anthony's* (116 W. Main St.), a grocery-store-turned-restaurant that still features the original meat coolers in the back of the main dining room. Dinner is an upscale affair, with a menu featuring seafood, steak, and poultry. Anthony's is open Tues through Thurs from 5 to 9:30 p.m., and Fri and Sat 'til 10 p.m. Call (662) 494-0316 or visit anthonysgoodfoodmarket.com.

Little-Known Facts about Mississippi

In 1839, the Mississippi legislature passed one of the first laws in the English-speaking world protecting the property rights of married women.

Mississippi was the first state in the nation with a planned system of junior colleges.

With a white-tailed deer population of two million, Mississippi boasts more white-tailed deer per capita than any other state.

Mississippi has a population of 2,872,000.

Some 78,000 Mississippians joined the Confederate military. By the Civil War's end, 59,000 were dead or wounded.

Mississippi has more certified tree farms than any other state.

TOP ANNUAL EVENTS IN THE EASTERN PLAINS

APRIL

Jimmie Rodgers Memorial Country Music Festival
Meridian
(888) 868-7720
jimmierodgersmusicfestival.com

Spring Pilgrimage/Tales from the Crypt
Columbus
(800) 327-2686

JULY

Choctaw Indian Fair
Philadelphia
(601) 650-7450
choctawindianfair.com

Neshoba County Fair
Philadelphia
(601) 656-8480
neshobacountyfair.org

SEPTEMBER

Prairie Arts Festival
West Point
(662) 494-5121
prairieartsfestival.org

Roast-n-Boast
Columbus
(662) 645-8291

The population of West Point triples on Labor Day weekend, when the *Prairie Arts Festival* brings more than 300 vendors and 30,000 festivalgoers to downtown. The high point of the festival is a juried art show, but shoppers may also choose from flea market trinkets and fine antiques. Non-shoppers enjoy live entertainment, food, and children's activities. The Prairie Arts Festival is held the Saturday before Labor Day. The Friday night prior to the Prairie Arts Festival, West Point hosts the *Black Prairie Blues Festival,* a tribute to the West Point native and blues legend. For more information visit blackprairie bluesfestival.com.

From West Point, take US 82 West to *Starkville,* the final point on the Golden Triangle and the home of *Mississippi State University.* Take the downtown exit, turn left on Main Street, and then head straight onto the sprawling campus. The state's largest university, MSU is a national leader in agricultural research. If a groundbreaking soybean study doesn't excite you, how about wine making? A tour of the *A. B. McKay Food and Enology Laboratory* takes wine lovers through the entire process from grapes to glass and concludes with a sampling of Mississippi muscadine juices.

Get a close-up-and-personal look at the world of creepy-crawlers at the *Mississippi Entomology Museum,* which features the third largest insect collection in the Southeast. A tour of the *Dunn-Seiler Earth Science Museum* may not be quite as exciting as a ride through Jurassic Park, but you will see a real triceratops skull and a saber-toothed tiger head.

"Starkville City Jail"

In the mid-1960s, *Johnny Cash* performed a concert at Mississippi State University. Afterward, he went back to his motel and had a few drinks, then decided to go out for smokes.

Maybe it was the few drinks or the intricacies of locating smokes in an unfamiliar town, but Cash wound up parked in a local family's flowerbed. On any other night the family might have been flattered by the country star's unexpected detour, but their daughter had planned to use the ill-fated flowers in her upcoming wedding and was most distraught to find them flattened.

Cash spent the remainder of his visit to Starkville in the city jail. But far from being humbled by the experience, Cash capitalized on his run-in with the local law, penning a tune called "Starkville City Jail." Cash soon returned to Starkville to sign copies of his new album, bringing with him gifts for the entire Starkville police force.

Don't leave campus without a hefty ball of Mississippi State's own Edam cheese. Manufactured at the dairy science plant on campus, this smooth, flavorful cheese is sold in one-, two-, and three-pound balls wrapped in red wax bearing the official university seal. Mississippi State cheese is sold by mail to Edam lovers around the world and in the Cheese Sales Office in the *Herzer Dairy Science Building.* The Herzer building is located on the campus on Stone Boulevard. The famous cheese is also available online at msucheese.com or by calling (662) 325-2338.

The *John Grisham Room* in the university's Mitchell Memorial Library houses the best-selling author's papers and publications. The collection includes literary manuscripts, legislative files, photos, signed works, and other materials from the popular author, including the original manuscript for his first novel *A Time To Kill.*

To schedule a tour of any or all of the university's laboratories or galleries, call (662) 323-3322.

Of course, there's more to life in a college town than just academics. Mississippi State brings the excitement of Southeastern Conference sports to Starkville, fielding teams in basketball, baseball, and football. In recent years, MSU has become a destination for women's college basketball fans with attendance at the Lady Bulldogs games ranked among the top ten in the nation. Game days at MSU are marked not only by tailgate parties and pom-poms, but also by the incessant clanging of cowbells, a tradition dating back to the university's days as an agricultural college.

The Natchez Trace Parkway

This section of the legendary **Natchez Trace Parkway** includes three major stops and dozens of smaller historic sites marked by the familiar brown and yellow signs. Don't let the European flair of town names like "French Camp" and "Kosciusko" fool you. This leg of the parkway still retains the frontier charm for which the route is famous.

From Starkville, continue on US 82 West approximately 20 miles to Eupora, where US 82 intersects the Natchez Trace. Head south on the Trace to mile marker 193.1 and **Jeff Busby Park**, a national park named for Congressman Thomas Jefferson Busby, who introduced the bill calling for the surveying of the Old Natchez Trace and the creation of the modern parkway.

Jeff Busby features nature trails, campsites, picnic areas, and a panoramic 20-mile view from the overlook atop Little Mountain, one of the highest points in Mississippi. A well-marked nature trail identifies native plants and describes their use as foods and medicines by early settlers. Be warned—the trail looks deceptively easy but will definitely leave you winded and ready for a cool drink from the convenience store at the park entrance. If you plan to continue along the Natchez Trace from here, gas up now. The service station at Jeff Busby is the only one located directly on the parkway.

Continue on the parkway 12 miles south of Jeff Busby to **French Camp**, a charming little village established in 1812. Nearly 200 years later, French Camp is still best described as a peaceful settlement on the rural frontier. Attractions just off the Natchez Trace include the 1846 **Colonel James Drane Plantation House**, a working blacksmith studio, and a sorghum mill that operates in the fall. The **French Camp Academy Historical Museum** displays tools, clothing, books, newspaper clippings, a 400-year-old Bible, a 1932 class ring, and dozens of photos and artifacts documenting the area's century-plus history as a Christian educational center. The French Camp information center and a gift shop selling sorghum, preserves, quilts, yard art, and other handicrafts are housed in an 1846 log cabin. And if you're strolling the settlement at noon, you'll be blessed by the peal of bells and joyous music emanating from the 1874 white clapboard **French Camp Baptist Church**.

Noon is also an excellent time to try the soup and sandwiches at the **Council House Cafe**, located in an authentic Choctaw Indian council house of the 1820s. Choose a table next to the fireplace, pull up a ladder-back chair, and sink your teeth into the best BLT you'll ever put in your mouth. The French Camp historic area is generally open 9 a.m. to 4 p.m. Mon through Sat. The cafe is open from 10:30 a.m. to 7 p.m. For more information, including a sorghum-making schedule, call (662) 547-9860.

A boardwalk leads from the Colonel Drane House to the **French Camp Academy Bed and Breakfast Inn**, a quiet frontier lodge where Daniel Boone would feel right at home. Made from two one-hundred-year-old hand-hewn log houses, the inn offers a wide back porch overlooking the Natchez Trace Parkway. When the tourists have left for the day and the sun sets slowly over the quiet Natchez Trace, it doesn't require too much imagination to picture a friendly Indian or weary trapper or missionary wandering up the road to become the inn's next guest. The ambience may be rustic, but rest assured the rooms are quite comfortable and modern. Rates begin at $110. Call (662) 547-6835 for reservations.

This tranquil setting is also home to the **French Camp Academy** boarding school. Marked by a sign reading "the heavens declare the glory of god," the academy's **Rainwater Observatory** houses the largest telescope in Mississippi. Gaze into the heavens through one of 25 powerful telescopes, five of which are designed for daytime viewing. A small planetarium offers educational programs for groups as large as thirty. Call (662) 547-7283 to schedule a free visit and a look at the stars.

Back on the Trace 20 miles south of French Camp, you'll spot the sign directing you to the **Kosciusko Museum and Information Center**. Kosciusko began as a community of taverns and inns established to serve travelers on the Old Natchez Trace. Listed in Norm Crampton's *The 100 Best Small Towns in America*, Kosciusko still welcomes visitors today.

Originally known as Redbud Springs, the town's name was changed to the easy-to-remember but impossible-to-spell "Kosciusko" in the late 1830s. The state representative in charge of choosing the name recalled an ancestor's colorful tales about Thaddeus Kosciuszko, a Polish engineer who served on George Washington's staff during the Revolutionary War. Kosciuszko never visited Mississippi, yet the town was named in his honor (minus the z), and the most prominent display in the Kosciusko Museum and Information Center is a life-size wax statue of the Polish freedom fighter. Dirt from Kosciuszko's grave in Krakow, Poland, was used in landscaping the town of Kosciusko's **Redbud Springs Park**.

The friendly volunteers at the information center (located at 124 N. Jackson St.) will be happy to tell you more about Kosciusko's history and to provide you with a walking and driving tour brochure showcasing the city's lovely Victorian architecture and numerous historic sites. Use caution exiting the information center—the peace and tranquility of the Natchez Trace gives way to a major highway bypass just off the property, and the sudden increase in traffic can be startling.

To avoid the traffic, take a right onto the bypass from the information center and then turn left onto Jefferson Street. Continue on Jefferson into downtown and then take a right on Huntington Street to the **Kosciusko City Cemetery**. Take the BoBo Street entrance into the cemetery; then continue straight until you come upon a stone woman in Victorian dress in the center of the Kelly family plot.

When Laura Kelly died in 1890, her devastated husband sent her photo and favorite clothing to a renowned sculptor in Italy, asking that the artist immortalize his beautiful wife in stone. The Kellys' house was under construction at the time of Laura's death, and her grieving husband's next instruction was to the builder. Mr. Kelly ordered a third story be added to the house so that he could look out across the cemetery and see the statue of his beloved wife gazing back at him. The **Kelly-Jones-Ivy House** still stands at 309 E. Jefferson St., though it's no longer visible from the statue site.

As you return to Huntington Street via BoBo Street, look to your left for a white marker labeled "Mother" and "Father." The names of Mr. and Mrs. W. E. Burdine's nineteen children are inscribed on the marker between their graves. With so many offspring, the prolific Burdines seem to have run out of names toward the end. Child number 17 was christened simply, "Seventeen."

As you leave the cemetery, turn left onto Huntington Street and then continue past the Jefferson Street intersection to the **Mary Ricks Thornton Cultural Center**. Built in 1898, this beautiful Gothic structure once served as a Presbyterian church, then fell into disrepair after years of abandonment and neglect. The building was destined for demolition until the late Mary Ricks Thornton spearheaded a campaign to save it, explaining that she became involved in the restoration because, "I was married in this church in 1930, and I couldn't bear to have it torn down for a parking lot."

After months of fundraising, the Kosciusko-Attala Historical Society purchased the building and restored it for use as a cultural center. The center features ornate stained-glass windows and unusual white-over-wood pews, curved to give every churchgoer a view of the pulpit. One of the stained-glass windows is dedicated to Laura Kelly, of statuary fame. The center also features a Delta Gamma room, honoring the three Kosciusko natives and Presbyterian church members who founded the national sorority in 1873. The building hosts performances, weddings, meetings, and other events, and is open for tours by appointment. For more information call (662) 289-2981.

Wrap up a tour of Kosciusko with a visit to the area where the town's most famous native, **Oprah Winfrey**, spent her childhood. Although her birthplace is no longer standing, fans can visit the spot where Oprah gave her first public performance; at a church in the Buffalo community, Oprah recited the Easter story. Buffalo Road, now Oprah Winfrey Road, makes a loop off MS 12 and passes the church (now the Buffalo Community Center), as well as Oprah's family cemetery and the site of her birthplace.

Reservations and Rails

If you expect to find Native Americans only "out west," you'll be surprised to stumble upon an Indian reservation here in the deep South. The legends and traditions of the Mississippi Band of Choctaw Indians dominate the culture in this part of the state, reminding visitors that Mississippi history did not begin on a cotton plantation or a Civil War battlefield.

Farther south near Meridian, history is forever intertwined with the railroad. The iron horses brought east Mississippi's first settlers, whose descendants still walk its streets today.

Leave the Natchez Trace Parkway at Kosciusko and take MS 35 South to **Carthage**, then follow MS 16 East toward **Philadelphia** and the **Choctaw Indian Reservation.** If you were expecting the Hollywood version of an Indian village, you're in for a surprise. The Choctaw are savvy businesspeople who've brought industry, commerce, and a comfortable lifestyle to their reservation. The tribe's most spectacular venture, the multimillion-dollar **Pearl River Resort,** rises from the red dirt prairie just west of Philadelphia on MS 16. Anchored by two dazzling casinos, the **Silver Star** and the **Golden Moon,** the resort also encompasses two luxury hotels, two award-winning golf courses, a $20 million water park, a nightly laser light and dancing water show, a full-service spa, live entertainment, restaurants, upscale shops and boutiques, and dozens of other diversions and amenities.

The members of the tribe residing on the reservation are descendants of the Choctaw who refused to leave their homeland following the 1830 Treaty of Dancing Rabbit, which ceded the last of Choctaw native land to the United States. Rather than relocate to Indian lands in the West, this small group of proud, determined Choctaw struggled against poverty and segregation to preserve their traditional culture on their native land.

Choctaw history before the coming of the "white man" and the tribe's subsequent struggles and triumphs are depicted in the **Chahta Immi Cultural Center,** a collection of exhibits and archives relating the tribe's long history in Mississippi, which dates back to the time of Christ. Located off MS 16 West, the museum is open Tues through Sat from 10 a.m. to 5 p.m. If you're near the reservation in July, stop for the **Choctaw Indian Fair,** a celebration of Native American culture that includes traditional dancing, crafts, stickball games,

Mississippi's Giant House Party

The first thing you'll notice as you approach the **Neshoba County Fairgrounds** are the houses—600 whimsical, crayon-colored cabins, most looking as though nothing more than good luck is holding them together. These ramshackle structures have usually been in the same family for generations and have been the subject of divorce disputes and contested wills on more than one occasion. The original cabins on "Founder's Square" are prime pieces of real estate, selling for as much as $100,000 each.

The price tag is only mildly astounding until you realize that for 51 weeks out of the year, the cabins are boarded up and the fairgrounds are deserted: That $100,000 is spent to enjoy a mere seven days at the fair in August. For that one week, the fair-grounds are jumping with a full-blown midway, harness races, musical acts, and the crowning of a teenage queen. The Neshoba County Fair is also famous for political stumping, attracting candidates for every office from dogcatcher to president of the United States.

Above all else, the Neshoba County Fair is famous for its hospitality. Many of the cabins have hosted overnight guests since the first Neshoba County Fair in 1889. Strangers will invite you to join them for lunch or lemonade on the front porch, or even to pass the night in one of the Technicolor cabins (be sure to choose one with air-conditioning—a nontraditional indulgence considered a fair faux pas as few as 15 years ago). This rare display of universal hospitality has earned the fair the nickname "Mississippi's Giant House Party." For this year's dates, call the Community Develop-ment Partnership at (601) 656-1000 or (877) 752-2643, or visit neshobacountyfair .org. Dress comfortably and bring a handheld fan.

foods, and entertainment. For this year's Choctaw Indian Fair dates, call the museum at (601) 650-7450 or visit choctawindianfair.com.

The land around Philadelphia is sacred to the Choctaw for good reason. According to Indian legend, the entire Choctaw Nation was born at the **Nanih Waiya Historic Site,** an ancient area marked by ceremonial Indian mounds and a sacred cave 20 miles north of Philadelphia off MS 21. The Choctaw refer to the large mound at the site as the "Mother Mound." During the mass Indian exodus that followed the Treaty of Dancing Rabbit, the Choctaw who remained in Mississippi vowed "never to leave their mother as long as she stood." A flight of steep, wooden stairs leads to the top of the Mother Mound, transporting visitors to an ancient world of myth and legend. Even in the hot stillness of a summer day, it's easy to imagine the ancient Choctaw ceremonies, to hear the beat of drums and smell the smoke of campfires.

The Nanih Waiya site includes a picnic area overlooking a cypress swamp and a park office directly across from the Mother Mound. Ask at the office for directions to the cave mound, marked by legend as the very spot where the first

Mississippi Burning

The most infamous chapter in Mississippi history unfolded in the summer of 1964, when three civil rights workers vanished in rural Neshoba County.

James Chaney, **Andrew Goodman**, and **Michael Schwerner** disappeared on June 21, 1964, while investigating the burning of a black church near Philadelphia. Forty-four days later, a still-unidentified informant led the FBI to their bodies, buried in an earthen dam just outside town. All three had been shot.

In 1967, after Mississippi officials failed to prosecute Ku Klux Klansmen suspected in the murders, a jury in federal court convicted seven men of conspiracy to violate the civil rights of the victims; none served more than six years in prison. After a reinvestigation, Edgar Ray Killen, a former Ku Klux Klansman, was convicted in 2005 of manslaughter in the deaths of the three civil rights workers. Killen died in prison in 2018.

Today, a monument honoring James Chaney, Andrew Goodman, and Michael Schwerner graces the grounds of Mt. Zion Church off MS 16 East in Neshoba County—the same place where the three young men gave their lives for the cause they believed in, and forever changed the future of the state where they died.

Choctaw Indian entered the world. The cave is partially hidden in a wooded area. It's possible to step inside, but the cave floor is muddy and dark, and spelunking is not encouraged. For more information on the Mississippi Band of Choctaw Indians, including their history, culture, and businesses, visit choctaw.org.

Philadelphia's heritage doesn't stop with the Choctaw. A self-guided driving-tour brochure of historic homes and architecture and an African-American Heritage driving-tour brochure are available by calling the Community Development Partnership at (601) 656-1000 or (877) 752-2643, and the *Neshoba County-Philadelphia Historical Museum* (303 Water Ave.) displays artifacts related to local history. But the town is most famous as the site of one of America's most unusual gatherings, the Neshoba County Fair (see sidebar, "Mississippi's Giant House Party").

On your way out of town, pick up a slice of hoop cheese and some slab bacon at the *Williams Brothers Store.* Founded in 1907, Williams Brothers still retains the old-fashioned charm that led *National Geographic* to feature the "needles to horse collars" emporium in a 1937 issue. Located at 10360 CR 375 off MS 16 west of Philadelphia, Williams Brothers is open Mon through Sat from 7 a.m. to 6 p.m. Call (601) 656-2651.

Take MS 39 South to *Meridian,* a historic railroad town and bustling industrial center. Occupying almost 60,000 square feet smack in the middle of downtown and built at a cost of more than $50 million, *The Mississippi*

Arts and Entertainment Experience, better known as *The MAX*, can't really be considered "off the beaten path," but a visit there will introduce you to little-known sides of Mississippi and some of the state's famous natives. This interactive, immersive experience invites visitors to take a virtual tour of Mississippi's rivers and hidden waterways in an open boat or create a virtual meal in an old-fashioned kitchen with some of the state's famous chefs. Visitors can throw virtual pots or paint virtual paintings, or use a "fantasy football" approach to build a band made up of Mississippi musicians from different eras and hear them perform together.

The MAX is also the place to learn more about famous Mississippians. For example, did you know that Darth Vader had a stutter? That's right, Mississippian James Earl Jones, who provided the voice for *Star Wars'* enduring antihero and for Mufasa of *The Lion King* had such a bad stutter as a child he didn't speak at all for eight years; acting gave him back his powerful voice. The MAX is full of little-known stories about actors, entertainers, musicians, writers, and other Mississippians who overcome the odds to become internationally famous and to build Mississippi's incredible creative legacy. Discover the stories behind the stories at The MAX, located at the corner of Front Street and 22nd Avenue. For more information, call (601) 581-1550 or visit msarts.org.

As you continue your drive around Meridian, you'll notice colorful carousel horses—more than 60—prancing in front of businesses citywide. The 5-foot fiberglass horses are part of the city's *Around Town Carousels Abound* program, a public art project inspired by the city's Dentzel Carousel. Each whimsical, rainbow-hued sculpture was sponsored by a Meridian individual or business, then decorated by a local or regional artist. Artists were given a stipend to cover materials, but donated their time and talents. Proceeds from the sponsorships benefited Hope Village for Children, a shelter founded by Meridian native and actor Sela Ward. Each horse was given a distinctive theme and name. You'll find "Horseplay" on the lawn of the Meridian Little Theatre, "Lightning" in front of the fire station, and "Horsecents" outside the local bank.

You Can Take the Girl Out of Meridian . . .

Golden Globe and two-time Emmy winner *Sela Ward* grew up in Meridian and still maintains a home in the area. Ward has proved a driving force in her hometown, spearheading renovation efforts at Meridian's Grand Opera House and founding Hope Village, a shelter for abused, neglected, and homeless children. If you miss Sela Ward's latest TV or movie project, look for her in reruns of the critically acclaimed television shows *Sisters*, *Once and Again*, and *House*.

The Father of Country Music

Meridian was the home of *Jimmie Rodgers*, the Father of Country Music. Born in Meridian in 1897, Rodgers recorded his first song in 1927. "Sleep, Baby, Sleep" sold more than a million copies and earned Rodgers national fame as an entertainer. Tragically, Rodgers was stricken with tuberculosis at the height of his career. In 1933, he recorded his last songs, performing from a cot set up in the studio. He died the day after he recorded his last song at age 36. In 1961, Jimmie Rodgers became the first inductee into the newly formed Country Music Hall of Fame.

At the time of this writing, Meridian's popular *Jimmie Rodgers Museum* was housed in a temporary location while its permanent home was under renovation. For current information, contact Visit Meridian at (888) 868-7720.

For a whirl on the carousel that inspired all this horseplay, follow I-20/59 to the Twenty-second Avenue exit, turn left on Eighth Street, and follow the signs to *Highland Park* (Forty-first Ave. and Nineteenth St.). Since 1909, Meridian's children (and more than a few adults) have flocked to the park for a spin on the rare *Dentzel Carousel.* Hand-carved, hand-painted ponies, goats, deer, giraffes, and lions whirl to cheerful circus music, accompanied

Meridian's Own Phantom of the Opera

The curtain first rose on Meridian's *Grand Opera House* on Fifth Street in 1890. Nicknamed "The Lady" after the hand-painted portrait of an unidentified "Gibson Girl" on the proscenium above the stage, this palatial theater hosted the finest talent in the country. Touring opera and Shakespearean companies, vaudeville shows, and minstrel acts all took the stage at the lavish Grand Opera House.

After 37 years of theatrical magic, the Grand Opera House closed, but it seems one of the performers never left. While the doors were kept locked and the curtain was down, a beautiful melody often rang through the empty theater—the crystal-clear voice of a woman singing. The sound seemed to come from the empty stage, behind the portrait of the unidentified Gibson Girl. Visitors to the long-dark theater reported cold spots on blistering summer days, the low murmur of a voice backstage, and the sound of shattering crystal—perhaps the spirit of a long-gone diva, practicing for her next performance. Over time, the ghost has also come to be known as "The Lady."

After a $25 million renovation, the Grand Opera House reopened in 2006 as part of the MSU Riley Center for the Performing Arts. In a nod to the Lady, the Meridan Carousels project includes a horse named "Lady" that prances across Fifth Street in Dumont Plaza facing the Riley Center. A silhouette of "The Lady" is reflected in the horse's eye, giving the impression that the horse is seeing the ghostly diva.

by the delighted shrieks and high-pitched giggles of children and grown-ups alike. The carousel was built by Gustav Dentzel in 1895. Meridian's city fathers bought the carousel for $2,000 in 1909 and built the present carousel house following a Dentzel blueprint. About twenty Dentzel carousels exist in the United States, but the Highland Park carousel is one of only a handful still populated by the original animals, and is the only two-row, stationary Dentzel menagerie carousel in existence. The carousel spins Saturdays year-round; also open Sun in Apr, May, and Aug through Oct; daily in June and July. Find out more at visitmeridian.com/index.cfm/play/all-play/dentzel-carousel. The price of a ride has gone up from the original nickel to fifty cents—a worthwhile investment for the nostalgic pleasure a ride is sure to bring.

Meridian offers tours of two historic homes, ***Merrehope*** and the ***F. W. Williams House,*** both located at 905 Martin Luther King Jr. Memorial Dr. Call (601) 483-8439 or visit merrehope.com for tour information. Be sure to inquire about Eugenia, Merrehope's resident ghost. Eugenia Gary died in Alabama just before her father purchased Merrehope in 1868. But if the stories are true, Eugenia moved into the house anyway—and continues to live there today. Several Merrehope visitors and employees have reported seeing a young woman in period dress moving about the house or gazing out the windows. All of the witnesses identified the specter as the same young woman whose portrait hangs in the museum room upstairs. The girl in the portrait is Eugenia Gary.

Those interested in Mississippi's civil rights and African-American heritage may wish to pay respects at the gravesite of James Chaney. Along with fellow civil rights workers Andrew Goodman and Michael Schwerner, Chaney gave

The King and Queen of the Gypsies

The events that brought **Kelly Mitchell**, the Queen of the Gypsies, to Meridian's **Rose Hill Cemetery** for burial in 1915 are unknown; some sources speculate that Meridian was the closest facility with adequate refrigeration to preserve her body while news of her death was sent to Romani people so they could travel to her funeral. Whatever the reason, it was in Meridian that the queen laid in state for 12 days while Romani people gathered from around United States for her funeral. When the hearse headed out to Rose Hill Cemetery, an estimated 5,000 mourners followed. When **Emil Mitchell**, the King of the Gypsies, died years later, he was buried next to his wife.

Today, the royal graves are visited frequently by people who leave fresh fruit and juices as a sign of respect. If you visit the graves at Rose Hill Cemetery (Fortieth Ave. off Eighth St.) yourself, be sure to bring along some fruit and fresh-squeezed juice as your own tribute.

mississippitrivia

Meridian's *E. F. Young Manu-facturing Company* is the oldest African-American-owned company in the United States. The firm was founded in 1933 by E. F. Young, a barber who developed and pat-ented one of the world's first lines of black hair-care products.

his life for the civil rights cause in 1964 (see sidebar, "Mississippi Burning," ear-lier in this chapter). When local black burial grounds refused to inter Chaney's body for fear of reprisals and vandal-ism, he was finally laid to rest in an isolated grave in the Okatibbee Baptist Church Cemetery in southwest Lauder-dale County. On the 25th anniversary of his death, a marble monument was erected at his grave. Chaney's marker bears the inscription, "There are those who are alive, yet will never live. there are those who are dead, yet will live forever. Great deeds inspire and encour-age the living." To get to the cemetery from I-20/59, take exit 151 (Valley Road). Travel 3.4 miles and then turn left at the church on Fish Lodge Road. The cemetery is on the right.

The cemetery is one of many sites on the ***Meridan Civil Rights Trail***, unveiled in 2014 during festivities honoring the 50th anniversary of Freedom Summer. The trail has markers at 18 sites, including James Chaney's grave and the courthouse where the "Mississippi Burning" trial took place. For more infor-mation, visit visitmeridian.com.

Little-Known Facts about the Eastern Plains

Columbus was originally christened "Possum Town" in a dubious tribute to early set-tler Spirus Roach, who bore an unfortunate resemblance to an opossum.

Before putting down roots on the Mississippi State University campus, a sycamore tree planted outside the university's Dorman Hall flew to the moon on an Apollo mis-sion as a sapling.

At its height in the early 1800s, the Mississippi Choctaw nation included fifty villages and more than 25,000 warriors. The word Choctaw means "charming voice."

Famed hatmaker *John B. Stetson* honed his skills at Dunn's Falls near Meridian. It was here the haberdasher designed his most popular creation, a men's hat known simply as "the Stetson."

Columbus's Sanderson Plumbing Products, Inc., is the exclusive supplier of toilet seats for the space shuttle.

The Mississippi School for Math and Science is one of only four state-supported resi-dential high schools for academically talented students in the nation.

Old Man Stucky's Ghost

A man named **Stucky** once ran an inn in the small community of Savoy near Dunn's Falls. Stucky was rumored to have been a member of the infamous Dalton gang. Unable to put his wicked ways behind him, he robbed and murdered as many as twenty of his patrons, burying his victims beneath a wooden bridge over the Chunky River. When his dastardly deeds were discovered, Stucky was hanged from the bridge, which came to be known as both The Hanging Bridge and Stucky's Bridge.

What became of Stucky's ill-gotten treasure isn't certain, but according to local legend and frightened witnesses, Stucky is still searching for it. The tale of **Old Man Stucky** may be shrouded in mystery, but one thing is clear—if your travels bring you to Stucky's Bridge in Savoy after dark, and if you see the swinging glow of a kerosene lantern crossing the bridge, the smartest thing for you to do is run.

Commemorate your visit to Meridian with a treasure from **Crooked Letter** (1020 Front St.), a downtown shop specializing in Mississippi-made products. Then admire your purchases over dinner around the corner at **Weidmann's Restaurant** (210 Twenty-second Ave.; 601-581-5770). This Meridian tradition began in 1870, when Swiss immigrant Felix Weidmann established a fruit and vegetable stand on this same downtown corner. As the business grew, Weidmann expanded his offerings and his property, until Weidmann's Restaurant evolved into one of the area's most popular eateries. The restaurant outlived its founder; while ownership has changed hands a few times, the restaurant has been continuously in business since 1870. For more information visit weidmanns1870.com.

If you're staying in Meridian overnight, consider a southern bed-and-breakfast with an English and Irish flair at **The Lion and Harp** (4432 State Blvd.). For rates and reservations at this lovely Victorian inn, call (601) 485-8235 or visit lionandharp.com. A neoclassical beauty overlooking the city, the 1902 **Century House Bed and Breakfast** (2412 Ninth St.) offers bed-and-breakfast accommodations within walking distance of several Meridian attractions. Call (601) 479-4291 or visit centuryhousebnb.com.

From the Meridian area, take I-59 South 11 miles to the Savoy exit at Enterprise, then follow the signs to **Dunn's Falls Water Park.** This crystal-clear 65-foot waterfall once served as a power source for a gristmill and for the manufacturing of Stetson hats. The historic Carroll Richardson Gristmill, complete with working waterwheel, is open for tours. Dunn's Falls also features a swimming area in the old millpond, hiking trails, campsites, and picnic areas with grills. Call (601) 655-8550 for seasonal hours and admission prices.

Continue on US 45 South to *Quitman* and another famous swimmin' hole, the *Archusa Creek Water Park* (540 CR 110; 601-776-6956 or 800-748-9403). Archusa Springs was a popular resort of the 1800s built around a "medicinal" sulfur spring. Located near the Civil War–era Texas Hospital, the spring was frequented by recuperating soldiers. The hospital and resort were destroyed by Union troops in 1864. A Texas Hospital memorial marker and Confederate cemetery are located 2 miles south of Quitman on US 45. The spring still flows into Archusa Lake today, and analyses reveal the water is still high in sulfur. Nearby Archusa Creek Water Park offers rustic cabin rentals and outdoor recreational activities in a wilderness setting.

In September, the water park hosts the annual *Clarke County Forestry and Wildlife Festival*, featuring arts and crafts, food, and live entertainment. Outdoorsy types will also enjoy a float trip down the *Chickasawhay River.* Information on cabin rentals at the park, the festival, and canoe rentals is available from the Clarke County Chamber of Commerce, (601) 776-5701. The chamber also offers a free brochure for a self-guided driving tour of lovely homes, a historic mill town, and other sites listed on the National Register of Historic Places. Call for your copy or pick one up at the chamber offices at 100 S. Railroad Ave.

Places to Stay in the Eastern Plains

COLUMBUS

Amzi Love
305 Seventh St. South
(662) 328-5413

Shadowlawn
1024 College St.
(662) 327-3600 or
(662) 425-2831
shadowlawncolumbus.com

KOSCIUSKO

The Maple Terrace Inn
300 N. Huntington St.
(662) 289-4131 or
(662) 792-9010 (after hours)
mapleterraceinn.com

PHILADELPHIA

Pearl River Resort
MS 16 West
(on the Choctaw Indian Reservation)
(866) 447-3275
pearlriverresort.com

STARKVILLE

Historic Hotel Chester
101 N. Jackson St.
(662) 323-5005 or
(866) 325-5005
historichotelchester.com

Places to Eat in the Eastern Plains

COLUMBUS

J. Broussard's
210 Fifth St. South
(662) 243-1480
jbroussards.com
New Orleans–style food

Proffitt's Porch
1587 Officer's Lake Rd.
(662) 327-4485
Po'boys, red beans and
rice, seafood gumbo,
homemade desserts

Thai by Thai
509 Main St.
(662) 327-4001
Thai

Zachary's
205 N. 5th St.
(662) 240-0101
American

KOSCIUSKO

Seasonings Catering & Eatery
307 N. Jackson St.
(662) 289-5244
Daily Southern menu
served in a historic home

PHILADELPHIA

Lump's Atomic Dog
274 Beacon St.
(601) 562-1309
Chicago-style hot dogs,
burgers, fries

Silver Star and Golden Moon casinos
13550 MS-16
(866) 447-3275
pearlriverresort.com
Offer several restaurants
ranging from coffee shops
to all-you-can-eat buffets to
fine dining

Ye Ole Deli
509 Main St.
(601) 656-7719
Sandwiches, old-fashioned
soda fountain treats

STARKVILLE

The Little Dooey
100 Fellowship St.
(662) 323-6094
littledooey.com
Barbecue

Oby's Deli
504 Academy Rd.
(662) 323-0444
Sandwiches, gumbo, red
beans and rice

The Veranda
208 Lincoln Green
(662) 323-1231
verandastarkville.com
Steaks, seafood

ALSO WORTH SEEING

Meridian Museum of Art, Meridian

Roosevelt State Park, Morton

Dancing Rabbit Golf Course, Philadelphia

Geyser Falls Water Park, Philadelphia

The Mississippi River Delta

According to writer David Cohen, "the Mississippi Delta begins in the lobby of the Peabody Hotel in Memphis and ends on Catfish Row in Vicksburg." Home to the richest farmland on earth, the Delta is a land and a people shaped by agriculture and ruled by the Mississippi River, a place where cotton was once king and its subjects sang the blues.

Cohen's statement may be geographically accurate, but a real description of the Delta reaches beyond mere geography. The Delta is not just a place, but a mind-set. Natives of the area will tell you that you can never really understand the Delta culture unless you were born into it, and you'll soon find that's not an exaggeration.

Some people can't bear a moment in this hot, flat land; others would wither up and die if they had to leave it. As you travel the Delta's back roads and get acquainted with its people and with the land itself, you can decide for yourself which group you belong to.

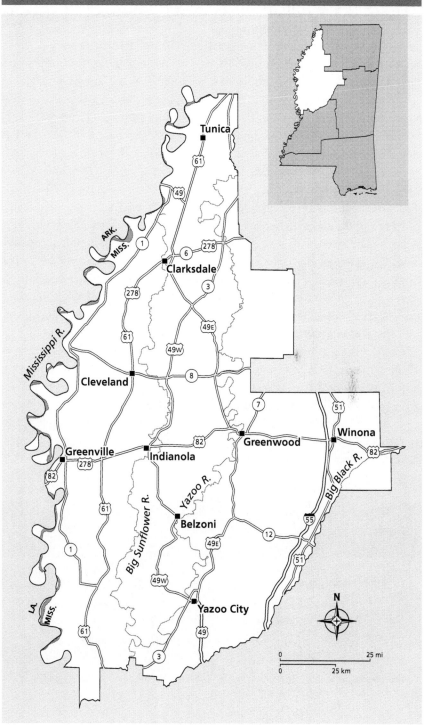

Blues Alley

Once the poorest county in the entire United States, **Tunica County** is now a tourist resort fueled by the nonstop action of casino gaming. The former agricultural villages of Tunica and Robinsonville are now a Vegas-style gambling destination. Of course, cotton is still planted right up to the slot machines, and the towering resorts share the Delta skyline with passing crop dusters.

Your first Blues Alley stop should be **The Hollywood Café** off US 61 in tiny **Robinsonville.** Housed in an 1860s plantation commissary, The Hollywood is mentioned in John Grisham's best-selling novel *The Firm* and in Mark Cohn's Grammy-winning song "Walking in Memphis." A native of New York, Cohn frequented The Hollywood Café whenever he was in the mid-South, often taking the stage to sing with Muriel the piano player. Not only did Cohn write the late Muriel into the song, he flew her to New York to play at his wedding. The Hollywood is open for lunch and dinner, serving up seafood, steaks, frog legs, catfish, and its famous fried dill pickles. The restaurant occasionally features live entertainment. The Hollywood is located at 1585 Old Commerce Rd. Call (662) 363-1225 or visit thehollywoodcafe.com for open days and times.

The **Gateway to the Blues Museum & Visitor Center** (13625 Hwy. 61 N.) is the place to begin a blues tour. Located on legendary Blues Highway 61 in a rustic 1890s train depot, the Gateway tells the remarkable story of how the blues was born and the role the Delta played in building the genre's legacy. You'll experience interactive exhibits, artwork, and more—including a recording studio where you'll learn the basics of blues music with a chance to record your own blues tune. For more information, call (888) 488-6422 or visit tunicatravel.com/blues.

AUTHOR'S FAVORITE ATTRACTIONS IN THE MISSISSIPPI RIVER DELTA

Cotton in bloom, as far as the eye can see

Catfish Pâté at **Crown Restaurant and Antique Mall**, Indianola

Doe's Eat Place, Greenville

Glenwood Cemetery, Final resting place of the Witch of Yazoo, Yazoo City

McCarty Pottery, Merigold

Cheese straws from the **Mississippi Cheese Straw Factory**, Yazoo City

Natural kudzu sculptures, just outside Yazoo City

Shack Up Inn, Clarksdale

Famous Deltans

Blues artists born in the Mississippi Delta include: Sam Chatmon, Billy Deaton, John Lee Hooker, Son House, Mississippi John Hurt, Skip James, Robert Johnson, B. B. King, Charlie Patton, Otis Spann, James "Son" Thomas, Ike Turner, Muddy Waters, Bukka White, and Sonny Boy Williamson.

The Delta was also home to a couple of country music stars. Sledge, Mississippi, was the birthplace of Charley Pride. Harold Jenkins, better known as Conway Twitty, grew up in tiny Friars Point.

The Reverend C. L. Franklin preached in Friars Point; his daughter, Aretha, was a member of the church choir.

Academy Award–winning actor Morgan Freeman, known for his roles in *Driving Miss Daisy*, *The Shawshank Redemption*, *Million Dollar Baby*, and *Invictus*, grew up in Tallahatchie County and still owns a farm in Charleston. Freeman is the owner of the **Ground Zero Blues Club**, a down-and-dirty, all-around-good-time juke joint in Clarksdale.

Food writer and former *New York Times* food editor Craig Claiborne grew up on home cookin' in the tiny town of Sunflower.

The late author Willie Morris immortalized his hometown of Yazoo City in his books *Good Old Boy* and *My Dog Skip*. Hollywood's version of *My Dog Skip* became an instant family classic.

Motivational speaker Zig Ziglar and the late comedian Jerry Clower also hailed from Yazoo City.

Pioneer TV producer Fred Coe was born in Alligator, Mississippi. Coe produced the 1950s live TV dramas *The Trip to Bountiful*, *Days of Wine and Roses*, and *Peter Pan*.

Just a few minutes' drive but a world away from the hustle and glitz of the casinos lies the quiet town of ***Tunica.*** Here visitors can stroll the peaceful streets of the turn-of-the-twentieth-century downtown area, browse the antiques and gift shops, or visit the restored ***Tunica County Courthouse,*** where the original marriage license of bluesman Robert Johnson is displayed. For an in-depth look at Tunica County before the casinos, visit the ***Tunica Museum,*** where exhibits focus on agriculture, music, and the county's famous sons and daughters. Step into the past at One Museum Blvd. (off US 61, north of Paul Battle Arena) in Tunica. Call (662) 363-6631.

Even before the casinos sprang up out of the cotton fields, the ***Blue & White Restaurant*** was a tourist attraction. The Blue & White has stood at the corner of US 61 and MS 4 in Tunica since 1937. Elvis Presley was once a frequent patron, and members of the ZZ Top band still stop by for a plate of old-fashioned

House of Blues

Many of Mississippi's most famous blues artists shared a common address—the Mississippi State Penitentiary, also known as *Parchman Farm*. This Delta correctional facility is a former residence of such blues notables as Bukka White, Son House, and Sonny Boy Williamson. Bukka White cashed in on his three-year stay in Parchman, recording the hit "Parchman Farm Blues" and a tribute to prison uniforms, "When Can I Change My Clothes?" Although accommodations and food are free and the current residents are usually happy to welcome visitors, Parchman is not high on the list of off-the-beaten-path vacation destinations.

country cooking whenever they play in Memphis. And country cooking it is. The Blue & White is the best place to get a quick introduction to some southern foods that even a lot of southerners might pass on. After all, it takes a special palate to appreciate turnip greens, country ham, and scrambled pork brains. The Blue & White is open for breakfast, lunch, and dinner. Call (662) 363-1371.

Continue along US 61 South through cotton fields and farmland to *Clarksdale.* The soil around Clarksdale is black, rich, and incredibly fertile. The topsoil thickness averages 132 feet and, in some spots, stretches as deep as 350 feet. Not one square inch of this precious earth goes to waste—where other towns have medians, Clarksdale has cotton. In some sections of the city, cotton is planted right up to the front doors.

Cotton notwithstanding, Clarksdale's biggest claim to fame is as a mecca for fans of the *Mississippi Delta Blues.* The blues is a combination of mournful wails and dryly humorous lyrics that's every bit as much a way of life as a musical form. Born from the chants of slaves who worked the cotton fields in this part of the state decades before the Civil War, the blues is recognized as America's only original music. As blues great B. B. King puts it, "the blues is the truth about life, how it was lived, and how it is lived today."

Clarksdale was the first stop on the "chitlin' circuit," a route through the Delta traveled by wandering bluesmen in the 1920s and 1930s. Blues legends W. C. Handy, Charlie Patton, Muddy Waters, John Lee Hooker, Robert Johnson, and Howlin' Wolf all called Clarksdale home. Weekends found Issaquena Avenue packed with sharecroppers who came to town to shop, socialize, and party in rough-and-tumble nightclubs known as "juke joints."

From these humble beginnings, the blues went on to influence every other form of American music. Polished and transplanted to nightclubs in Chicago, urbanized blues became jazz, and Elvis Presley combined the blues with country music to give the world rock 'n' roll.

The best place to begin a blues tour is the ***Clarksdale Station and Blues Alley,*** an old railroad depot renovated and transformed into an entertainment complex featuring shopping, dining, and live musical performances, all with a blues theme.

In this complex, 1 Blues Alley is home to the ***Delta Blues Museum,*** the definitive repository of the blues. In creating the museum, founder Sid Graves said, "I don't want a museum that swims in formaldehyde—I want something vibrant and alive." Vibrant and alive it is. Tucked among the expected guitars, harmonicas, and photographs, you'll find oddities like the folk-art sculpture *Woman in Coffin* by bluesman James "Son" Thomas, who also worked as a gravedigger. An 8-foot-tall, one-hundred-pound, Technicolor egg depicting blues scenes rests in the center of the display area. Inherited from a mock Fabergé exhibit in Memphis, the *Beale Street Blues Egg* is covered in paintings of blues artists and overlaid with bottle caps and coins collected from Beale Street.

But the most intriguing display is what's left of blues great Muddy Waters's cabin from the old Stovall Plantation. Muddy Waters (born McKinley Morganfield) grew up in this humble cabin and worked on the plantation as a young man. In 1941 and 1942, a researcher studying the blues for a project sponsored by the Library of Congress recorded Waters's music in this cabin. The recordings were later released as *Muddy Waters: Down on Stovall's Plantation.*

A Huck Finn Adventure

The Mississippi River winds some 2,350 miles from the central United States to the Gulf of Mexico. One of the most scenic and exciting ways to explore the lower Mississippi River, which includes the entire western boundary of the state of Mississippi, is by canoe.

Clarksdale's **Quapaw Canoe Company** offers wilderness expeditions on the lower Mississippi River, its backwaters, tributaries, bayous, oxbow lakes, and floodplains. Adventurers camp on secluded sandbars, come eyeball-to-eyeball with river wildlife, and navigate swirling eddies the size of a city block, all under the leadership of an experienced river guide.

Float trips are available along any section of the river between Cairo, Illinois, and the Gulf of Mexico. Trips may last anywhere from a single day to several weeks.

A word of warning: Clients must be willing to paddle and to endure nature's extremes, not the least of which is intense heat during the summer months.

For more information or to plan your Mississippi River adventure, contact Quapaw Canoe Company, (662) 627-4070, or visit the website at island63.com.

Musicians from Eric Clapton to ZZ Top have credited Muddy Waters as a primary influence on their music; The Rolling Stones even took their name from the lyrics of a Muddy Waters song. Clapton once said, "Muddy took the music of the Delta plantation, transplanted it in a Chicago nightclub, surrounded it with an electric band, and changed the course of popular music forever." In 1989, ZZ Top's Billy Gibbons took several pieces of wood from Muddy Waters's dilapidated cabin and had them fashioned into the "Muddywood guitar." The instrument toured the country as a fundraiser for the Delta Blues Museum.

For decades Waters's cabin remained on the Stovall Plantation grounds, enduring exposure to the elements and vandalism by souvenir seekers. Preservation came in the form of the House of Blues restaurant/nightclub chain, which "restored" the cabin to its original outer appearance, then loaded up the structure and took it on tour. Upon its return to Clarksdale, the cabin became a permanent exhibit in the Delta Blues Museum. The cabin houses a lifelike wax statue of Waters, and the Muddywood guitar is displayed near the very section of the wall from which its wood was harvested. A scrap of the newspaper used as original wallpaper is framed on the cabin wall. As the museum guide explains, "They had no money for wallpaper, insulation, or entertainment. The newspaper provided all three."

Posted quotations from Muddy Waters himself offer insight into this blues great's personality. "When you say blues, you know what the average guy is looking for," one reads, "half-slouching, raggedy, bottle of wine in your pocket. I wasn't that kind of blues singer. I stayed sharp . . . They might say I can't play or can't sing, but damn it, they'll say I'm a gentleman."

The museum gift shop sells books, magazines, photos, and, of course, recordings of America's only original music. Pick up a CD for the road; you'll

The Mississippi Blues Trail

The Mississippi Blues Trail is a series of historical markers that combine words and images to tell the story of the blues, America's only original music. The markers recount the lives of bluesmen and women and explain how the places where they lived and the times in which they lived influenced their music. The markers are found throughout the state, from city streets to cotton fields, train depots to cemeteries, juke joints to churches. A project of the Mississippi Blues Commission, the Blues Trail represents the combined work of the world's foremost blues scholars and historians.

For a map of the hundred-plus marker locations (new markers are still being added), visit msbluestrail.org. Then tune into a blues station or pop in a CD and begin your journey into the history of American music.

find the blues offer a history lesson, cultural experience, and audio tour of the Delta in every note.

Attracting fans from around the world, the Delta Blues Museum can't really be considered off the beaten path. In one 10-day period, visitors from Australia, Italy, Colombia, Egypt, Russia, Portugal, Thailand, Spain, Syria, Ireland, Iceland, and England all signed the guest register. To add your name to the list, follow the many signs to 1 Blues Alley. The museum is open Mon through Sat, from 9 a.m. to 5 p.m. Mar through Oct, and 10 am. to 5 p.m. Nov through Feb. Admission is $10 for adults, $8 for children six through twelve, and free for kids under six with an adult. Call (662) 627-6820 or visit deltabluesmuseum.org.

Downtown Clarksdale is filled with significant blues landmarks. Take a stroll down Sunflower Avenue, paying close attention to the row of shotgun houses backing up to the Sunflower River. A sign on one of these modest buildings identifies it as the ***Riverside Hotel.*** Originally Clarksdale's black hospital, the building became a blues landmark when Bessie Smith, the "Empress of the Blues," died there after a car wreck in 1937. The old hospital became a boarding house and hotel in 1944 and has been home to many blues greats over the past fifty years. While any blues enthusiast will enjoy a daytime visit to the Riverside Hotel, the $25 overnight accommodations are modest to say the least, and require guests to share common bathroom facilities.

Any bluesman worth his salt once strolled and played on the stretch of road called Issaquena Avenue. While it's harder to catch a street performance these days, a handful of landmarks points to the area's bluesy heritage.

A guitar painted on the outside wall and a sign proclaiming no cameras or recording devices hint that there was once more than haircutting going on at ***Wade Walton's Barbershop.*** A personal friend of W. C. Handy, Sonny Boy Williamson, and John Lee Hooker, the late Wade Walton was given to impromptu blues performances and gifted storytelling sessions. Patrons who spent time in Walton's chair left with not only a spiffy new look, but also a better understanding of the lifestyle called the blues. When Walton died, he took his music and his stories with him. But peeking in the windows of the now-silent shop, it's easy to imagine Walton wielding both a comb and a harmonica as his customers hummed along.

A number of the modest dwellings in this area were once home to the famous or semi-famous. A marker near the barbershop on Issaquena Avenue points out the spot where W. C. Handy's house once stood. Sam Cooke spent his childhood at 2303 Seventh St. Ike Turner's father's name is inscribed in the cornerstone at New Centennial Church, where he served as church secretary and pastor; Ike himself grew up at 304 Washington St.

After hearing so much about it, you're probably ready for your own taste of the blues. The staff at the Delta Blues Museum can usually direct you to a juke joint (also spelled "jook" joint), or you can check the utility poles around town for homemade flyers announcing performances. Don't expect live music during the week; most blues artists hold day jobs and save their music for Friday and Saturday nights. There are juke joints all over the Delta, but arrangements with the artists are often last-minute and never binding. Since most of these establishments don't have telephones, the only sure way to confirm a blues performance is to show up and wait for the music to start. A word of warning—the best blues are played in juke joints where people may warn you not to go. **Red's** is a popular juke joint that's welcoming to tourists.

odetobilliejoe

Visitors to rural Tallahatchie County can drive over the Tallahatchie bridge where the fictional Billie Joe McAllister jumped to his death in Bobby Gentry's sad country ballad "Ode to Billie Joe."

If you can't make it to a juke joint, tune in to WROX Radio instead. One of the country's first blues stations, WROX hired Mississippi's first black disc jockey. The late Early Wright began spinning blues (as the "Soul Man") and gospel (as "Brother Early") in Clarksdale in 1947 and continued until his retirement in 1997, just two years prior to his death at the age of 84. The University of Mississippi honored Wright's contributions to southern culture by establishing a scholarship in his name in 1988.WROX also claimed a pre-fame Ike Turner as both a DJ and a janitor, and legend has it a young Elvis Presley used to hang around the station in hopes of getting a chance to sing on the air.

You'll find WROX, now a satellite music station, at 1450 AM on your radio dial. The former WROX studios used from 1948 to 1954 are housed in the historic **Hopson 1920 Building** at 257 Delta Ave. The studio is periodically open for tours.

For the best in live blues, plan a Clarksdale visit that coincides with the **Sunflower River Blues and Gospel Festival.** This free, three-day open-air party is internationally recognized as one of the purest and bluesy-est of all festivals celebrating the art form. Be warned—the festival is held in August, and while the music is cool, the temperatures are scorching. For this year's dates, call the Clarksdale & Coahoma Chamber of Commerce at (662) 627-7337.

Just when you think there's nothing in Clarksdale but the blues, someone will invite you to the **Tennessee Williams Festival.** Young Tom Williams attended school in Clarksdale and spent summers visiting his grandfather, who was the pastor of St. George's Episcopal Church and lived in the rectory next door. The playwright's mother wrote of finding a scrap of paper upon which

Williams had scrawled, "Before I was eight, my life was completely unshadowed by fear. I lived in a small Mississippi town. My sister and I were gloriously happy."

Many of Clarksdale's landmarks and citizens reappeared years later in Williams's works. Now owned by Delta State University, Clarksdale's elegant **Cutrer Mansion** was originally the home of flamboyant attorney J. W. Cutrer and his equally colorful wife, Blanche. The couple's legendary yard parties, masked balls, and madcap antics made quite an impression on young Tom Williams. The playwright used the Cutrers as models for characters in *A Streetcar Named Desire, Cat on a Hot Tin Roof,* and *The Glass Menagerie,* and named his most famous heroine, Blanche DuBois, after Mrs. Cutrer. The 1916 Cutrer Mansion is not open for tours, but is visible from Clark Street.

Held each October, the Tennessee Williams Festival stars Clarksdale's own citizens, who act out short scenes from his plays on their front lawns and front porches. Festivalgoers receive a map telling them which plays will be performed on which lawns at what time. The festival also includes dinner parties at the old Moon Lake Casino (now Uncle Henry's Place), seminars on Williams's work, musical entertainment, and home tours in the grand historic district between Clark and Court Streets—quite a contrast to the bluesy side of life. For this year's festival dates, call the Clarksdale & Coahoma Chamber of Commerce at (662) 627-7337.

Williams is not the only writer to grow up in Coahoma County. Thomas Harris, author of the chilling *Red Dragon, Silence of the Lambs,* and *Hannibal,* spent his childhood in nearby **Rich.** Of course, if Harris's characters, including the infamous "Hannibal the Cannibal," are based on real people, the locals would probably rather not know about it.

Back in downtown Clarksdale, Delta Avenue is lined with specialty and antiques shops and locally owned boutiques well worth an hour (or two) of browsing. **Cat Head Delta Blues & Folk Art** (252 Delta Ave.) is an example of just how addictive the blues can be. After several memorable vacations to the Delta, St. Louis resident Roger Stolle left a high-powered career in Missouri, moved to Clarksdale, and opened this quirky little music and art shop.

"A year ago, I was meeting with the CEOs of major companies and taking business trips to Hong Kong," Roger said shortly after Cat Head opened. "This week, I booked a blues musician named T-Model Ford to play for our grand opening and set up a store display that included a chair made out of painted cow bones. You tell me which sounds like more fun."

Cat Head features a full selection of blues CDs, videos, DVDs, books, and collectibles, as well as an affordable, completely unique selection of southern folk art. The shop's "Sounds Around Town" chalkboard offers up-to-the-minute performance schedules for clubs and juke joints around Clarksdale, and Roger is on hand to talk with visitors about the magic of the Delta. With live music often performed in the store, the overall effect is one of shopping in a juke joint. Cat Head is open Mon through Sat from 10 a.m. to 5 p.m. and on Sun from 11 a.m. to 3 p.m. You can also visit Cat Head online at cathead.biz. Call (662) 624-5992.

For a town its size, Clarksdale offers a surprising number and diversity of restaurants. A Clarksdale staple since 1924, **Abe's Bar-B-Q** is listed as one of the best pork joints in the South in the books *Roadfood* and *Goodfood*. Abe's occupies a modest building at 616 N. State St., at the intersection of US 61 and US 49. Call (662) 624-9947 or visit abesbbq.com. A little farther south on US 61, **Chamoun's Resthaven** (419 State S. St., 662-624-8601) serves up stuffed grape leaves, kibbeh, baklava, and other Lebanese and Mediterranean delicacies.

For some lively after-dinner entertainment—and a chance at a **Morgan Freeman** sighting—head to the **Ground Zero Blues Club,** the actor's juke joint. Adorned with plastic tablecloths, Christmas lights, and sublime-to-ridiculous graffiti (be sure to add a word of your own), the cavernous club is a prime place to party. Ground Zero does a hopping lunch and dinner business, but is better known as the place to hear live music every weekend. Patrons and employees—including Ground Zero's famous owner—have been known to dance on the bar. The Ground Zero Blues Club is located in an old cotton warehouse at 0 Blues Alley, across the road from the Delta Blues Museum. For a lineup of performances, call (662) 621-9009 or visit groundzerobluesclub.com.

If you're planning to party extra hard at Ground Zero, you'd be wise to rent one of the **Ground Zero Blues Club Apartments** above the club. Located in an area of the old warehouse formerly used for grading cotton fiber, each of the seven apartments takes its name from a cotton grade. But don't let the names fool you—every unit, from "Strict Low Middling" to "Good Ordinary," is comfortable and well appointed. The most popular apartment, "Good Middling," overlooks Blues Alley and features a funky, retro decor complete with a Warhol-style painting of Morgan Freeman. Ground Zero Blues Apartments feature living areas and kitchens, but are not equipped with telephones, cable TV, or Internet access. And while it probably goes without saying, when there's a band playing at Ground Zero Blues Club, it's not exactly quiet upstairs. Then again, you really should be downstairs enjoying the party anyway. Rates at the Delta Cotton Company Apartments start at $125. For reservations call (662) 645-9366.

In addition to high-profile projects like Ground Zero Blues Club and the Delta Cotton Company Apartments, Morgan Freeman quietly supports libraries, public schools, and a number of community projects in Clarksdale and throughout the Delta.

Little-Known Facts about the Mississippi River Delta

In 1992, Tunica County boasted twenty hotel rooms. A dozen Las Vegas–style casinos later, the county is home to more than 6,000.

Topsoil in the Mississippi Delta is an average of 132 feet deep and, in some spots, reaches as deep as 350 feet.

The world's first franchised Holiday Inn opened its register in Clarksdale.

The Norris Bookbinding Company of Greenwood is the largest Bible-binding plant in the nation.

The national 4-H Club was founded in Holmes County in 1907.

Twenty-nine ships sunk during the Civil War lie beneath the waters of the Yazoo River.

Greenwood's Grand Boulevard was once named one of America's ten most beautiful streets by the US Chambers of Commerce and the Garden Clubs of America.

Just 2 miles apart, the Yazoo and Tallahatchie Rivers run parallel to each other, yet flow in opposite directions.

"I've been just about everywhere, and there's no place better," Freeman says. "What the state offered me, I got growing up. Now, I have something to offer the state."

For a Delta cultural lesson that's equal parts fun, funky, and fascinating, head for the *Hopson Commissary* on the historic *Hopson Plantation.* The country's first cotton crop produced entirely by machine—from plantin' to balin'—was grown and harvested in 1944 on 28 acres owned by the Hopson Planting Company. Today the historic Hopson Commissary houses a sometime "social club" and mini-museum packed with farming memorabilia, statuary, an old post office, and a complete barbershop. A huge banner draped on one wall features a likeness of the King of Rock 'n' Roll and the proclamation "Elvis will never leave this building." Owner James Butler, whose wife inherited the Hopson family property, collected the memorabilia for preservation from small towns all over Mississippi.

Evenings at the Commissary usually find a genial mix of locals and tourists gathered 'round the volunteer-run bar (a rescued antique soda fountain) or chatting at a handful of tables covered with red-and-white-checkered cloths. On occasion, the Commissary features live musical entertainment, often of the blues variety. The Commissary is open to the public Mon through Fri from 5 to 9 p.m., and Sat from 5 p.m. to 1 a.m. Beer and setups are available.

Make a visit to Clarksdale even more memorable with an overnight stay at the **Shack Up Inn** adjacent to the Hopson Plantation property. A handful of business partners known as "the Shackmeisters" salvaged a six-pack of authentic sharecroppers' shotgun shacks from around the countryside, relocated them to the property, added electricity and plumbing, and rent them out to overnight guests. Don't worry—while the exterior of each ramshackle shanty is authentically dilapidated, rickety, and rustic, the interiors are modern, clean, and comfy, with amenities you just won't find at the local Holiday Inn. A copper coil from a previous tenant's still has been recycled as a bathroom fixture, the circa-1970 television sets pick up only the blues channel, and your kitchenette might feature an old Coke machine converted into a refrigerator. Landscaping on the grounds includes Christmas lights, plenty of pink flamingos, a rusted storage tank, and a bottle tree designed to keep away evil spirits (the bottle tree prompted one guest unfamiliar with southern folklore to inquire, "What's with the vodka tree?"). Turndown service replaces the traditional chocolates with—what else—moonpies on your pillow. And each shack comes complete with an authentically musty aroma that would be impossible to replicate. With amenities like these, who needs room service?

For those suffering from shack shock, the property is also home to the **Cotton Gin Inn,** an old cotton gin that's been completely renovated into a one-of-a-kind motel. Each modern, comfortable room (or "bin") features a bathroom mural hand-painted by a different local artist. The murals depict Delta scenes ranging from landscapes to cotton plantations to blues clubs. As one guest said, "You haven't lived 'til you've sat on the john in the middle of a juke joint."

As an added bonus, a stay in "Mississippi's Oldest B&B (Bed & Beer)" is such an affordable experience that you'll have enough left over to buy a Shack Up Inn T-shirt. The Shack Up Inn is located at the Clarksdale city limits on US 49 South at Hopson Road. For rates and more information on shacking up, call (662) 624-8329 or visit shackupinn.com.

Fans who didn't get their fill of blues lore in Clarksdale should continue down US 49 South to **Tutwiler,** where a message on the water tower proclaims the town to be "Where the Blues Was Born." Drivers are welcomed to Tutwiler by three-dimensional billboards designed to look like juke joints. Created by horticulturist Felder Rushing and acclaimed Mississippi folk artist Earl Simmons, the billboards were funded through a grant from the Mississippi Arts Commission.

The billboards direct visitors from the highway into downtown Tutwiler and **Railroad Park.** A marker where the railroad depot once stood commemorates W. C. Handy's "discovery" of the blues—the spot where the "Father of the Blues" heard a man playing guitar and singing a mournful tune about

"Goin' where the Southern cross the Dog"—that's a railroad intersection in nearby Moorhead. The walls of Railroad Park next to the site are adorned with sweeping murals depicting Handy's chance meeting with the bluesman, as well as scenes from Tutwiler's history. Created by Delta artist Cristen Craven Barnard, the mural also features images of bluesman Aleck Miller, better known as Sonny Boy Williamson. Miller/Williamson is buried near Tutwiler beside the old **Whitfield M. B. Church** under a new marker erected by Trumpet Records. The grave site is easy to spot—it's the one littered with beer cans, whiskey bottles, spare change, and a dozen rusty harmonicas.

From Tutwiler, continue on US 49 South approximately fifteen miles to the tiny community of **Glendora**, the home of the **Emmett Till Historic Intrepid Center** (ETHIC), located at 235 Thomas St. In 1955, Emmett Till, a fourteen-year-old African-American boy visiting Mississippi from Chicago, allegedly whistled at Carolyn Bryant, a white woman in a grocery store. Four days later, Till was dragged from his bed by two white men who beat him and shot him to death, then dumped his body in the Tallahatchie River near Glendora. Emmett's mutilated remains were returned to Chicago, where his mother, Mamie Till Bradley, held an open casket funeral to show the world the horrors of racial violence in Mississippi. Two white men, J. W. Milam and Roy Bryant, were tried for Till's murder, but acquitted by an all-white jury; they later confessed to the horrific crime in an article in *Look Magazine,* for which they were paid. Till's brutal murder and the hasty trial and acquittal shocked the nation and helped mobilize the civil rights movement.

mississippitrivia

Based on income tax returns documenting charitable donations, Mississippians are the most generous citizens in the United States.

The new Emmett Till museum in Glendora is housed in an old cotton gin near the site where Till's body was dumped into the river. Among the items on display are family snapshots and the photograph of Till's mutilated body that stunned the nation in 1955. The museum also houses exhibits honoring the late Sonny Boy Williamson, a native of Glendora. The Emmett Till Historic Intrepid Center is a tribute to Emmett Till and to his mother's courage. Call (662) 375-7333.

From Glendora, head back up US 49 North to Clarksdale and pick up US 61 South, or continue on US 49 South to MS 8; then head west. Either route will lead you to the charming Delta communities of Mound Bayou, Merigold, and Cleveland.

If you choose the US 61 South route, be careful not to blink. You'll miss the MS 161 cutoff that leads to **Mound Bayou,** a town founded by freed slaves who once chopped cotton on Jefferson Davis's brother's plantation. The grounds of the **Mound Bayou City Hall** feature a carved wooden plaque depicting famous African Americans, including Martin Luther King Jr., Fannie Lou Hamer, and Malcolm X.

A favorite stop in Mound Bayou is **Peter's Pottery.** Peter Woods and his three brothers learned the fine art of pottery from the master at McCarty Pottery in Merigold (the next town down the road). The Woods brothers left McCarty in 1998 with plans to pursue new careers, but soon realized that clay was in their blood. Together they established Peter's Pottery, the place to find animals, candlesticks, dinnerware, crosses, and vases crafted of Mississippi clay and finished with the brothers' exclusive glaze, Bayou Blue. Peter's pottery is collected worldwide; former president George W. Bush is the proud owner of a Bayou Blue elephant. The brothers' work is sold at their gallery (301 Fortune Ave.) and in upscale gift shops statewide. To get to the gallery, turn right at the big blue industrial building across from New Salem Baptist Church; then follow the gravel road to the brown building at the end. Browse the pottery or place a custom order during regular business hours (Mon, Tues, and Thurs through Sat, 10 a.m. to 4 p.m.), call (662) 741-2283, or visit peters-pottery.net.

The entire town of **Merigold** covers a mere 6 blocks but packs a lot of charm into such a small space. This Delta village (population 383) is home to a handful of quaint restaurants and specialty shops, including **McCarty Pottery.** Turn right at the post office on MS 161, then left on North St. Mary Street to No. 101, the low cypress building surrounded by bamboo. There's no sign, but as soon as you open the door you'll know you've found the McCarty gallery and tour gardens. The late Lee and Pup McCarty founded the business, which is now operated by members of their extended family. The McCarty collection includes dinnerware, vases, wind chimes, and candlesticks, but the McCartys are best known for their family of pottery rabbits. Each inquisitive bunny has a name, and whether you choose Lettuce, Easter, or Baby Bunny, you'll take home one of Mississippi's most popular souvenirs. Obsessed McCarty collectors can be found all over the world. Even Nikita Khrushchev had a collection of McCarty pottery, supposedly received as a gift from Armand Hammer. McCarty Pottery is open 10 a.m. to 4 p.m. Tues through Sat. Call (662) 748-2293 or visit mccartyspottery.com.

The Gallery restaurant, 2 blocks from the studio (again, there's no sign), is also owned by the McCarty family and serves light lunches on dinnerware fashioned by the artists. Nearby **Crawdad's** (104 S. Park St.; 662-748-2441) is a popular spot for dinner, and sometimes features live music on weekends.

The next stop on US 61 is **Cleveland,** listed in Norm Crampton's *The 100 Best Small Towns in America*. W. C. Handy wrote about Cleveland in his autobiography, describing a pivotal incident at a dance held in the Cleveland Courthouse. When the audience demanded blues tunes, Handy and his orchestra were at a loss. A local trio stepped in and saved the day, performing bawdy, soulful music the likes of which Handy had never heard, but which he would later incorporate into his own songs. "My enlightenment came in Cleveland, Mississippi," Handy wrote years later. "That night, an American composer was born."

Attractions in Cleveland include the small-but-scenic campus of **Delta State University,** excellent shopping in more than thirty-five boutiques along historic Cotton Row and Sharpe Avenue.

Cleveland is also home to the **GRAMMY Museum Mississippi**, the only GRAMMY museum located outside of Los Angeles and the most technologically advanced, music-themed museum in the South. So, what's a high-tech tribute to the best of the music industry doing in this sleepy little college town? The decision to locate this very high-profile museum in this off-the-beaten-path town was based on Mississippi's legacy as the birthplace of the blues, America's only original music, and as the birthplace of so many GRAMMY winners. It's been said that Mississippi has more GRAMMY winners per capita than any other state. The GRAMMY Museum is located at 800 W. Sunflower Rd. on the campus of Delta State University. For more information, call (662) 441-0100 or visit grammymuseumms.org.

Airport Grocery (3608 US 61 N; 662-843-4817) bills its burgers, barbecue, hot tamales, and other hearty fare as "out-of-this-world food at a down-to-earth place." Visit airportcleveland.com. Lunch and shopping go hand-in-hand at **A la Carte Alley** (111 S. Court St.; 662-545-4229; alacartealley.net), a delightful southern bistro and gift gallery.

Located on MS 8 East between Cleveland and Ruleville, **Dockery Farms,** the most famous of the old Delta cotton plantations, is included on a long list of places as the possible birthplace of the blues. Blues great Charlie Patton called the plantation home. Patton's presence at Dockery Farms is believed to have drawn dozens of other blues musicians to the area. A barn bearing the plantation name and dates of operation is visible from the highway and is a popular photo opportunity.

On the other side of Cleveland, MS 8 West intersects MS 1 at **Rosedale,** a thriving port on the **Mississippi River.** With acres of riverfront and a 75-foot-high observation tower, **Great River Road State Park** offers spectacular views of the mighty Mississippi and enjoys the distinction of being the world's longest park. Visitors can hike a trail that winds down to the riverbank, or rent a Frisbee and play the Deer Meadow Disc Golf Course. The restaurant at the park's visitor center fries up a scrumptious catfish lunch, with panoramic views of the river on the side.

Fishing is good at the park's **Perry Martin Lake**, named for an infamous moonshiner of Mississippi's Prohibition era. Perry Martin lived on a houseboat on the lake, keeping a watchful eye on the highly productive, highly illegal stills he had hidden in the woods nearby. The trails visitors roam freely today were never prowled after dark in Perry Martin's heyday. You won't find any of Martin's potent moonshine at Great River Road, but one of his prized stills is on display.

Continuing on MS 1 South, the next stop is **Benoit**. Take a left at the four-way stop (yes, there's only one), go about a mile past the residential district, and take the gravel road to the right. That antebellum mansion rising out of the field is locally referred to as the Baby Doll House, but officially known as **The Burrus House at Hollywood Plantation**. The movie *Baby Doll* was filmed on location here in 1956. Based on a play by Tennessee Williams, *Baby Doll* was so scandalous it was condemned by the Legion of Decency. For as long as anyone around Benoit can remember, no one has lived in the Baby Doll House—at least not officially. The house is widely regarded as haunted and boasts a shadowy, convoluted past involving an escaped John Wilkes Booth. The estate was renovated in 2012 and is available for events and guided tours by appointment only. For more info call (601) 807-1856 or visit thebabydoll house.com.

Cotton Row

This flat, fertile section of the Delta that stretches from Greenville east to Green-wood is virtually devoid of trees, but you won't need spring buds or fall foliage to tell you what season it is.

In the summertime the heat shimmers so thickly off the highway you can actually catch it on film. Even the most resilient crops look parched without a daily drenching. Those huge, spidery pieces of machinery spanning the fields are pivot irrigation systems, designed to give each precious acre of cotton and soybeans a good soaking.

Fall sees Cotton Row at its peak, when the fields are white with "Delta Gold." When harvesting takes place in early autumn, trucks loaded with the fluffy stuff travel every Delta highway, leftover strands float lazily in the welcome breeze, and out-of-state visitors pull over to swipe a souvenir boll.

In the winter, the Delta seems determined to relive its prehistoric days as a swamp—the rain never seems to stop, the fertile soil turns to mucky gumbo, and flash floods can literally wash away the back roads.

In the spring, the whole process begins anew. And no matter how many years a particular field is worked, the land continues to reveal new treasures

No Mistaking It

I'd like to say I stumbled upon the **No Mistake Plantation** by accident, but to find yourself in **Satartia**, the smallest incorporated town in Mississippi, you really have to be looking for something.

The town lies just off MS 3, 25 miles south of Yazoo City. I had directions to the No Mistake, but as it turned out I didn't need the hand-drawn map after all—the explosion of color was a dead giveaway. The antebellum plantation home was surrounded by daylilies—thousands upon thousands of daylilies, in every hue and shade imaginable.

After lunch in the tearoom, the plantation's owner told me about the first mistress of No Mistake, a planter's wife who had raised a single bale of cotton every year, then used her modest earnings to build this scenic masterpiece—one garden at a time. My host concluded the tour by offering me a well-worn garden trowel and an invitation to take a living reminder of the No Mistake home.

The No Mistake Plantation has changed hands since my visit there and, sadly, no longer allows outsiders to explore its kaleidoscopic grounds. But every summer, when those generations-old daylilies burst into bloom in my own backyard, I relive that afternoon at the No Mistake Plantation—one flower at a time.

---

with every pass of the plow. The rich black earth sparkles with glass—once part of a window in a sharecropper's shack. Wild daffodils spring up where a long-ago garden once bloomed, and plows turn up shards of ancient Indian pottery, arrowheads, and even an occasional dinosaur bone or human skeleton.

Dozens of Indian artifacts are displayed at the **Winterville Indian Mounds State Park and Museum,** 5 miles north of Greenville on MS 1. The mound builders' metropolis at Winterville includes fifteen earthen structures, one of them a massive six-story temple mound. The mounds were built one basketful of earth at a time by the women of the tribe, while the men worked the fields and hunted for dinner. A museum on the Winterville property houses Indian artifacts recovered from all over the Delta. The museum is open Tues through Sat from 9 a.m. to 5 p.m. Call (662) 334-4684 or visit mdah.state.ms.us.

Continue into **Greenville,** the state's largest city on the Mississippi River. MS 1 intersects with US 82 here, providing an easy way to navigate the city; virtually every point of interest is located a block or two off US 82.

Your first stop should be the **River Road Queen Welcome Center,** a replica of a nineteenth-century stern-wheeler that made its debut at the 1984 New Orleans World's Fair, then returned to Greenville to greet visitors arriving in Mississippi from Arkansas. This landlocked stern-wheeler is located at the intersection of US 82 West and Reed Road, just past the US 82 and Main Street intersection. Stop to admire the miniature cotton patch planted out front, then head inside where a knowledgeable staffer will provide you with brochures and directions to Greenville attractions, hotels, and restaurants. Call (662) 332-2378.

From the *River Road Queen,* head back east on US 82 to Main Street, which dead-ends at the **Mississippi River levee,** a marvel of engineering longer and taller than the Great Wall of China. Barges headed for the bustling **Port of Greenville** are visible just beyond the casinos that line the levee's edge. For a close-up view of the mighty Mississippi, stop at the observation tower at **Warfield Point Park,** nestled inside the levee off US 82, 5 miles south of Greenville. The park offers the only public riverbank campsites on the Mississippi between St. Louis and New Orleans. Call (662) 820-8630 or visit warfield pointpark.com to reserve your spot.

At the end of Main Street, 1 block east of the levee, you'll spot the **Old Number One Firehouse Museum** (230 Main St.). It's not surprising that Greenville would open a museum honoring firefighting—in the late 1800s, the city burned to the ground not once, not twice, but on three separate occasions. Exhibits include old fire engines, call boxes, and "fire marks"—plaques displayed only on those homes that carried fire insurance. In the old days, if firemen arrived at a burning home and didn't see the appropriate mark, they would head back to the station and leave the house to burn. The Firehouse Museum is a favorite with kids, who can dress in firefighting garb, pull a real fire alarm, and pretend to douse the flames with a working hose. Open by appointment; call (662) 334-2711 or (800) 467-3582.

Those with a literary bent will find the **Greenville Writers Exhibit** at the William Alexander Percy Memorial Library (341 Main St.) of interest. According to the local chamber of commerce, Greenville boasts more published writers per capita than any other town in the nation. The list of distinguished authors includes Ellen Douglas, Walker Percy, Hodding Carter, and Civil War historian Shelby Foote, who gained national notoriety as a featured commentator in Ken Burns's epic PBS series, *The Civil War.* The Greenville Writers Exhibit includes

The Mississippi Delta Tamale Trail

In the Mississippi Delta, hot tamales are as ubiquitous as fried catfish and iced tea. Fans of this Latin American/Deep Southern American delicacy should visit tamaletrail .com for a list of Delta establishments famous for their tamales.

photographs, original manuscripts, and displays celebrating Greenville's rich literary heritage.

Dinnertime in Greenville calls for a trip to **Doe's Eat Place** (502 Nelson St.), where you'll find the biggest, best steaks in Mississippi, and quite possibly in all of America. In fact, *Men's Journal* proclaimed Doe's porterhouse steak "the best thing to eat in America," period. With maps to the restaurant distributed in every convenience store and hotel lobby in Greenville, Doe's can't really be considered off the beaten path, but its stubborn refusal to conform to any level of restaurant normalcy is what puts Doe's on everyone's "must see" list.

For starters, the restaurant is housed in a dilapidated 1903 grocery-store-turned-honky-tonk-turned-tamale-stand-turned-restaurant that looks as though it should be condemned, if not by the building commission, then at least by the local health department. Patrons enter through the kitchen, where the owner ("Little Doe," son of restaurant founder "Big Doe") will turn to you with a hefty steak in each hand and say, "Aunt Florence will seat you." Aunt Florence will indeed lead you to a rickety table, where a friendly waitress will soon appear with a bowl of anchovies or a sample of Doe's famous hot tamales. While you wait for the main course in the cramped little room, you can eavesdrop on the conversations of other diners, who range from Doe's regulars chatting with the staff to first-time patrons wondering if the restrooms might actually be outside somewhere.

Be warned—dinner at Doe's could put you in a coma. The smallest steak on the menu weighs in at a whopping two pounds and comes with French-fried potatoes and fresh bread. The food is nothing short of delicious, and though the atmosphere seems a little rustic at first, it soon becomes quite comfortable. Doe's is open Mon through Sun from 5 p.m. until 9 p.m. Call (662) 334-3315 or (662) 254-8081, or visit doeseatplace.com.

The restaurant is located on **Nelson Street,** which is also home to some down-and-dirty blues clubs. Although it's true that some of these establishments have a reputation for vice and violence, visitors who stick to the blues and stay out of the street life aren't likely to run into trouble.

For a daylong dose of the blues, follow the crowds to a forty-acre patch in the Delta outside Greenville on the third Sat in Sept. Once you've attended the **Mississippi Delta Blues and Heritage Festival,** nothing but a live performance will ever do again. The festival brings the biggest names in blues for an all-day blowout—the Woodstock of the blues world. Bring a lawn chair or blanket and an ice chest and be warned—late Sept in Mississippi is still hot and humid. For this year's lineup of performers, call (662) 335-3523 or visit deltabluesms.org.

From Greenville, take US 82 East toward Greenwood, or backtrack to MS 1 and pick up a few more attractions farther south.

Located 5 miles off MS 1 South on MS 12, **_LeRoy Percy State Park_** is home to the only hot spring in Mississippi, but it's not the place for a leisurely soak—the 94-degree water has already been claimed by the local alligator population. You can enjoy a not-too-up-close-and-personal visit with the scaly reptiles from a raised boardwalk above their hot artesian spring home. A nature trail through the park offers a look at the Delta of old—a steamy jungle of a place overrun by Spanish moss and cypress trees.

MS 1 intersects with US 61 South at **_Rolling Fork,_** birthplace of blues great Muddy Waters. A bend in the road near Rolling Fork is home to a growing collection (or herd) of wire-sculpted dinosaurs fashioned by a local resident. Rolling Fork is also home to **_Mont Helena,_** a private home built in 1896 by Helen and George Harris. Constructed atop an Indian mound—the only rise in the pancake-flat land for miles—the Colonial Revival–style mansion is clearly visible from US 61. Mont Helena is lovely in its own right, but the house is most famous because its original mistress, Helen Johnstone Harris, is widely believed to be the ghostly Bride of Annandale (see sidebar in "The Heartland" chapter).

US 61 North and US 82 intersect just outside Greenville near **_Leland._** As you head east on US 82, keep a sharp eye out for talking frogs, fashion-conscious

The Birth of the Teddy Bear

One of the world's most popular toys was born in tiny Onward, Mississippi, as the result of a presidential pardon.

In 1902, President Theodore Roosevelt participated in a black bear hunt in the Onward area. The hunt was led by former slave, Confederate soldier, and skilled hunting guide Holt Collier. When a 235-pound bear attacked one of Collier's prized hunting dogs, the guide clubbed and lassoed the bear, tied it to a tree, and invited the president to shoot it. Roosevelt refused to kill the tethered animal, claiming it would not be sportsmanlike. A cartoonist with the *Washington Post* captured this noble gesture on paper, and the story of "Teddy's bear" quickly spread nationwide.

Soon after, a savvy New York merchant named Morris Michton made toy history by creating a cuddly toy christened "the Teddy bear." Michton went on to found the Ideal Toy Company, starting the entire business with revenues generated by the original teddy bear.

Guide Holt Collier went on to become known as the greatest bear hunter in the South, and in an interesting footnote (pawnote?) to the story, the 2002 Mississippi legislature passed a bill naming the teddy bear the official state toy of Mississippi.

pigs, and perennial roommates Bert and Ernie. This Delta town is home to the **Birthplace of the Frog,** a museum honoring Leland native *Jim Henson*, the creator of the beloved Muppets. You'll find original Muppets and Muppet memorabilia at this fanciful exhibit on South Deer Creek Drive, 1.5 miles west of the intersection of US 82 and US 61. Fans will delight in learning the inspiration behind their favorite Muppets; for example, Kermit the Frog is affectionately named after Henson's boyhood best friend. Hobnob with the stars of *The Muppet Movie* and *The Muppets Take Manhattan* Mon through Sat from 10 a.m. to 4 p.m. There is no admission, but donations are appreciated. Be sure to add your name to the guest register, which already lists Muppet fans from Australia, England, and Japan. Call (662) 686-7383.

Like most Delta communities, Leland's music of choice is the blues. Several of Leland's downtown buildings are adorned with colorful murals celebrating the blues. Located at 307 N. Broad St., the **Highway 61 Blues Museum** showcases bluesmen from this area of the Delta and their contributions to American music. The museum is open Mon through Sat from 10 a.m. to 5 p.m. Call (662) 686-7646 or visit highway61blues.com.

Broad Street is also home to the **Mississippi Wildlife Heritage Museum** (804 N. Broad St.), a tribute to all things hunting, fishing, wildlife, and the great Mississippi outdoors. In addition to artifacts and memorabilia, the museum houses a Hall of Fame honoring Mississippi's greatest outdoorsmen and outdoorswomen. The museum is open Mon through Sat, 10 a.m. to 5 p.m. Admission is $10 per person, $7 for seniors, and free for children 16 and under. Call (662) 686-7085 or visit mswildlifeheritagemuseum.com.

Pick up a fluffy souvenir from your visit to Leland at **Little Bales of Cotton,** a specialty shop offering miniature cotton bales, grapevine wreaths covered in cotton bolls, cotton boll dolls, and other gifts and decorative items fashioned of Delta gold. You can stop by the shop at 116 E. Third St. in Leland and watch the merchandise being made from fresh-picked cotton, or place an order online at littlebalesofcotton.com. Call (662) 686-2372.

Your next stop on US 2 East is **Indianola,** the hometown of late blues great Riley B. King, better known as **B. B. King**. King began his musical career singing gospel, but as he explained, "Gospel songs got me encouragement. Blues tunes got me a tip and a beer. Do I really need to say anything else?"

The high point of a trip to Indianola is the **B. B. King Museum and Delta Interpretive Center.** This spectacular, interactive museum houses exhibits from King's phenomenal, sixty-plus-year career. In addition to hundreds of photographs and thousands of artifacts, scenes from King's childhood and early career have been painstakingly re-created, creating a sense of place that transcends the museum and puts visitors into the heart of the blues culture.

Visitors can spend hours studying the detailed displays, taking in archival performance videos, listening to soulful recordings, or viewing short films in which modern musicians credit B. B. King's influence as instrumental to their success. The museum complex includes meeting space in an old brick cotton gin where B. B. King himself once worked as a boy. Even non-blues fans will find themselves moved by the story of B. B. King and his contributions to American music. The museum is also B. B. King's final resting place. As the legendary Eric Clapton says in one of the museum films, "I can tell B. B. from one note. He's the master—the grand master." For museum hours and admission fees, visit bbkingmuseum.org or call (662) 887-9539.

The museum isn't the town's only tribute to its beloved B. B. A mural of King and his guitar "Lucille" adorns a brick wall at the corner of Front Street and Second Street in downtown Indianola. The town also features a park and a street named after its most famous resident. Indianola is a far cry from Hollywood, but you will find King's handprints, footprints, and autograph in the sidewalk at the corner of Second and Church Streets.

If you'd like a taste of the music B. B. made famous, visit **Club Ebony** (404 Hanna St.), an authentic juke joint once owned by the King of the Blues

The Buried Treasure and the Headless Horseman

Schlater, Mississippi, is a tiny town full of big tales. If the legends are true, this modest agricultural community is home to both buried treasure and a headless horseman.

The tale of the buried treasure dates back to the Civil War. When the county treasurer was warned of approaching Union soldiers, he gathered up all of the county's gold, silver, and currency, stuffed them into his saddlebags, and whisked the riches away to a "secret hiding place." He returned—saddlebags empty—just in time to see the Union troops gallop into town. The treasurer planned to return the money after the war, but died before he could retrieve it, taking the secret location of his hiding place to the grave. Despite the best efforts of professional treasure hunters, local kids, and even Teddy Roosevelt, the treasure has never been found.

Schlater's headless horseman is the ghost of Red Elm, an Indian brave who fell in love with a married woman named Mrs. Janes. Ignoring her repeated rebuffs, Red Elm pursued Mrs. Janes relentlessly—even, it seems, after her husband decapitated him. Shortly after Red Elm's murder, Mrs. Janes herself died of typhoid fever; the headless ghost made its first appearance wailing near her grave. If you visit Schlater, you'll find Mrs. Janes's grave in **McNutt Cemetery**—under two red elm trees that have grown together as one.

and donated to the B. B. King Museum. Call (662) 887-9539 to check on the performance schedule.

Another popular Indianola attraction is the ***Gin Mill Galleries*** (109 Pershing Ave.), an art gallery/restaurant located just next door to the B. B. King Museum. The Gin Mill Galleries showcases the work of artists from around the Delta, including pottery, photography, and wood carvings. The Gin Mill Galleries doubles as a restaurant, serving up steaks, salads, and the house specialty, fried bologna sandwiches. Call (662) 887-3209.

A memorable dining experience also awaits at the ***Crown Restaurant and Antique Mall,*** the birthplace of catfish pâté. Open for lunch only, the restaurant offers a menu starring owner Evelyn Roughton's world-famous catfish recipes. You'll have a choice of several entrées, one of which is always an exotic concoction like catfish thermidor, shrimp-stuffed catfish, or black-butter catfish. You'll also be required to sample Evelyn's award-winning catfish pâtés. Purchase a tub or two of the scrumptious pâté to serve to your friends back home—but don't tell them what they're eating until after they've licked the bowl clean.

Lunch includes a catfish entrée, sampling of the pâté, and your choice of any or all of the Crown's collection of homemade pies. Lunch is served 11 a.m. to 2 p.m. Tues through Sat. Visit the Crown at 112 Front St. in downtown Indianola or at thecrownrestaurant.com, or call (662) 887-4522 or (800) 833-7731 to order a catalog. You can buy a tub of the pâté or any of the pie mixes at the restaurant, or take home one of the Crown's mail-order catalogs.

On your way out of Indianola, stop by the ***Indianola Pecan House*** on the left side of US 82 just west of the 82–49 intersection and pick up a snack for the road. The Pecan House offers gourmet nuts, candies, spices, desserts, and dressings and usually has a tableful of samples that's worth a stop in itself. Call (662) 887-5420. The Pecan House also does a thriving online business; visit pecanhouse.com.

From Indianola continue on 82 East to ***Greenwood.*** Just as you come into town, you'll spot signs pointing you toward the ***Museum of the Mississippi Delta*** (US 82 West). The $10 admission buys a look at several rooms of artifacts dating all the way back to the Ice Age. Exhibits include Indian pottery, 10,000-year-old mastodon bones, historic trade beads, a swamp diorama, an Apr 15, 1865, news clipping with the headline "President Dead," and pieces of the Union gunboat *Star of the West* recovered from the waters near Greenwood. The museum is open Mon through Sat from 9 a.m. to 5 p.m. Call (662) 453-0925 or visit museumofthemississippidelta.com.

Greenwood has always seen itself as a genteel town of cultured Delta folk; this concern with propriety and appearances helped make ***Lusco's*** (722

Carrolton Ave.) one of the most popular dining establishments of the Prohibition era. Restaurateur Charles Lusco built private, partitioned rooms that
allowed his guests to imbibe without fear of being observed. Even today, guests
at Lusco's enjoy delicious seafood and steaks in private cubicles, summoning
discreet waiters with the touch of a buzzer. Of course, the rules concerning
alcohol are a little more relaxed today—the restaurant serves beer and wine
coolers and allows guests to bring their own wine and liquor. But don't over-
indulge—remembering which cubicle is yours after a trip to the restroom can
require all of your wits. Reservations are recommended; call (662) 453-5365.

Even if you weren't planning to stay overnight in Greenwood, just stepping
into the lobby of *The Alluvian Hotel* hotel and spa is enough to make you
change your mind. Nestled in the heart of downtown Greenwood, the Alluvian
bills itself as a "cosmopolitan boutique hotel deep in the Delta," and it's an
accurate description. The contemporary hotel's forty-five luxurious rooms and
five spacious suites feature custom-designed furnishings, sinfully plush bed
and bath linens, and custom artwork by Mississippi artists. Just across the street
from the hotel, the *Alluvian Spa* offers a full menu of pampering face and
body treatments with a southern flair. The Alluvian Hotel and Alluvian Spa are
located on Greenwood's historic Howard Street. To book a decadent escape,
call (662) 453-2114 or (866) 600-5201, or visit thealluvian.com.

The Lady in Red

One of the strangest mysteries in Mississippi history began on April 24, 1969, when a
backhoe digging on the *Egypt Plantation* unearthed the *Lady in Red*.

At a depth of a few feet, the backhoe struck a fitted, cast-iron coffin with a glass lid.
Inside was the perfectly preserved body of a petite young woman. She was clad in
an expensive red velvet dress with a frilly lace collar. Her small hands were encased
in white gloves, her dainty feet in stylish black boots. She had been dead for more
than a century.

The workers who unearthed the woman's body described her as "miraculously preserved, with long auburn hair and the beautiful skin of a young woman."

Her body had been preserved in alcohol, an unusual funeral practice of the early
1800s. Based upon the embalming technique and style of her clothing, it is believed
that the Lady in Red died in the late 1830s.

No one ever came forward to claim the body, and no record of her burial was ever
found. With no clue as to her identity, the owner of Egypt Plantation had the lady
interred at Odd Fellows Cemetery in nearby Lexington, where she remains today. The
marker on her grave reads simply, "Lady in Red . . . Found on Egypt Plantation . . .
1835–1969."

The Alluvian was the brainchild of Fred Carl, the founder of Greenwood's most famous business, Viking Range Corporation. Across the street from the hotel, the **Viking Cooking School** offers cooking classes conducted by trained chefs, while the **Viking Kitchen Center** sells the latest in Viking cookware, cutlery, and small kitchen appliances, as well as the same lavish linens found in the guest rooms of the Alluvian. For a schedule of upcoming cooking classes, call (662) 451-6750 or visit vikingcookingschool.com.

Do not, repeat, do not leave Greenwood without a stop at **The Mississippi Gift Company.** Owned by Greenwood residents Tim and Cindy Tyler, The Mississippi Gift Company is the only retail store in the entire state that carries only products made in Mississippi. The Mississippi Gift Company offers more than 750 food and gift items, including gourmet snacks, sauces, and Mississippi-shaped chocolates; artwork; books; note cards; pottery; candles; and cotton-, catfish-, and magnolia-themed souvenirs. The Mississippi Gift Company specializes in gift baskets, and they'll gladly ship a Mississippi souvenir to your friends back home. Visit The Mississippi Gift Company's retail store at 300 Howard St. in historic downtown Greenwood, shop on the web at themississippigiftcompany.com, or request a free catalog packed with goodies by calling (662) 455-6961 or (800) 467-7763.

From Greenwood, take US 82 East to MS 7 North and the small hamlet of **Avalon.** From MS 7, take CR 41 to Rural Road 109 and the **Mississippi John Hurt Museum.** This area of Carroll County was once the stomping ground of blues great Mississippi **John Hurt**, who paid tribute to the area in his song "Avalon Blues." Hurt's granddaughter, Mary Frances Hurt Wright, moved her grandfather's modest shotgun house to its present location (about 3 miles from the original homesite) and opened it as a museum. The museum is open by appointment only; to schedule a visit, call (662) 299-1574. For more information visit mississippijohnhurtfoundation.org.

Following your side trip into blues history, take MS 7 back to US 82 and continue east fifteen miles to charming **Carrollton,** where the stately mansions and cozy cottages built by Carroll County's original settlers still stand. Visitors will also discover a collection of antebellum churches (one built with funds raised through a chain letter), and a town square that looks more like a movie set than anything from the real world.

Once you've explored the eastern edge of the Delta in Carroll County, backtrack about 25 miles on US 82 West to MS 7 South. The **Itta Bena** area is home to two of the three churchyards rumored to be the final resting place of blues great **Robert Johnson.**

As a rule, bluesmen lived a rough life, often dividing their time between playing the blues, romancing other men's wives, and engaging in "cuttin's" and "shootin's." Johnson was no exception. He was living in Greenwood when he was poisoned by a jealous lover (or a lover's jealous husband, the story isn't clear which) at a local juke joint and died a horrible death at age twenty-seven—a fitting end, some said, for the man who sold his soul to the Devil for the ability to play the blues.

In spite of this wicked pact and his wicked ways, Johnson was buried in a churchyard—or at least, it's believed he was buried in *some* churchyard, *some*where. Conflicting stories place Johnson's grave in either the ***Payne Chapel M. B. Churchyard*** at ***Quito,*** the ***Mount Zion M. B. Church*** just north of ***Morgan City,*** or the ***Little Zion M. B. Church*** north of Greenwood.

One of Johnson's ex-girlfriends claimed to have witnessed his burial in an unmarked grave at the Quito location. She further stated that Johnson was in Hell and wouldn't appreciate flowers, much less a tombstone. Nevertheless, a Georgia rock band contributed a marker bearing Johnson's name and the inscription resting in the blues.

The Mt. Zion site features an elaborate, four-sided obelisk engraved with the words, "his music struck a chord that continues to resonate." his blues addressed generations he would never know and made poetry of his visions and fears. To get to the Mt. Zion church, take a left at the sign on MS 7 that says Matthew's Brake National Wildlife Refuge. Mt. Zion is the white frame church on the left.

Robert Johnson's Deal with the Devil

"I went down to the crossroad,
fell down on my knees.
Asked the Lord above, 'Have mercy,
Save poor Bob, if you please.'"

The lyrics to Robert Johnson's "Cross Road Blues" may ask for mercy from the Lord, but according to legend, Johnson actually got his talent from the Devil.

As the story goes, Johnson met with the Devil at the crossroads of US 61 and US 49 on a dark summer night, and agreed to sell his soul for the ability to play the blues.

Most Delta residents scoffed at the notion of the Devil giving music lessons, but Son House, Willie Brown, and other noted bluesmen of the day were amazed by how quickly Johnson learned to play the guitar. No other resident of Clarksdale has ever claimed to see the Devil hanging around in the area, but standing at a Delta crossroads on a hot, black summer night, it's easy to imagine a dark figure in the dusty road, waiting for the next aspiring musician.

Lyric excerpt from Robert Johnson's "Cross Road Blues" © (1978) 1990, 1991 King of Spades Music. All rights reserved. Used with permission.

In recent years, an eyewitness came forward to swear she watched as her own husband buried Johnson at the Little Zion location. That gravesite, too, now bears a marker honoring the King of the Delta Blues.

Although Johnson's actual resting place may forever remain a mystery, all three gravesites draw their share of whiskey bottles, rusty harmonicas, and well-worn guitar picks, left by blues fans from around the world.

Catfish Corridor

The **Catfish Corridor** reaches from Belzoni through Yazoo City and south to the Delta's end at the kudzu-covered hills near Vicksburg. Here the green-and-white fields give way to catfish farms—square ponds where Mississippi's whiskered crop swims.

Continue on MS 7 South to **Belzoni** and **Humphreys County**, nicknamed the World Catfish Capital. The **Catfish Capitol Visitors Center** (111 Magnolia St.) honors the bewhiskered crop with exhibits tracing the industry from pond to plate. Things in Belzoni get really, really fishy the first Saturday in April, when the entire county turns out for the **World Catfish Festival**. Activities include live entertainment, the crowning of Miss Catfish, and the world's largest fish fry (2,500 pounds, plus hush puppies). For more information on the Catfish Capital and all things fishy, visit worldcatfishfestival.org or call (662) 247-4838 or (800) 408-4838.

Before you leave Belzoni, take a break from the road at **Wister Gardens**, a 14-acre park on the northern outskirts of town. Be sure to snap a picture of the statue of Johnny Appleseed, presented to Wister Henry, the garden's founder, by the Men's Garden Club of America.

After those long, flat roads stretching to the horizon, the hill that signals the entrance to Yazoo County looks more like a small mountain. The county bills itself as the spot "where the Delta meets the hills," and indeed, one side of the county touches the flat edge of the Delta while the other rolls gently into the loess bluffs.

For a unique dining, shopping, and conservation experience, stop by the **Hines Grocery** on US 49 just west of Yazoo City. Hines smokes their own sausage, among other Delta delicacies. Hines Grocery is open 6 a.m. to 5:30 p.m. Mon through Thurs. and 6 a.m. to 10 p.m. Fri and Sat. Call (662) 746-5566 to see what's cooking.

In addition to a Delta side and a Hill side, **Yazoo City** boasts a dark side. The tale of the **Witch of Yazoo** has been kept alive not only by local residents, but by late author Willie Morris, a Yazoo City native who repeated the spooky story in his books of childhood reminiscences, *Good Old Boy* and *My Dog Skip*.

When Morris died in 1999, he was buried in Glenwood Cemetery, 13 paces from the witch's grave.

Make your first stop in town the *Triangle Cultural Center*. Take US 49 to Broadway Street, go down the steep hill, then take a right at the first traffic light. Housed in the old Main Street School built in 1905, the building houses a collection of small museums and a gallery with rotating exhibits. At the time of this writing, some changes were planned for the center, including a possible name change and added exhibitions.

The homes in the *Sam Olden Yazoo City Historic District* aren't open for tours, but a stroll along wisteria-lined streets offers a look at charming examples of Victorian, Queen Anne, Gothic, Italianate, and Greek Revival architecture.

As you head out of town, you'll notice a profusion of green vines covering everything—everything—in sight. This rampant vegetation is *kudzu,* described by writer Lewis Grizzard as "the vine that ate the South." You'll find natural kudzu sculptures all over Mississippi, but the tenacious vine is especially prolific in the area between Yazoo City and Vicksburg. Once hailed as the remedy for the erosion of valuable farmland, kudzu became a nuisance, then an example of nature gone wild, when its growth could not be contained. The stuff grows an average of 6 inches per day, so fast you can almost watch it spread. The thick vine eagerly swallows up telephone poles, trees, buildings—virtually anything in its path. Don't stand in one place too long!

The Witch of Yazoo

In the late 1800s, Yazoo City was home to a self-proclaimed witch, a crazy old woman who lured fishermen to their deaths in her home on the banks of the Yazoo River.

Eventually, a group of vigilantes chased the old woman into a nearby swamp, where she met her death in a pool of quicksand. Just before her "ghastly, pockmarked" head was sucked below the surface, she vowed to return from the grave and burn the entire town on the morning of May 25, 1904. The old woman's body was pulled from the quicksand and buried in Glenwood Cemetery, the plot surrounded by a thick iron chain, each link 15 inches long.

You guessed it. On May 25, 1904, all of downtown Yazoo City was indeed destroyed by fire, and visitors to the old woman's grave found a link missing from the chain. You'll find the century-old chain and a new marker inscribed "The Witch of Yazoo" near the fountain in the center of the old section of the cemetery at the intersection of Lintonia and Webster Streets. Visit the witch and give the chain a tug yourself—if you dare.

The Legend of Casey Jones

Shortly after midnight on April 30, 1900, the train *Cannonball* left Memphis, Tennessee, with Jonathan Luther "Casey" Jones at the throttle of engine No. 382. Trying to make up time on his run to Canton, Jones barreled through a stop signal only to spot a freight train stalled on the track ahead. Realizing a crash was inevitable, Jones ordered his fireman to jump clear, but stayed on board himself to try and brake the train. Casey's heroic effort cost him his life.

The tale of Casey Jones and the ill-fated *Cannonball* might have ended that night if not for the musical skills of an engine wiper named Wallace Sanders, who composed "The Ballad of Casey Jones" as a tribute to his friend. The song became a hit, and Casey Jones became a legend.

As for engine No. 382, it was repaired and put back in service on the same route. Just three years later, the 382 crashed again, killing the train's fireman and critically injuring its engineer. All told, the doomed 382 took five lives before it was finally retired from service in 1935.

Wrap up your visit to the Delta by heading east on MS 16, then north up I-55 to **Vaughan** and ***Harkins Woodworks,*** where Greg Harkins makes rocking chairs and primitive furniture by hand using techniques passed down from the mid-1800s. Harkins's famous chairs have graced the homes of Presidents Bill Clinton, Ronald Reagan, George W. Bush, and Jimmy Carter, as well as those of Pope John Paul II, Paul Harvey, Bob Hope, and George Burns. Place your own order on your way through Vaughn; then leave a shipping address and be patient—Harkins spends about thirty hours on each chair, even hand-picking the tree he starts with. Harkins has turned down offers to automate and mass produce, preferring to stick with the exquisite craftsmanship that makes each chair a signed, dated, one-of-a-kind work of art. From the Vaughn exit on I-55, head west and take the first paved road to the left (Bend Road). Follow the road about 2 miles to Harkins's shop on the left. Harkins also operates a business in nearby Canton, Mississippi, Harkins Chairs. For more information, visit harkinschairs.com.

Places to Stay in the Mississippi River Delta

CLEVELAND

Cotton House
233 Cotton Row
(662) 843-7733

GREENWOOD

Tallahatchie Flats
58458 CR 518
(662) 453-1854 or
(877) 453-1854
tallahatchieflats.com

TUNICA

The Columns of Tunica
1120 Hickory Ln.
(662) 363-3659 or
(866) 363-3659
thecolumnsoftunica.com

The casinos of Tunica and Tunica Resorts offer hotel rooms in every price range. For a complete list of casino resorts, visit tunicatravel.com

YAZOO CITY

M. J. Cabins
2419 Deerfield Rd.
662-528-9125 or
662-836-7162 (after hours)
Mjcabin.weebly.com

The Main Street Hotel
203 S. Main St.
(662) 751-8886
mainsthotel.com

Places to Eat in the Mississippi River Delta

CLARKSDALE

Hicks Famous Hot Tamales and More
305 State St./Hwy 61
(662) 624-9887
Tamales and home-style Southern cooking

CLEVELAND

Mississippi Grounds
219 S. Court St.
(662) 545-4528
mississippigrounds.com
Specialty coffees, sandwiches, desserts

Hey Joe's/Mosquito Burrito
118 E. Sunflower Rd.
(662) 843-5425
"Sister" restaurants with a patio overlooking downtown; burgers and beer; Mexican

Lost Pizza Co.
3425 MS 61 N
(662) 846-1300
lostpizza.com
Signature pizzas with homemade sauce

The Pickled Okra
201 Sharpe Ave.
(662) 843-8510
Grill, full bar

GREENVILLE

Frostop of Greenville
1654 MLK Blvd. 1 S.
(662) 378-2078
pasquales-frostop.com
Lot-o-burgers, catfish, rib tips

Walnut Street Blues Bar
128 S. Walnut St.
(662) 378-2254
Sandwiches, salads, appetizers

GREENWOOD

Crystal Grill
423 Carrollton Ave.
(662) 453-6530
crystalgrillms.com
Sandwiches, steaks, seafood, desserts; a menu best described as "vast" and "scrumptious"

Giardina's
(inside The Alluvian hotel)
314 Howard St.
(662) 455-4227
thealluvian.com/giardinas
Steaks, seafood, incredible French fries

Veronica's Custom Bakery
707 W. Park Ave.
(662) 451-9425
veronicas-custom-bakery
.business.site

Webster's
216 W. Claiborne Ave.
(662) 455-1215
Steaks, seafood

ALSO WORTH SEEING

Blue Front Café, Bentonia
The oldest juke joint in Mississippi; showcasing blues performers since 1948

Harlow's Casino Resort & Spa, Greenville

Juanita's Beauty Shop, Bail Bonds, and Bridal Salon, Greenwood
Surely you need something from this establishment, even if it's only a photo of the sign

Sky Lake Wildlife Management Area, Belzoni
A natural wonder, Sky Lake is home to bald cypress trees estimated to be more than 1,000 years old; the oldest of these denizens is 47 feet in circumference and 70 feet tall. A 1,700-foot boardwalk winds through this watery wonderland.

Trop Casino Greenville, Greenville

Tunica casinos, Tunica
including 1st Jackpot Casino Tunica; Fitz Tunica Casino & Hotel; Gold Strike Casino Resort; Hollywood Casino & Hotel Tunica; Horseshoe Tunica Hotel & Casino; Sam's Town Hotel and Casino

Tunica RiverPark & Museum, Tunica

ROLLING FORK

Big Fellas
34178 MS-1
(662) 873-9356
Restaurant and butcher shop serving lunch and dinner in a rustic atmosphere; domestic and craft beers

ROSEDALE

White Front Cafe
902 Main St.
(662) 759-3842
Hot tamales

TUNICA

The casinos of Tunica and Tunica Resorts offer dozens of restaurants ranging from coffee shops to all-you-can-eat buffets to fine dining.

The Heartland

The Heartland stretches from Jackson, Mississippi's capital city and geographic center, through several rural communities south of the "big city" limits, then west to the historic towns that line the bluffs of the mighty Mississippi River.

As explorers of this area of the state soon discover, the Heartland manages to be urban and rural, Old South and New, and cosmopolitan yet down-home friendly—all at the same time.

The Jackson Metro Area

Ask out-of-state visitors to name a city in Mississippi and they'll usually pick Jackson, recalled from that often-recited list of state capitals learned in elementary school. But adventures in the Jackson Metro Area aren't limited to the capital city. Many of the region's genuine pleasures lie in the spirited college towns, quaint country villages, and folksy town squares just outside the city limits.

A tour of the Metro Area begins just off I-55 South in *Canton*, where the focal point is the antebellum *Madison County Courthouse,* built between 1854 and 1858. Make your first

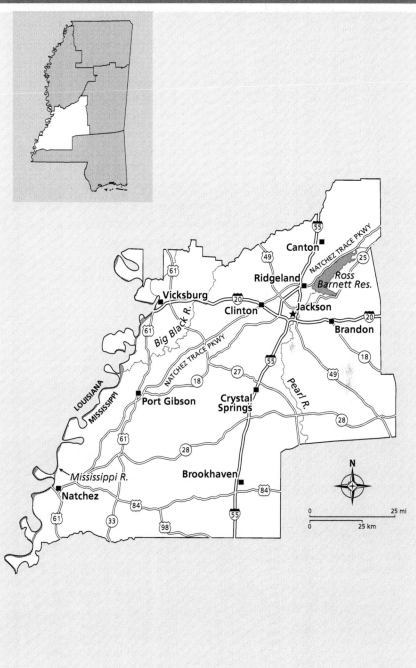

stop in this charming southern hamlet the Canton Convention and Visitors Bureau, housed in the lovely old ***Trolio Hotel*** on the west side of the Canton Courthouse Square. The friendly bureau staff will provide brochures and help you plan a day exploring the town. The Convention and Visitors Bureau is open Mon through Fri from 10 a.m. to 5 p.m., and on Sat from 10 a.m. to 2 p.m. Call (800) 844-3369 or (601) 859-1307, or visit cantontourism.com.

Its picturesque square and small-town charm have made Canton a popular location for films. *A Time to Kill* (based on the novel by Mississippi author John Grisham), *My Dog Skip* (based on the book by the late Mississippi author Willie Morris), *The Ponder Heart* (based on the novel by the late Mississippi author Eudora Welty), *The Rising Place*, and *Oh Brother, Where Art Thou?* (believe it or not, not based on books by Mississippi authors) were all filmed entirely in Canton. Scenes from the films *Mississippi Burning*, *The Chamber*, and *The Ghosts of Mississippi* were also shot within the city limits.

The ***Canton Movie Museums*** (141 N. Union St.), also referred to locally as "the Museum at Wohner's Corner," showcases props and sets from several of the films. Visitors can pay a call to Jake Brigance's law offices or the coffee shop from *A Time to Kill*, take a seat in the beauty salon from *The Ponder Heart*, or risk a peek at the spooky crypt from *My Dog Skip*. The museum also includes a Willie Morris tribute section featuring a replica of the late author's writing desk, complete with notes transcribed word for word from his own. To tour the museum, call or stop by the Canton Convention and Visitors Bureau at 147 N. Union St.; (601) 859-1307 or (800) 844-3369.

AUTHOR'S FAVORITE ATTRACTIONS IN THE HEARTLAND

Antebellum homes and bed-and-breakfast inns, Natchez

McClain Safari Park and Restaurants, Brandon

The Mississippi Civil Rights Museum, Jackson

The Museum of Mississippi History, Jackson

Mississippi River Bridge, Vicksburg

Cocktail hour at **Natchez-Under-the-Hill**, Natchez

The Natchez Trace Parkway as it runs alongside the Ross Barnett Reservoir, Ridgeland

The Old Capitol, Jackson

Old Court House Museum, Vicksburg

Sunday mornings in the **churches of Port Gibson**

Vicksburg National Military Park, Vicksburg

Windsor Ruins, Port Gibson

The Howcott Memorial

Canton is home to the only Civil War monument constructed by a white family in honor of the slave of a Confederate solider. Willis Howcott followed his master, William Howcott, into battle; it is speculated that Willis tried trying to save William, who survived the Civil War and had the 20-foot-high, granite monument erected to honor Willis in the 1890s. An inscription on the monument reads, "A tribute to my faithful servant and friend, Willis Howcott . . . whose memory I cherish with deep gratitude."

If you're in Canton on a Wednesday, book yourself into the **Old Canton Jail Museum**. Built in 1870 and fully functional until 1969, the Old Canton Jail is now the headquarters of the Canton-Madison Historical Society and is open for tours on Wednesdays and on the second Saturday of every month. In all the years the jail "welcomed' temporary residents, there was only one escape. A patient and industrious inmate chipped his way out of his cell using nothing but his toothbrush. The jail welcomes noncriminal visitors at 234 East Fulton Street.

Even before Canton hit the silver screen, the town was famous as the home of the **Canton Flea Market**. Held twice yearly, this juried economic extravaganza attracts 1,100 vendors from twenty-nine states and thousands of shoppers from around the country. Wares include fine art, paintings, pottery, jewelry, crafts, antiques, and plants displayed around the Courthouse Square, in the old jailhouse, and on the grounds of Grace Episcopal Church, Sacred Heart Catholic Church, and other area churches. Come prepared to fight the traffic and pay a premium price for a good parking spot, and don't forget your flashlight—the best deals are made before dawn. The Canton Flea Market is held the second Thurs of May and Oct. Call (800) 844-3369 or (601) 859-8055 for more information, including details on shuttle-bus packages featuring highly coveted and well-worth-it restroom privileges. Visit cantonmsfleamarket.com.

If you prefer shopping as a leisure activity instead of an extreme sport, visit the **Canton Square** on one of the 363 other days of the year. You'll find a number of antique and gift shops and specialty boutiques, and can browse sans the crowds.

The rationale behind Canton's slogan, "the city of lights," becomes abundantly clear each December, when the town launches its monthlong **Victorian Christmas Festival**. From Thanksgiving to New Year's, downtown Canton is ablaze with more than 200,000 white lights. The celebration includes the annual opening of the **Christmas Animation Museum,** a child-pleasing display of 125 moving figures set in vignettes depicting the town's history. An old-fashioned carousel and horse-and-buggy rides round out the winter wonderland atmosphere.

From Canton it's just a short drive south along US 51 to **Madison,** one of Mississippi's premier residential communities. *Southern Living* magazine hails Madison as the place to find "fun shops and casual dining . . . with boutiques, galleries, and restaurants that are drawing a lot of attention." Many of those "fun shops" are located on Main Street (MS 463) just off US 51 in Madison's historic depot district. Shops worth a stop include **Persnickety** (2078 Main St.), an elegant yet funky establishment packed with distinctive, upscale home accessories, fine china, pottery, candles, and gifts. For a handcrafted souvenir, stop by **Pickenpaugh Pottery,** located at 2034 Main St., near the depot area. The Pickenpaugh pottery shop is also the Pickenpaugh residence; visitors to Pickenpaugh will usually find a landscaping project in progress that's every bit as unique as the pottery. Call (601) 856-4985 or (601) 896-3978 or visit pickenpaughpottery.com.

An excellent dining option within walking distance of Madison's shops is the **Strawberry Café** (107 Depot Dr.). Lunch here is creative salads and sandwiches—including the Train Car sandwich, a hefty combination of prime rib and fried shrimp on French bread—with a side order of sweet-potato fries. In the evening, the lights go down, the candles are lit, and the Strawberry Café is transformed into a fine-dining experience, complete with full bar. The Strawberry Café is open Mon through Sat from 11 a.m. to 9 p.m., and Sun for brunch from 10:30 a.m. to 2:30 p.m. Dinner reservations are recommended; call (601) 856-3822 or visit strawberrycafemadison.com.

The Bride of Annandale

Annandale was a huge Madison County plantation built in the 1840s. The plantation owner's daughter, Helen Johnstone, fell in love with the dashing Henry Vick, and their wedding was planned for May 21, 1859, at the Chapel of the Cross. But mere days before the nuptials, Henry was killed in a duel. He was buried at midnight in the churchyard behind the chapel, and the devastated Helen wore her wedding gown to the funeral. Helen eventually married, but never forgot her first love. The last words uttered from her deathbed were, "He's coming back for me."

Visitors to the Chapel of the Cross often report sightings of a sad woman clad all in white, sitting on a bench near Henry Vick's grave. If you go, don't wait for Helen past twilight. It's illegal to prowl the cemetery after dark, and as a number of unfortunate ghost-hunters can verify, it's a law that's strictly enforced.

From downtown Madison, cross I-55 and travel along MS 463 to the **Chapel of the Cross.** The tranquility that envelops this tree-shaded churchyard and antebellum chapel is reason enough for a visit, but if you're in the mood for a mystery, drop by around twilight. You might be lucky enough to bump into the Bride of Annandale—the chapel's resident ghost.

MS 463 intersects MS 22 just northeast of **Flora** and the only petrified forest in the eastern United States. The **Mississippi Petrified Forest** was designated a National Natural Landmark by the National Park Service in 1966. According to geologists, the giant trees embedded in the earth here are some 36 to 38 million years old. A well-marked trail through the wooded park can be easily explored in half an hour. The path ends in the earth science museum and gift shop, where visitors may purchase sparkling crystals, chunks of petrified wood, fossils, and other geological souvenirs. The Petrified Forest is open Mon through Sat from 9 a.m. to 5 p.m. Labor Day through Apr 1; 9 a.m. to 6 p.m. Apr 1 through Labor Day. Admission is $7 for adults and $6 for children and seniors. Call (601) 879-8189 or visit mspetrifiedforest.com.

Double back to Mississippi 463, then follow US 51 south of Madison to **Ridgeland.** A must-stop shopping experience in this busy town is the **Bill Waller Mississippi Crafts Center** (950 Rice Rd.; 601-856-7546). The Crafts Center displays and sells one-of-a-kind masterpieces made by the members of the **Craftsmen's Guild of Mississippi,** including basketry, pottery, woodwork, and jewelry. The crafts center also stages frequent live demonstrations—visitors may arrive to find artisans whittling, weaving, carving, or quilting outside the ultracontemporary building or in one of the many gallery spaces inside. Keep in mind, the work shown and sold here is art, and is priced accordingly. But for those in search of a one-of-a-kind Mississippi gift or collectible, this is the place.

mississippitrivia

Kathryn Stockett's best-selling novel *The Help* is set in Jackson, Mississippi, in the days just before the civil rights movement. *The Help* recounts the story of a group of black maids and their relationships with their white employers.

The Madison–Ridgeland stretch of the Natchez Trace Parkway borders the 33,000-acre **Ross Barnett Reservoir.** Take the parkway north from Ridgeland and you'll arrive at the **Reservoir Overlook,** a grassy plateau that offers a lovely view of the water and provides the perfect setting for a picnic. The "Rez" is a hot spot for power boating, skiing, sailing, and fishing.

From the reservoir area, take Spillway Road (which turns into Lake Harbor Drive as it crosses the reservoir back into Ridgeland) to Old Canton Road; then head south into **Jackson.** You'll know you've left Ridgeland and entered

TOP ANNUAL EVENTS IN THE HEARTLAND

MARCH

Hal's St. Paddy's Day Parade
Jackson
(800) 354-7695
halsstpaddysparade.com

Spring Pilgrimage
Natchez
(800) 647-6742
natchezpilgrimage.com

APRIL

Crossroads Film Festival
Jackson
(601) 345-5674
crossroadsfilmfestival.com

MAY

Canton Flea Market
Canton
(800) 844-3369 or
(601) 859-8055
cantonmsfleamarket.com

Vicksburg Civil War Siege Reenactment
Vicksburg
(800) 221-3536

JUNE

Civil War Reenactments
Vicksburg
(800) 221-3536

JULY

Vicksburg Civil War Siege Reenactment
Vicksburg
(800) 221-3536

Mississippi Championship Hot-Air Balloon Festival
Canton
(800) 844-3369 or
(601) 859-1307
ballooncanton.com

OCTOBER

Canton Flea Market
Canton
(800) 844-3369 or
(601) 859-8055
cantonmsfleamarket.com

Fall Pilgrimage
Natchez
(800) 647-6742
natchezpilgrimage.com

Natchez Balloon Festival
Natchez
(800) 647-6724 or
(601) 442-2500
natchezballoonfestival.com

NOVEMBER

Angels on the Bluff
Natchez
(800) 647-6724
visitnatchez.org

Mistletoe Marketplace
Jackson
(601) 948-2357
mistletoemarketplace.com

DECEMBER

The Chimneyville Arts Festival
Jackson
(601) 856-7549
mscrafts.org

Mississippi's capital city when you cross County Line Road, a major thoroughfare lined with retail shops and restaurants. Located at the intersection of I-55 and I-20, Jackson is hardly off the beaten path, but even this busy city nicknamed the "crossroads of the South" offers a few undiscovered treasures.

Follow County Line Road west to the small but significant campus of **Tougaloo College** (500 W. County Line Rd.). Located on the old Boddie Plantation, Tougaloo is a historically black private liberal arts college founded in 1869. Tougaloo played a vital role in the civil rights movement of the 1960s. Researchers and history buffs will appreciate the Lillian Pierce Benbow Room of special collections in the Coleman Library, where thousands of documents, tapes, photographs, and other artifacts tell the compelling story of the struggle for equal rights.

The civil rights movement also helped create one of the most impressive art collections in Mississippi. In the early 1960s a student from Brown University visiting Tougaloo College described the limited opportunities for black students in Mississippi to study art to his sister, Dore Ashton, a former art critic for the *New York Times*. Ashton organized a group of artists, critics, and collectors who put together the permanent **Tougaloo Art Collection,** the first contemporary art collection in the state. Ashton's group also established a fund for future purchases. Today the Tougaloo Collection includes more than 1,000 paintings, sculptures, and wood carvings valued at between $3 and $5 million. The collection is housed in the college's Coleman Library. Call (601) 977-7706 for viewing hours.

From County Line Road, pick up I-55 South and head toward downtown. The Frontage Road runs along either side of I-55 near the Northside Drive and Meadowbrook exits. Located on the eastern side of I-55, upscale **Highland Village** offers a number of clothing stores, home accessory shops, and galleries worth an afternoon's exploration.

Highland Village is also home to one of Mississippi's most celebrated restaurants, **Bravo! Italian Restaurant and Bar.** Co-owned by high school buddies Dan Blumenthal and Jeff Good, this exceptional restaurant serves innovative Italian cuisine and fine wines. Call (601) 982-8111 or visit bravobuzz.com.

That striking art deco building on the western side of I-55 at Meadowbrook is **Banner Hall,** home to one of Mississippi's premier independent bookstores. Boasting a cozy, friendly atmosphere and a knowledgeable staff of bookworms, **Lemuria** is the place to pick up the latest best seller or a classic literary masterpiece, often signed by the author. The walls are decked with photos of famous writers who've held readings or signings in this popular gathering spot for bibliophiles. Call (601) 366-7619 or visit lemuriabooks.com to check on your favorite title or inquire about authors' appearances.

Be warned—the tempting aroma of fresh-baked bread emanating from Banner Hall's first-floor **Broad Street Bakery** (the sister restaurant of award-winning Bravo!) is impossible to resist. If you really want to concentrate on browsing in the bookstore, give in to the temptation and enjoy a hearty made-to-order sandwich before heading upstairs. Call (601) 362-2900 or visit broad stbakery.com

Back on I-55, continue south to the Lakeland Drive exit, then head west to the *Fondren District,* a neighborhood marked by specialty shops, galleries, and a rich sense of history and character that's impossible to duplicate in a modern mall or strip shopping center. Dating to the 1890s, the eclectic area near the intersection of North State Street and Old Canton Road was Jackson's first suburb; residents traveled back and forth to downtown via streetcar. Today, the Fondren District is a shining example of neighborhood revitalization. Interesting stops here include the *Treehouse Boutique* (3000 N. State St.), featuring unusual gifts and ladies' apparel; the *Everyday Gardener* (2905 Old Canton Rd.), a paradise for green thumbs; *Interiors Market* (659 Duling Ave.), where more than thirty antiques, accessory, and gift shops share display space under a single roof; and *Brown's Fine Art and Framing* (630 Fondren Pl.), an upscale gallery showcasing original paintings and sculpture.

Take a shopping break at *Brent's Drugs and Soda Fountain* (655 Duling Ave.), a Jackson tradition featuring cherry Cokes, milkshakes, and burgers at the counter since the 1940s. Call (601) 366-3427 or visit brentsdrugs.com.

Three of Jackson's most popular museums are found just off Lakeland Drive on the eastern side of I-55. Just five minutes from downtown, the *Mississippi Museum of Natural Science* seems worlds away from city life. The museum complex is nestled in a wooded 300-acre site featuring 2.5 miles of winding nature trails, a woodland pond, and a forest area that serves as a natural habitat for native birds, animals, and plants. Inside the 73,000-square-foot facility, vast windows and a huge central skylight provide a visual link to the outdoors. Exhibits showcasing Mississippi's natural heritage include a white-tailed deer exhibit, a "wall of fossils" display, and a 100,000-gallon, twenty-tank aquarium system swimming with 200 species of native fish, reptiles, and amphibians. "The Swamp," a 1,700-square-foot greenhouse and 20,000-gallon aquarium, is home to alligators and turtles. A 200-seat auditorium screens natural-science films and hosts speakers and special events.

mississippitrivia

Upon its completion in 1925, the ten-story Lamar Life Building (317 E. Capitol St.) was hailed as Jackson's first skyscraper.

The Mississippi Museum of Natural Science is located in *LeFleur's Bluff State Park* at Lakeland Drive and Riverside Drive just past the Lakeland Drive exit on I-55. The museum is open Mon through Fri from 8 a.m. to 5 p.m.; Sat from 9 a.m. to 5 p.m.; and Sun from 1 to 5 p.m. Admission is $6 for adults,

$5 for senior citizens 60 and over, and $4 for children ages 3 to 18. Children under 3, as well as members, are free. For information on changing exhibits and special programs, call (601) 576-6000 or visit mdwfp.com/museum.

Another distinctly Mississippi museum awaits just down Lakeland Drive. The *Mississippi Agriculture and Forestry Museum* (1150 Lakeland Dr.) includes living-history re-creations of life on an 1860s farm (watch out for those chickens!) and in a 1920s small town. The museum and grounds are open 9 a.m. to 5 p.m. Mon through Sat. Admission is $5 for adults; $4 for seniors, military, and children ages 3 to 18; free for children under 3. Family passes and group rates are available. Call (601) 432-4500.

Located just behind the Agriculture Museum, *The Mississippi Sports Hall of Fame and Museum* (1152 Lakeland Dr.) pays tribute to Mississippi's many professional athletes, including Dizzy Dean, Walter Payton, and Archie Manning. Interactive kiosks allow visitors to access archival footage and photos capturing the greatest moments in Mississippi sports history. The Sports Hall of Fame is open Mon through Sat from 10 a.m. to 4 p.m. Admission is $5 for adults and $3.50 for seniors age 60 and over and children ages 6 to 17. Children 5 and under are free. Group rates are available. Call (601) 982-8264 or visit msfame.com.

Jump back on I-55 South and head toward downtown Jackson. Take the Fortification Street exit, head right to North Jefferson Street, and then turn left to tour *The Oaks* (823 N. Jefferson St.; 601-353-9339), the oldest house in the capital city. Built in 1846, the house served as General William Tecumseh Sherman's headquarters during the Civil War. Period furnishings include the sofa from a young Abraham Lincoln's Illinois law office. Tours are available by appointment, with the last tour beginning at 2:15 p.m. Admission is $4.50 for adults, $4 for seniors 65 and over, and $3.50 for children. Visit theoakshouse museum.org for more information.

Back on Fortification Street, you may be surprised to spot a white picket fence smack on the corner of one of Jackson's busiest intersections. The fence surrounds the 1857 *Manship House* (420 E. Fortification St.), home of Jackson's Civil War–era mayor, Charles Henry Manship. In addition to his civic involvement, Manship was an early practitioner of ornamental painting, specializing in the same type of "faux finish" work popular in homes today. Manship transformed the inexpensive lumber used to trim the home's interior into rich wood grains and fine marble. The stenciled floors in the nearby Mississippi Governor's Mansion are also believed to be Manship's work. The Manship House is open by appointment for group tours. For more information or to schedule a group tour, call (601) 961-4724.

Head just a couple of blocks south of Fortification Street, and you'll find yourself in the heart of downtown Jackson. The city was originally laid out following Thomas Jefferson's checkerboard plan, which alternated squares of urban development with public squares or "greens." The result is a downtown district in which trees outnumber utility poles, and it's actually possible to hear birds singing above the traffic. Mississippi's version of a "bustling metropolis" is green and smog-free, with high-tech business conducted in buildings that witnessed the Civil War and sociable natives always ready to extend a gracious southern welcome.

From the historic to the ultramodern, attractions in Jackson share a cultural flair. In addition to antebellum City Hall and the "new" Capitol building (dedicated in 1903), the handful of city blocks that make up downtown are home to no fewer than a dozen historic buildings and museums, all within easy walking distance.

The centerpieces of the Jackson museum scene are the *Mississippi Civil Rights Museum* and the *Museum of Mississippi History*, both located at 222 North Street and often sharing billing under the banner "Two Mississippi Museums." While these multimillion-dollar facilities attract thousands of visitors annually and cannot be considered "off the beaten path," they showcase vital aspects of Mississippi's culture and history and are must-stops for any visitor interested in a deeper understanding of the state. The Mississippi Civil Rights Museum sets the stage for the Civil Rights Movement with a look at the dark history of slavery and segregation, celebrates the heroes who championed Civil Rights in Mississippi and nationwide, and asks visitors to look to the challenges ahead. The Museum of Mississippi History presents the Mississippi story from 13,000 BC to the present through artifacts, interactive exhibitions, and film presentations. Both museums evoke emotional reactions; it the rare visitor who leaves the Civil Rights Museum without shedding tears. To find out more, call (601) 576-6800 or visit mcrm.mdah.ms.gov or mmh.mdah.ms.gov.

In the 1860s, Union troops reduced the capital city to a smoking ruin, earning Jackson the dismal nickname "Chimneyville." More than 130 years later, the handful of antebellum structures that survived the Civil War are still among the city's most impressive. The home of Mississippi's governors since 1842, the proud Greek Revival–style *Governor's Mansion* at 300 E. Capitol St. served as a hospital during the war and was the scene of General Sherman's victory dinner following the fall of Vicksburg. When the state legislature recommended destroying the deteriorating mansion in the early 1900s, public outcry saved the building. Rescued by cries of "Will Mississippi destroy that which even Sherman would not burn?" the mansion was instead renovated to its former glory, opened for public tours, and designated a National Historic Landmark. Free tours are conducted on the half-hour Tues through Fri from 9:30 to 11 a.m. Call (601) 359-6421.

Capitol Street dead-ends at the **Old Capitol,** a favorite landmark of Mississippians. Built in 1833, this magnificent Greek Revival statehouse houses exhibits chronicling Mississippi history, but the real attraction is the building itself. Much of Mississippi's past is preserved in the corridors of this proud old building. It was here that the Ordinance of Secession was passed in 1861, in a hall "crowded to the point of suffocation with visitors who beckoned the state to succession." Jefferson Davis, president of the Confederacy, spoke here on more than one occasion, and the governor was arrested on the staircase at the war's end. There's no charge to tour this grand old museum, which is open 9 a.m. to 5 p.m. Tues through Sat and 1 to 5 p.m. on Sun. Call (601) 576-6920.

Housed in the first school for African-American children in Mississippi, the **Smith Robertson Museum and Cultural Center** (528 Bloom St., 1 block off High Street) celebrates the state's African-American history and heritage. The museum is named for Smith Robertson, a former slave who became a successful businessman and respected community leader, and eventually served as a Jackson alderman. Acclaimed novelist **Richard Wright**, author of *Native Son* and *Black Boy,* was a student at Smith Robertson from 1923 to 1925. The school was closed in 1971 during public school desegregation. In 1984 the building was reopened as a museum to interpret the history of African-American Mississippians. Exhibits document the contributions of African Americans to education, politics, business, and the arts in Mississippi. Smith Robertson schedules regular folk-art demonstrations and workshops and operates a gift shop featuring locally crafted African-American artworks. The museum is open weekdays from 9 a.m. to 5 p.m., and on Sat from 10 a.m. to 1 p.m. Admission is $7 for adults; $5 for seniors and college students; $1.50 for children. Call (601) 960-1457.

The **Farish Street Historic District** just west of downtown was an important African-American residential and business district of the late nineteenth century. Prior to desegregation, Farish Street was the center of the African-American professional and trade community. Bounded by Amite, Fortification, Lamar, and Mill Streets, this 125-acre area features more than 600 listings in the National Register of Historic Places. A drive through the district offers a look at Creole, Queen Anne, shotgun, and bungalow-style cottages constructed by the premier African-American contractors of the day.

Visitors particularly interested in African-American heritage may want to take a side trip to northwest Jackson to see the **Medgar Evers Home Museum**. Evers and his wife, Myrlie, bought this modest home with a GI mortgage in 1957. Shortly after midnight on June 12, 1963, Medgar Evers was shot in the driveway as he returned home from a meeting at a nearby church, his arms full of "Jim Crow Must Go" T-shirts. (See sidebar, "Justice for Medgar Evers"). Myrlie Evers donated the house (located at 2332 Margaret Walker Alexander Dr.) to Tougaloo College, which is preserving it as a historic and cultural site. The humble house itself is far from awe-inspiring. But along with the modest neighborhood surrounding it, the Medgar Evers home stands as a symbol of the simple longing for freedom and opportunity that inspired the civil rights movement, and the ultimate sacrifice made by a leader for the cause. Guided tours are available to the public by appointment. Call (601) 977-7706 or (601) 977-7935, or email libraryservices@tougaloo.edu.

The street on which Evers's home is located, ***Margaret Walker Alexander Drive,*** was named for another famous African American, the late author of the novel *Jubilee,* often referred to as the African-American version of *Gone With the Wind.*

The city of Jackson dedicated both the library in Evers's neighborhood and the street on which it stands to his memory. Neighborhood residents raised funds and erected a life-size bronze ***statue of Evers*** in front of the ***Medgar Evers Boulevard Library*** at 4215 Medgar Evers Blvd.

The Evers home and library and more than 50 other sites related to African-American heritage are included in the ***Jackson Civil Rights Movement***

Justice for Medgar Evers

On June 12, 1963, **Medgar Evers**, a field secretary for the NAACP, was shot and killed by a sniper in his own driveway. A white supremacist named Byron De La Beckwith was tried twice for the murder in 1964. Both trials ended in hung juries.

In 1989 the Hinds County district attorney's office reopened the case when new evidence revealed that the now-defunct state Sovereignty Commission, created in 1956 to preserve segregation, aided Beckwith's defense by screening potential jurors. Beckwith, now 70 years old, was prosecuted for the third time in 1994. Thirty-one years after the murder, Beckwith was found guilty. He died in 2001 after being transferred from prison to a Jackson hospital.

The reopening and retrying of the Beckwith case was the subject of the 1996 feature film *Ghosts of Mississippi*, which starred Alec Baldwin, James Woods, and Whoopi Goldberg. Evers's sons, Darrell and Vann, played themselves in the movie; his daughter Reena was played by Yolanda King, daughter of the late Martin Luther King, Jr. The film was shot on location in Jackson.

Describing the scene in which the guilty verdict is finally returned, the late Darrell Evers said, "It was like reliving the entire thing . . . I always wondered if I'd be able to cry in that scene. It was no problem."

Driving Tour available on the Jackson Convention and Visitors Bureau website at visitjackson.com. The tour includes descriptions of and directions to public buildings, businesses, residences, and churches where history was made. Highlights include the Mississippi state fairgrounds, where demonstrators were held behind hog-wire fences when local jail cells reached capacity; the former site of Woolworth's, where a peaceful sit-in turned into one of the most violent confrontations of the movement; Collins Funeral Home, where 4,000 mourners gathered to pay tribute to slain hero Medgar Evers; and the former home of white civil rights movement supporter Jane Schutt, who transformed a cross burned on her front lawn in December 1963 into a beautiful and enduring Christmas decoration. Marked with blue-and-yellow tour signs, sites are located in downtown Jackson, the Medgar Evers historic district, and on or near the campuses of Jackson State University and Tougaloo College.

After you've completed your tour of downtown, cross back to the north side of Fortification Street and drive through the lovely old residential area known as ***Belhaven.*** Towering trees, generations-old southern gardens, and an eclectic collection of architectural styles are the hallmarks of this gracious old neighborhood. Belhaven's most famous resident was the late Pulitzer Prize–winning author ***Eudora Welty.*** The creator of *The Ponder Heart, The Optimist's Daughter, The Robber Bridegroom,* and other classic southern tales spent most of her life in the Tudor-style house at 1119 Pinehurst St. A young Eudora and her parents moved into the house in 1923; other than a few years in New York and time spent traveling, Miss Welty resided and wrote in the house until her death in 2001 at the age of 92.

Eudora Welty's literary career spanned six decades, beginning in 1936 with the publication of her first short story, "Death of a Traveling Salesman."

mississippitrivia

Author ***Eudora Welty***'s birthplace at 741 N. Congress St. is located directly across the street from the childhood home of novelist ***Richard Wright***. Only in Mississippi, the state known for its literary heritage, will you find the childhood homes of two award–winning authors across the street from one another.

Her novel *The Optimist's Daughter* captured the Pulitzer Prize in 1973. Welty was also the winner of the Guggenheim Award, the O. Henry Award, the National Book Award, the William Dean Howell Medal from the American Academy of Arts and Letters, and countless other awards for her writing. She was given honorary degrees from both Harvard and Yale Universities and received France's highest civilian honor, The French Legion of Honor (1996).

Although she achieved international fame, Welty will always be intrinsically linked to Jackson, her hometown and the city she immortalized in so many pages. As a child, Eudora Welty often roller-skated through the marbled halls of the State Capitol on her way to the downtown library. She was usually greeted at the door by a frowning librarian, who would send little Eudora back home to put on her petticoat, a lecture on library etiquette still ringing in her ears. In an ironic twist, the main branch of the Jackson Public Library system is now known as the Eudora Welty Library. In later years, the famous author was a strong benefactor of performing and cultural arts in Jackson. "Miss Eudora" could still be spotted shopping at the Jitney 14, a local Belhaven grocery store, until shortly before her death.

In a gesture typical of her well-known generosity, Welty deeded her Pinehurst Street home to the Mississippi Department of Archives and History, which operates the house as a literary house museum. The **Eudora Welty House** has been meticulously restored and interpreted to the mid-1980s, the period in which Welty made her decision to bequeath her home to the state of Mississippi and during which time she was still actively writing.

Visitors to the house step into an intimate setting alive with the presence of Eudora Welty. Highlights of the guided tour include the comfortable living room where Welty entertained both her legendary circle of friends and the many fans who appeared at her door seeking autographs; the sitting room, where the handsome secretary displays a first edition set of Welty's works autographed to her mother; and the dining room table where Welty edited her manuscripts, literally cutting them into pieces and reassembling the passages with straight pins. The tour concludes in the upstairs bedroom where Welty worked at her desk beside a bank of windows, creating the characters and stories that won her literary awards and fans worldwide.

Welty's beloved garden is also on the tour, restored to its late 1930s appearance using the original plan developed by Welty's mother. Welty readers and gardening enthusiasts walk among the heirloom camellias and spider lilies and breathe the sweet perfume of the gardenias, roses, and hyacinths referenced in Welty's prose.

Filled with Welty's furniture, overflowing with her cherished books, and surrounded by her garden, 1119 Pinehurst is one of America's most intact literary house museums. The Eudora Welty House is open for tours by reservation Tues through Fri, four times a day at 9 a.m., 11 a.m., 1 p.m., and 3 p.m., and 9 and 11 a.m. the second Sat of each month. To make a reservation for individual or group tours, email tours@eudoraweltyhouse.com. For more information, call (601) 353-7762 or visit eudorawelty.org.

Downtown Jackson offers a couple of down-home diners straight out of the 1940s. Operating under the motto, "It's the food that counts," **The Elite** (141 E. Capitol St.) has been pleasing the palates of discerning diners for more than a century. Just down the street, *The Mayflower* (123 W. Capitol St.), also in business for decades, has perfected the art of homemade roll baking. The Jackson restaurant scene also includes dozens of casual and formal establishments serving everything from barbecue to sushi, Chinese to Indian, white tablecloth to paper plate. Choices are citywide and too many to list; for a few recommendations, see the end of this chapter.

If you're interested in good food *and* the Jackson nightlife, your next stop is *Hal 'n Mal's* (200 Commerce St.). Local politicians, entertainers, and movers and shakers gather at Hal 'n Mal's for a cup of gumbo or an ostrich sandwich or to hear live music. The fictional Adam Cayhall and Hez Kerry planned their legal strategies over a plate of red beans and rice here in John Grisham's *The Chamber*. To find out who's playing, call (601) 948-0888 or visit halandmals.com

Overnight visitors to the capital city will find luxurious bed-and-breakfast accommodations in the heart of downtown. Located within steps of the building for which it was named, the *Old Capitol Inn* (226 N. State St.) is an elegant bed-and-breakfast housed in the old YMCA building. Call (601) 359-9000 or (888) 359-9001 or visit oldcapitolinn.com.

Upscale accommodations are also available downtown at the *King Edward Hotel/Hilton Garden Inn*. The King Edward Hotel originally opened its ornate doors on West Capitol Street in 1923. For the next 40 years, the elegant hotel was the focal point of the Jackson political and social scene. The hotel's ballrooms were the scene of lavish galas, and Mississippi's political leaders discussed matters of state in the grand bar. In 1967 the King Edward closed its doors, and the hotel quickly fell into a state of disrepair. The windows overlooking Capitol Street were boarded over, the sweeping staircase was robbed of its spindles by vandals, and the once-grand ballrooms were visited only by flocks of pigeons. In 2007 a group of developers began the daunting, multimillion-dollar process of restoring the King Edward. Meticulous research was conducted into the hotel's original design; plaster casts were made so that the millwork could be meticulously duplicated. In December 2009 the Hotel King Edward once again opened its doors. While the property is officially operating as a Hilton Garden Inn, the old King Edward sign once again lights up the night. For reservations at this grand old, new-again hotel, call (601) 353-5464.

Belhaven is home to the *Fairview Inn* (734 Fairview St.), a Colonial Revival mansion named the 2003 North America & Caribbean Most Outstanding Inn by Condé Nast. Dinner is served in the Fairview's formal restaurant Mon through Fri from 5 p.m. to 9:30 p.m, and on Sun for brunch only from 10 a.m. to 2 p.m. Call (601) 948-3429 or (888) 948-1908 or visit fairviewinn.com.

Just west of Jackson off I-20, the college town of *Clinton* features a historic "Olde Towne" district marked by brick streets and specialty shops. Olde Towne is home to the **Wyatt Waters Gallery** (307 Jefferson St.). Phenomenally talented watercolorist and all-around nice guy Wyatt Waters is one of Mississippi's most admired and collected fine artists. Waters paints on location and can often be spotted around the Jackson area behind his easel, palette in hand.

Founded in 1826, Clinton's **Mississippi College** (200 S. Capitol St.) is one of the oldest in the nation and was the first college in the United States to graduate a woman. The **Provine Chapel** on campus served as a combination hospital-and-horse stable during the Civil War.

Located on thirty-two acres of wooded land near the Olde Towne district, the **Clinton Nature Center** features hundreds of labeled trees and shrubs, a peaceful 2-mile nature trail, and a butterfly garden. The Nature Center property encompasses portions of the original Natchez Trace, largely unchanged since the first explorers set foot there more than three centuries ago. The Nature Center is located at 617 Dunton Rd. in Clinton. Call (601) 926-1104 or visit clintonnaturecenter.org.

Tiny **Byram**, located just south of Jackson on I-55, made history in Japan when the town's swinging bridge was featured on the popular Japanese television program *Bridges of the World*. One of only four suspension bridges left in Mississippi, the 360-foot, graffiti-plastered, wooden plank bridge was built

Out of Africa, into Mississippi

It's not quite as adventurous as an African safari, but a day spent at *McClain Safari Park and Restaurants* in Brandon, Mississippi, will introduce you to exotic animals from Africa and other worldwide destinations. Owners Buddy and Joni McClain transformed 2,000 acres in Rankin County, Mississippi, into an adventure destination. Visitors board safari wagons for a guided tour that includes up-close-and-personal encounters with zebras, a giraffe, camels, lemurs, buffalos, kangaroos, and dozens of other exotic animals. At the safari's end, guests can enjoy a drink in the well-appointed Tavern, which features live music almost every night, followed by a delicious meal in one of the lodge's two restaurants.

McClain is also home to a well-stocked general store and gift shop, butcher shop, bakery, and farmers' market. The friendly staff, curious animals, and variety of foods makes McClain a popular day trip for adults and children alike. And if you want to extend your visit, McClain also offers a variety of overnight accommodations. At nearby *McClain Lodge*, guests relax in the rustic yet modern lodge or in guest cabins, enjoying a retreat that's close to Jackson yet feels a world away.

McClain Safari Park and Restaurants is located a few miles east of Jackson at 874 Holly Bush Rd. in Brandon. McClain Lodge is located nearby at 314 Clark Creek Rd. For information on either property, call (601) 829-1101 or visit mcclain.ms.

in 1905 by Mississippi engineers who dubbed it the "mini–Brooklyn Bridge." The bridge is open to pedestrian traffic only, offering a pleasant stroll across the Pearl River.

Farmland and Festivals

Follow the signs from I-55 South to US 49 South, where the cityscape quickly gives way to rural Mississippi. Communities just outside the Metro Area are known for their festivals, which usually honor a favorite local crop, and for their folk art, pieces of which are perceived as cultural masterpieces or dressed-up junk, depending on whom you ask and how much it costs.

Eskimos and catfish probably have nothing in common except **Jerry's Catfish House**, an igloo-shaped restaurant located right on the highway in **Florence**. Jerry's claim to fame is an all-you-can-eat deal on Mississippi's favorite bewhiskered treat that has crowds lining up for dinner before the doors open at 5 p.m. Call (601) 845-8860.

Continuing south on US 49, you'll spot signs directing you to **The Piney Woods School**. This Christian boarding school for disadvantaged African-American students has attracted national attention for its old-fashioned teaching philosophy and phenomenal success.

The school was founded in 1909 by Dr. Laurence Jones, who came to Mississippi with nothing but a Bible, $1.65 in change, and a dream of a school where a "head, heart, and hands" education would be available for poor, rural black children. Dr. Jones taught his first classes under a cedar tree and was nearly lynched by a group of men who thought he was preaching against whites. After talking with Dr. Jones, the men were so inspired that they not only put away their rope, but donated $50 to the school. The tree is still standing, marked by a plaque reading "a log, a dream, a vision, a restless urge, a young man, laurence c. jones". Nearby is the log cabin that served as Piney Woods' first schoolroom by day and as Dr. Jones's quarters and a sheep shed by night.

In 1954, Dr. Jones was a guest on Ralph Edwards's television show, *This Is Your Life*. Edwards asked every viewer who was impressed with Piney Woods to send in $1. This call raised more than $700,000, and was the beginning of the school's endowment program.

Dr. Jones's dream is now a national model that's been featured in numerous publications and on more than one segment of *60 Minutes*. More than 90 percent of Piney Woods graduates go on to college, many on scholarships. Visitors are welcome to tour the fifty-acre campus and the surrounding 1,950 acres of farmland, lakes, and pinewoods and to view exhibits chronicling the school's inspiring history. Dr. Jones is buried on the Piney Woods campus, under a cedar tree near the spot where he taught his first lesson. Call (601) 845-2214 for an appointment to tour the campus.

The catchy country tune "Watermelon Crawl" was surely inspired by a visit to nearby *Mize*. The population of this small Smith County community nearly doubles in July, when locals and out-of-towners alike cool off at the Mize *Watermelon Festival*. This daylong celebration includes a flea market, seed-spitting contest, greased-watermelon races, watermelon-eating contest, and the obligatory crowning of the Watermelon Queen. The Watermelon Festival is held the third Saturday in July unless the month has five Saturdays; then the festival moves to the fourth Saturday. To get your juicy slice, take US 49 South to MS 28 and then follow the signs a few miles east to Mize. For more information visit mswatermelonfestival.com.

If you travel west of US 49 on MS 28, you'll find yourself in *Hazlehurst*, the setting for Beth Henley's Pulitzer Prize–winning play *Crimes of the Heart*. The dark comedy was later made into a movie starring Jessica Lange, Sissy Spacek, and Diane Keaton.

Take I-55 20 miles south of Hazlehurst to *Brookhaven*, proclaimed by one of the first electric street signs in Mississippi as "a homeseeker's paradise." According to an account from the period, when the two-story sign was originally switched on in 1915, "all sound stopped. It was as if the people were awe-stricken." The sign continued to amaze and astound visitors until 1943, when it was donated to the war effort. Fifty-three years later, the sign was re-erected at its original location at the intersection of West Cherokee Street and South Whitworth Avenue in downtown Brookhaven, where it continues to welcome "homeseekers" today.

mississippitrivia

Country music superstar *Faith Hill* grew up in Star, Mississippi, and was briefly enrolled at nearby Hinds Community College.

One of Brookhaven's private homes also features a unique mini-museum. Take your cheatin' heart to the residence of Benton Case (410 S. Whitworth Ave.), where you can see and hear the *Hank Williams Sr. Collection*. Case's fascination with the late country superstar began in 1947 when Case, a country music performer himself, heard his first Hank Williams song, "Never Again." He's been an avid fan ever since. Case's collection includes all of Hank Williams's 45 and 78 LP records (in mint condition), posters, photographs, T-shirts, and a hand-cranked phonograph and battery-powered radio.

A member of the Hank Williams Sr. National Society and Fan Club, Case is more than happy to share his wealth of knowledge and his appreciation for Williams with other fans. As Case explains it, "Hank Williams' music will live on because there will always be a cheatin' heart, someone so lonesome they could cry, or someone who can't help it if they're still in love with you." To schedule an appointment to see the collection, call Benton Case at (601) 833-5138.

A beautiful artifact from a faraway land hangs in the sanctuary of the ***First Baptist Church*** on Monticello Street. The magnificent tapestry of Christ praying in the Garden of Gethsemane, a generous 22 feet wide by 24 feet long, was handwoven in a small village in Beijing, China. Local Mississippi artist Asem Zeini created an oil painting to use as a guide. Church members then hand-carried the painting to China. Initially, the Chinese artisans were reluctant to undertake the project because of its size. But upon learning that the man in the painting was a spiritual leader and the tapestry would hang in a place of worship, they expressed honor at being chosen to create the work. According to the weavers, the tapestry is the largest ever made in their area. The finished piece contains one hundred hand-tied knots per square inch, for a total of 7.6 million. As many as 18 weavers worked on the piece at a time, laboring for more than two years. The finished tapestry was hung in the sanctuary in 1996, with the hope that all those who view it will see not dyed wool and knots, but a loving, caring Savior. To view the tapestry, call (601) 833-5118.

Brookhaven is the home of gifted sculptor, illustrator, and mixed-media artist Dr. Kim Sessums. A fine artist whose work graces collections nationwide, Sessums's welcomes serious art enthusiasts to his studio by appointment. Sessums's work also graces the rooms of The Inn on Whitworth, a small Brookhaven hotel. To see his work and schedule a visit, go to jkimsessums.com.

Coffee's On

Located on South First Street in tiny Bogue Chitto, Mississippi, **The Coffee Pot** no longer serves food or coffee, but it's worth driving by to snap a photo of the larger-than-life coffeepot perched atop the roof—a caffeine addict's dream come true. The building was constructed in the 1920s, and has been referred to as the first fast-food restaurant in the South. In the 1930s, The Coffee Pot staged one of fast food's earliest promotions when a pianist played on the roof for 24 hours straight.

That's the Tea

The South is famous for its sweet iced tea, but most people who enjoy a glass don't think about where their tea comes from or how it's grown. Located just outside Brookhaven, **The Great Mississippi Tea Company** is committed to growing tea ethically and sustainably. This working tea farm offers tours and tastings by appointment. For more information, visit greatmsteacompany.com.

If you're in the Brookhaven area on the last Saturday in June, head back north about 35 miles to **Crystal Springs**, home of the annual **Tomato Festival**. The celebration recalls Crystal Springs's history as the "Tomato-polis of the World" with live entertainment, a flea market, children's activities, and, of course, tomatoes. Fried green tomatoes, tomato sandwiches, stuffed tomatoes, salsa—even tomato gravy ladled over hot tomato biscuits. Ketchup, anyone?

From Crystal Springs, continue on I-55 North toward I-20 and the towns and cities that fell in the path of the Civil War assault on Vicksburg. General Ulysses S. Grant's campaign for the "Gibraltar of the Confederacy" left a swath of destruction through this area of the state. But what seemed an unfortunate location in the 1860s is now a business advantage; the cities and towns that suffered Civil War destruction now welcome thousands of Yankees and Rebels drawn to the area for its rich Civil War history.

One of many skirmishes took place in **Raymond**, a small community located on MS 18. Despite the careful plans of the women of the community, the Battle of Raymond was no picnic. When the Rebels marched out to meet the Yanks on May 12, 1863, they were counting on a quick victory. Tables at the **Hinds County Courthouse** and **St. Mark's Episcopal Church** were laden with food in anticipation of a celebratory post-battle feast.

But the 2,500 Union troops the Rebs were expecting turned out to be 12,000. The ensuing battle was fierce, bloody, and, for the South, disastrous. The retreating Confederates fled past the buffet, although legend has it that a few Yankees did stop for a snack before returning to the Rebel rout. The gaily decorated tables intended for cheerful feasting and toasting instead became the scene of ghastly field surgeries and amputations; century-old bloodstains still mar the church floors.

The courthouse and the church, both located on West Main Street, are among the many landmarks listed in a driving-tour guide to Raymond available at raymondms.com. Other sites listed include **Waverly**, which served as temporary headquarters of General Ulysses S. Grant during the Vicksburg campaign; the **Confederate Cemetery**, where many of the soldiers killed in the battle were buried; and the ***Dupree House and Mamie's Cottage***, a historic property and bed-and-breakfast inn.

Little Big Store, a specialty shop located in the historic ***Raymond Depot Building*** at 201 E. Main St., specializes in rare and out-of-print records. Spend a day browsing among the real vinyl albums and nostalgia-inspiring 45s, or call (601) 857-8579 to inquire about your favorite oldies. Little Big Store is open Mon through Sat from 10 a.m. to 5 p.m., and on Sun from 1 to 5 p.m. Visit littlebigstore.com.

Head north to I-20 West and ***Edwards***, site of the ***Battle of Champion Hill***. On May 16, 1863, the Confederate loss at Champion Hill led to the fall of

"What'd you expect from an old broke down store?"

If you're in the Raymond area on a Thursday, Friday, or Saturday, a detour to the unincorporated village of *Learned* (8 miles south of Raymond, population around 100) will lead you to a dinner you'll never forget. The *H.D. Gibbes & Sons Old Country Store* was built in the late 1800s and judging from the exterior, it appears very few enhancements have been made to the bulding since. The store began life as a general mercantile and still sells chips, gas, and soft drinks.

Three nights a week, Gibbes offers a dinner menu, serving up steaks, lamb, and seafood—all presented on groaning paper plates and accompanied by plastic utensils—for hundreds of diners who begin to form a crowd on the porch before 5 p.m., waiting for a seat at one of the community tables. The eclectic crowd typically includes everything from celebratory groups in cocktail wear to bikers on Harleys taking a break from riding the Natchez Trace to hunters in full camo. All sit elbow-to-elbow at long tables designed to encourage conversation with new friends. The store is still owned by members of the Gibbes family and the waitstaff is made up of cheerfully brusque locals who've fielded every kind of comment about the uniqueness of the place and can give as good as they take. When my husband jokingly said he'd prefer cheese and crackers over a juicy steak, our waitress brought him a basket of saltines—still wrapped in plastic—covered with grated cheese. It seems everyone at Glbbes is determined to live up to the motto, "What'd you expect from an old broke down store?"

The old doors open for dinner at 5 p.m. on Thurs and Fri; 4:30 p.m. on Sat. Gibbes & Sons is located at 140 Main St. in Learned. Call (601) 885-6833 or visit hdgib besandsons.com.

If you don't feel like driving back to civilization after that huge meal at Gibbes, cozy accommodations for two are available just two miles down the road at *Harmony Farm*, a tranquil horse farm with a guest cottage for rent. Harmony Farm also welcomes well-behaved dogs, and offers stables for those traveling with horses. Call (601) 946-7482 or visit harmonyfarmofms.com.

Vicksburg, which ultimately cost the Confederacy the Civil War. A noted military historian emphasized the importance of the battle to the war's outcome, writing that "the drums of Champion Hill sounded the doom of Richmond." The 1852 **Coker House** near the battle site was used as a hospital by both Union and Confederate forces. More than 6,200 wounded and dead soldiers littered the grounds of the Coker House; a "limb pit" in the yard hides scores of amputated arms and legs. The battle for Champion Hill is reenacted from time to time; call (601) 446-6502 for the next battle date.

The River Cities

A tour of the River Cities begins in Vicksburg, home of the Vicksburg National Military Park, and ends in Natchez, where you'll find the highest concentration of antebellum mansions in the United States.

This section of the state features at least one historic bed-and-breakfast mansion, Civil War monument, or well-preserved battlefield every 10 miles. Reminders of the antebellum South and the War Between the States dominate not only the landscape, but the very mindset of the people here, reminding visitors that soil once fought and died for is never again an ordinary plot of ground.

From Edwards, follow I-20 West toward the Mississippi River, through steep loess bluffs, gently rolling hills, and ever-encroaching kudzu to the Civil War time capsule that is **Vicksburg**.

President Abraham Lincoln called this river city "the key . . . let us get Vicksburg and all that country is ours. The war can never be brought to a close until that key is in our pocket." A victory at Vicksburg would sever Texas, Arkansas, and Louisiana from the Confederacy and give the Union complete control of the Mississippi River. For over a year, Vicksburg seemed impregnable as Union forces made several fruitless attempts by land and water to capture the city.

When direct charges failed, Grant decided to starve the city into submission. For 47 days and nights, the Union forces engaged in "the grand sport of tossing giant shells into Vicksburg." Accompanied by their slaves and taking their furniture and possessions, the frightened citizens sought shelter from the constant rain of shells in caves dug into the hillsides. (Six of these shelters remain hidden in the bluffs surrounding Vicksburg, but the caves aren't easily accessible, and the locals advise against any spelunking.)

Soldiers and citizens suffered alike as the siege wore on. The summer heat was terrible, water supplies dwindled, and mule meat became a delicacy. As the long, sweltering days passed, the distance between the lines shrank, until aggressors and defenders were virtually eyeball-to-eyeball. During lulls in the shelling, Union and Confederate soldiers exchanged jokes and stories along with coffee and tobacco, and two brothers from Missouri who were fighting on opposite sides were reunited.

On July 3, with his army and the civilian population starving, General John C. Pemberton met with Grant to discuss the terms of surrender. When Grant demanded "unconditional surrender," Pemberton replied, "Sir, it is unnecessary that you and I hold any further conversation. We will go to fighting again at once. I can assure you, you will bury many more of your men before you will enter Vicksburg." Grant relented, offering parole to the city's defenders. On July 4, 1863, the Confederate flag over the courthouse was lowered, and the Stars and Stripes flew once again in Vicksburg. It would be more than one hundred years before the city again observed the Fourth of July.

The Confederates defending the city were outraged by the surrender. Many of the Southern soldiers destroyed their rifles, scattered their ammunition on the ground, and tore their battle standards into shreds. In a remarkable show of respect for the defenders, the occupying Union forces refrained from taunting the vanquished. According to one witness, the Federal troops instead entered the war-torn city with a "hearty cheer for the gallant defenders of Vicksburg," and offers of food were extended with the sentiment, "Here, brave Reb, I know you are starved nearly to death."

With the fall of Vicksburg, the Union regained control of the Mississippi River from Cairo, Illinois, to the Gulf of Mexico. Upon hearing of the surrender, President Abraham Lincoln wrote, "the Father of Waters again goes unvexed to the sea."

The final days of siege and battle are replayed endlessly on the green expanses and rolling hills of the *Vicksburg National Military Park*, where 1,800 acres of fortifications and earthworks lined with monuments tell the dramatic story of the defense and fall of the "Gibraltar of the Confederacy." The Confederate and Union lines are identified, and markers trace the progress of the Union soldiers as they pushed uphill under fire in the thick heat of the

"Giddy up, Jeff Davis!"

Throughout the Civil War, General Ulysses S. Grant rode a horse named Cincinnatis. In his memoirs, however, the northern general owned up to stealing a horse from Confederate president Jefferson Davis's Brierfield plantation near Vicksburg. What did the Union general christen the stolen mount?

Jeff Davis, of course.

Mississippi summer. Generals made of stone lead the charge, bronze horses eternally race into battle, and moss-covered cannons guard the city against a final attack.

Nearly all of the 28 states that sent soldiers to Vicksburg erected markers, statues, and monuments in the park, the largest of which is the ***Illinois Memorial,*** an imposing dome-topped structure inscribed with the names of every Illinois soldier present at Vicksburg. Forty-seven stone steps leading into the monument represent the forty-seven days of siege. Of the thousands of names listed inside, two are of particular interest. Fred Grant, the general's 12-year-old son, is listed as his aide. Also listed is Albert D. Cashire, who served throughout the Vicksburg campaign. When Cashire was hospitalized years later, he was discovered to be a *she*—an immigrant named Jennie Hodgers, who had masqueraded as a man for nearly half a century.

Also displayed at the Military Park is the ***USS* Cairo**, a Union ironclad sunk by the Confederacy and raised after a hundred years underwater. Remarkably intact artifacts recovered from aboard ship, including a running watch, dishes, photos, and clothing, are displayed in an adjoining museum. The National Military Park is located at 3201 Clay St.; for information on guided tours, tapes, and events, call (601) 636-0583. The Military Park is open seven days a week from 8 a.m. to 5 p.m. Admission is $20 per car; a personal guide will ride along with you for an additional fee. For details, visit nps.gov/vick.

Vicksburg's Civil War story is reenacted in May and again in July during the ***Vicksburg Civil War Siege Reenactment.*** The Memorial Day Reenactment includes Union and Confederate tent camps, truce periods during which soldiers barter for coffee and information and attend church services, and bloody assaults on the Confederate lines. Smaller in terms of the number of participants but equally stirring is the Fourth of July Reenactment, which concludes when Union troops take control of the city, lower the Confederate flag, and raise the Stars and Stripes over the courthouse.

The reenactors themselves are a serious bunch, often refusing to acknowledge they're playing a part. Their clothing, campsites, ammunition, even their conversation with spectators, is authentic to the 1860s. Many of the reenactors who make the annual trek to Vicksburg travel thousands of miles to participate in the campaign—much as their ancestors did nearly a century and a half ago.

Relive the siege any time of year through *The Vanishing Glory,* a 30-minute wide-screen production that relies on the eyewitness accounts, letters, and diaries of citizens and soldiers to tell the Vicksburg story. Showtimes are every hour on the hour 9 a.m. to 5 p.m. daily at the ***Old Depot Museum.*** Admission is $5.50. The museum also houses the Gray and Blue Naval Society collection of model gunboats, the largest collection of its kind in the world, as well as original paintings, a detailed siege diorama, and other exhibits related to the city's history. The museum is located at 1010 Levee St.; call (601) 638-6500.

A number of Vicksburg's antebellum mansions survived the siege and are open for tours; about a dozen operate as bed-and-breakfast inns. Many of the homes played significant roles in the war and still bear the scars of battle. A Union cannonball tore through the front door at **Cedar Grove** and is still embedded in the parlor wall. Cedar Grove was built in 1840 as the home of John and Elizabeth Klein. Mrs. Klein was a relative of the much-loathed Union General William Tecumseh Sherman. Soon after the shelling began in Vicksburg, General Sherman personally escorted the Klein family to safety, and Union forces occupied the house until the end of the siege. Grant himself is said to have slept in the master bedroom.

But even though Cedar Grove bore the scars of shelling, the residents of Vicksburg never forgave the Kleins for their affiliation with the hated Union general. When the Kleins' 16-year-old son Willie was accidentally shot to death on the back stairs, townspeople reportedly told Elizabeth Klein she had placed a curse on the child by naming him after the despised Sherman.

Union affiliations aside, Cedar Grove stands as a testimony to the antebellum South. In addition to bed-and-breakfast accommodations and daily home tours, Cedar Grove offers romantic gourmet dining by candlelight, a cocktail hour in the five-acre formal gardens or in the **Mansion Bar,** and sweeping views of the Mississippi River from the rooftop gardens. Cedar Grove may even harbor a ghost. Mr. Klein was fond of smoking a pipe in the gentlemen's parlor each evening, and guests and staff alike have reported the distinct odor of pipe tobacco lingering in the empty room at twilight.

With rooms available in the mansion, carriage house, and poolside garden cottages, Cedar Grove is the largest bed-and-breakfast in Mississippi. For rates and reservations, call (601) 636-1000 or visit cedargroveinn.com.

Vicksburg is home to more than a dozen historic bed-and-breakfast inns. Vicksburg's casinos also offer hotel rooms in every price range. For a complete list of casino resorts and bed-and-breakfast inns in Vicksburg, call the Vicksburg Convention and Visitors Bureau at (800) 221-3536 or visit visitvicksburg .com.

Overnight guests at nearby **Anchuca,** another mansion-turned-bed-and-breakfast, can sleep in the same bed where Jefferson Davis, president of the Confederacy, often passed the night.

Several additional homes welcome visitors during the annual **Spring and Fall Pilgrimages.** For a complete list of the many historic tour homes and bed-and-breakfast inns and this year's Vicksburg Pilgrimage dates, stop by the welcome center located near the scenic **Mississippi River Bridge,** call the Vicksburg Convention and Visitors Bureau at (800) 221-3536, or visit visit vicksburg.com.

Prominently situated atop a hill on Cherry Street, the 1858 Vicksburg courthouse was a favorite target for Union shells until all of the Federal prisoners in Vicksburg were moved into the courtroom—a ploy credited with saving the building. The **Old Court House** is now one of the state's best historical museums, filled to the rafters with an extensive collection of Civil War letters, soldiers' diaries, period clothing, and other artifacts related to Vicksburg history. Exhibits include the tie worn by Confederate president Jefferson Davis upon his inauguration, a never-surrendered Confederate flag, and a minié ball that supposedly impregnated a local woman when it passed through a soldier's "private parts" before striking her own. Nicknamed "Vicksburg's Attic," the Old Court House is literally packed with artifacts—some items are even suspended from the ceiling. The **Old Court House Museum** is located at 1008 Cherry St, in the heart of historic downtown. The museum is open Mon through Sat from 8:30 a.m. to 4:30 p.m., and on Sun from 1:30 to 4:30 p.m. Admission is $6 for adults, $5.50 for seniors 65 and over, and $4 for students grades 1 through 12. Call (601) 636-0741 or visit oldcourthouse.org.

Several historic homes and the **Vicksburg Garden District** are located on Washington Avenue, which also runs into a quaint area of shops and small museums. The **Biedenharn Museum of Coca-Cola Memorabilia** (1107 Washington St.) is housed in the building where Coca-Cola was first bottled in 1894. The museum chronicles the history of the world's most popular soft drink and serves up "the real thing" in floats from the old-fashioned soda fountain. For more information visit biedenharncoca-colamuseum.com.

The **Attic Gallery** (1101 Washington St.) lives up to its name, bursting with an eclectic collection of pottery, paintings, carvings, and other local and regional art. "Attic" is an apt description of the gallery. The place is packed with colorful artwork, and if you hunt, poke, and rummage long enough, you're sure to find something that seems painted, sculpted, or thrown just for you. Owner Leslie Silver has operated this Vicksburg treasure trove for more than 30 years and is one of Mississippi's foremost experts on folk art. Call (601) 638-9221.

Vicksburg does offer more than Civil War attractions. The **Jacqueline House African American Museum** (1325 Main St.) celebrates the city's African-American history and culture. The museum is open on Sat from 10 a.m. to 5 p.m., or by appointment. Call (601) 636-0941. The **Southern Cultural Heritage Center** (1302 Adams St.), an art gallery and bookstore with an African-American emphasis, also offers exhibits and cultural programs. Call (601) 631-2997.

That wonderful, ramshackle structure built of colorful masonry on US 61 a few miles north of the center of Vicksburg is **Margaret's Grocery,** a Mississippi folk art icon recently named the Weirdest Roadside Attraction in Mississippi by Thrillist.com. The pink, yellow, red, and white archways, pillars, and towers sprinkled with Bible verses were built by the late Rev. H. D. Dennis as a loving tribute to his wife, Margaret Dennis. In 1984, the minister promised Margaret if she married him, he'd turn her simple country store into a palace, and he was true to his word. For many years, Rev. Dennis continued to add on to the Lego-like structure, taking time out from his work to greet visitors and share a word of inspiration. His roadside sermons often revolved around the simple truth that "God ain't got no black church and God ain't got no white church. He's got one church and all are welcome." When visitors admired his artistic construction project, the humble Reverend replied, "God is the greatest architect. I'm only his assistant." For years the couple ran the site as a combination grocery store and religious outreach center; Rev. Dennis continued to operate the site after Margaret died in 2009. When Rev. Dennis followed his beloved wife in 2012, it seemed Margaret's Grocery might die, too. Fortunately, Rev. Dennis was not the only person who had made a promise connected to the property.

One of the many visitors to Margaret's Grocery was a freelance photographer named Suzi Altman. Altman first visited the site in 2000, and fell in love not only with the grocery, but also with its proprietors. Altman grew so close to the couple that she spoke at Margaret's funeral. Near the end of his own life, the Reverend—known to Suzi and those close to him as "Preacher"—asked a promise of Altman. "Promise me, Suzi. Promise me that you'll take care of my place."

Altman agreed and has been true to her word. In 2013, she established the **Mississippi Folk Art Foundation**, a nonprofit dedicated to preserving Margaret's Grocery. Altman has worked tirelessly to preserve both the building and Preacher's art, cataloguing every piece of his work and moving much of it from the grocery to climate-controlled storage for preservation, with the hope of one day establishing a museum in Preacher and Margaret's honor. Altman is also working to maintain and restore the grocery building/folk art environment outside Vicksburg, handling every task from security to roof repair to cutting the grass. Her role as the founder of the Mississippi Folk Art Foundation has required Altman to learn the ins and outs of art preservation, grant application, and managing a nonprofit on a slimmer-than-shoestring budget. Her ultimate goal is to preserve Margaret's Grocery as a permanent roadside attraction and a tangible reminder of the irreplaceable value of outsider art to Mississippi's culture. It's a demanding labor of love for Altman, who on the day she first stepped beneath the sign proclaiming "All is welcome, Jews and Gentiles," could never have imagined she would someday be entrusted with saving the property. "It's made me a better person," Altman says. "It's reminded me what's real. If this is what I'm remembered for, it's not a bad thing."

Margaret's Grocery is closed while Altman works on the extensive repairs needed to preserve this treasure, but Altman offers tours by appointment. The experience of a guided tour by the knowledgeable Altman, who not only understands and appreciates the art, but also intimately knew and loved its creators, is a truly unique opportunity. For information, contact Suzi Altman at (601) 668-9611. Learn more about Margaret's Grocery and see Altman's photos of this iconic landmark on Facebook pages for Margaret's Grocery and the Mississippi Folk Art Foundation.

Continue south on US 61 to the all-but-extinct town of **Grand Gulf**. Once one of the busiest ports between New Orleans and St. Louis, Grand Gulf endured a series of disasters that eventually wiped out the town. Grand Gulf stoically survived citywide fires, a yellow fever epidemic, and a devastating tornado before the Mississippi River changed its course, gobbling up 55 city blocks in the late 1850s. What little was left of the once-thriving city was burned to the ground by the Union army during the Civil War.

Though you'll still find it on the map, Grand Gulf is so small it doesn't even warrant a zip code. This isolated hamlet's sole claim to fame is its rich nineteenth-century history, preserved in the **Grand Gulf Military Monument Park.** The 400-acre park includes Fort Wade, where heavily armed Confederates repelled Grant's initial landing attempt; the **Grand Gulf Cemetery,** where black Union troops who occupied the town are buried and the headstones offer a synopsis of Grand Gulf's tragic history; well-preserved earthworks built by the Grand Gulf defenders; and several restored buildings moved to the park from other sites in Mississippi, including the Sacred Heart Catholic Church, which was moved from the ghost town of Rodney. The park museum—named one of the best small museums in the nation by *Reader's Digest*—contains hundreds of Civil War artifacts, including soldiers' letters and diaries, guns, and bloodstained uniforms. An outbuilding houses a collection of carriages and wagons, including a rare Civil War ambulance and a one-man submarine used to smuggle whiskey during Prohibition. The Mississippi River is visible for miles from the park's observation tower, and it's easy to imagine Grant's troops assembling for the attack.

The park also includes nature trails and facilities for tent and RV camping. Admission is charged only for the museum and RV camping. Grand Gulf Military Monument Park is located 10 miles northwest of Port Gibson and US 61 on Grand Gulf Road. The office is open daily from 8 a.m. to 5 p.m., and the park is open until dusk. Call (601) 437-5911.

Lakemont's Perfumed Lady

When William Lake was killed in a duel in 1861, his wife was watching through a spy-glass from the second floor of their Vicksburg home. Today the home, still known as *Lakemont*, is thought to be haunted by Lake's widow.

The present owners claim to hear the rustle of petticoats and smell the overpowering scent of sweet, old-fashioned perfume. The presence is strongest during the month of October—the same month in which William Lake died.

Nearby **Port Gibson** is probably the only town in the South that uses a quote from the much-loathed General Grant as its slogan. In a rare departure from his scorched-earth policy, General Grant declared Port Gibson "too beautiful to burn" and left the town's picturesque collection of homes and churches unscathed. Port Gibson was the first town in Mississippi designated a National Historic District.

Most of the antebellum homes and churches that so enchanted the general are located directly on US 61 South, which turns into Church Street in Port Gibson. Drive as far as the visitor center located at the south end of the street, where a helpful volunteer will provide you with maps, brochures, and background information on the homes and churches; then leave your car parked at the visitor center and enjoy a walking tour of Church Street.

Port Gibson's most striking structure is the ***First Presbyterian Church,*** its steeple topped by a 10-foot gold hand pointing heavenward. The church was built in 1859 under the dynamic leadership of the Reverend Zebulon Butler. Butler himself labored with the workers and craftsmen during the church's construction, but he died just before the building was completed. Ironically, the first service held in the new church was his funeral. The original hand atop the steeple was fashioned of wood—to the delight of area woodpeckers, who showed little respect for this holy symbol. The present metal hand topping the church has become Port Gibson's most famous landmark. Notable features inside the church include the original slave gallery and the chandeliers from the steamboat Robert E. Lee; each chandelier features a figure of General Lee on horseback.

Just down the street is ***St. Joseph's Catholic Church,*** where an eerie trick of the light and stained glass makes the very air inside the church seem blue at any hour of the day. Exquisite panels carved of walnut depict religious symbols, including the Ten Commandments and the Lamb of God, and enhance the solemn atmosphere of reverence that permeates this 1849 house of worship.

St. Joseph's is open for tours through Southern Magnolia Tours (1601 Church St.; 601-715-7214) and for worship Sun mornings at 9 a.m. Church Street is also home to the oldest synagogue in Mississippi, Temple Gemiluth Chessed, which is open on Sat from 10 a.m. to 2 p.m.

Civil War buffs will want to stop by **Wintergreen Cemetery** (613 Greenwood St.), where Confederate general Earl Van Dorn is buried facing his beloved South and a section known as "Soldier's Row" is the final resting place for Union and Confederate soldiers. True Blue-and-Gray buffs can pick up a map of **General Grant's March Route** through the county, available at the visitor center on Church Street. Sections of the route have been left undisturbed for more than 140 years; the dirt road and steep ravines navigated by Grant's 20,000 troops remain largely untouched. The road is impassable during inclement weather, and explorers are advised to check in with the Port Gibson–Claiborne County Chamber of Commerce before setting out (601-437-4351).

Guided tours of the Port Gibson area, including antebellum homes, churches, cemeteries, battlefields, haunted spaces, and more, are available through **Southern Magnolia Tours**, operated by husband-and-wife team Josh and Jessica McCraine. Call (601) 715-7214 or visit southernmagnoliatourspg.com.

The local Port Gibson arts agency known as the **Mississippi Cultural Crossroads** was formed to promote local arts and culture and to preserve and celebrate the African-American art form of quilting. Work by the Crossroads Quilters is displayed in galleries across the South. Colorful patchworks and vivid murals line the walls of the Cultural Crossroads headquarters at 507 Market St. in downtown Port Gibson. Cultural Crossroads sponsors **Pieces and String,** an annual quilting exhibition and contest held the last full weekend in Apr. For more information, contact the Cultural Crossroads at (601) 437-8905.

African-American history of a later era is preserved in the exhibit **No Easy Journey,** a permanent collection of photographs and artifacts commemorating the civil rights movement in Claiborne County. Haunting images of African Americans facing billy clubs and guns, picketing local businesses, and marching the streets of a 1960s Port Gibson in search of equal rights remind visitors of the turbulent era and celebrate the progress that has been made over the past 40 years. Housed in the Claiborne County administration building, this free exhibit is open Mon through Fri from 8 a.m. to 5 p.m.

No visit to the Port Gibson area is complete without a side trip to the **Windsor Ruins.** A dusty road winding through the quiet countryside leads to the crumbling remains of what was the largest antebellum mansion in Mississippi. Following the Battle of Port Gibson, Union troops claimed the house as a hospital, and the eloquent pleas of the mistress of Windsor saved the mansion from destruction at their hands on three separate occasions. Windsor survived the war only to burn to the ground at the hands of a careless smoker in 1890. Twenty-three towering Corinthian columns are all that remain of the once-opulent mansion, and a sketch drawn by a Union soldier in May of 1863 is the only known image of the house in its heyday. The dramatic ruins have been featured in a number of movies, including *Raintree County,* which starred Elizabeth Taylor and Montgomery Clift. A map indicating the shortest route to the Windsor Ruins is available from the visitor center on Church Street, or you can take US 61 South, then follow the signs to Mississippi 552 West and the ruins.

Heading back to US 61 on Mississippi 552, you'll pass **Alcorn State University.** Founded in 1871, Alcorn was the nation's first land-grant college for African Americans. Alcorn's **Oakland Chapel** features the iron staircase that once led to the front doors of the Windsor mansion.

Just south of the intersection of Mississippi 552 and US 61 in **Lorman** is the **Old Country Store,** which first opened its doors to shoppers in 1875. Today,

Travels with Frosty

One of the best research tools I've discovered for travel writing isn't a guidebook, an Internet listing, or even a well-marked map.

It's my dog, Frosty.

An American Eskimo spitz, Frosty is forty pounds of fluffy white fur, intelligent brown eyes, and adventurous spirit. The Eskimo spitz is a striking dog and a rather uncommon breed for Mississippi—traits that turned out to be invaluable during the researching of *Mississippi Off the Beaten Path*.

When I drove into small towns with Frosty hanging out the window, we caused quite a stir. People invariably wanted to pet him, offered him water, and, as an afterthought, talked to me, too.

I was made privy to local legends, received detailed directions to out-of-the-way attractions, and soaked up the local color, all from people who shared freely with me while petting my dog. I gathered critical information not because I was a skilled field researcher, but because I was Frosty's traveling companion.

As for Frosty himself, I'd like to believe he put up with all the attention as a favor to me and out of dedication to the project, not simply because he enjoyed being doted on by strangers all over Mississippi.

Since he worked so hard on this book, it's only fair that I tell you Frosty's favorite spot in *Mississippi Off the Beaten Path*. It was the Windsor Ruins, paws down. It seems those twenty-three towering Corinthian columns have a lot more doggy appeal than an ordinary fire hydrant.

the Old Country Store is a combination restaurant and flea market where you'll find some of the best fried chicken in the South, an array of quirky artifacts for sale, and a colorful, friendly owner who serenades his delighted guests while serving said chicken with side orders of red roses. Call (601) 437-3661.

For an adventure way, way, way off the beaten path, take the first road to the right on the south side of the Old Country Store and head for the **Rodney Ghost Town.**

Incorporated in 1828, Rodney was known for its high level of culture and business activity. The Mississippi River flowed past Rodney, rendering the town a bustling center of commerce and distribution. In its heyday, Rodney was home to two banks, two newspapers, 35 stores, a large hotel, an opera house, and several saloons. By 1860, with a population approaching 4,000, Rodney was one of Mississippi's most prosperous towns.

mississippitrivia

The late actor **Michael Clarke Duncan** attended college at Alcorn State University in Lorman. His heartbreaking performance in *The Green Mile* earned Duncan an Oscar nomination.

Then the Civil War depleted Rodney's wealth, and the town was nearly wiped out by a series of disastrous fires. But it was Mother Nature who dealt the final blow. Around 1869 the Mississippi River changed its course, leaving Rodney high and dry. The population dwindled over the coming decades, and in 1930, Mississippi Governor Theodore Bilbo issued an executive proclamation abolishing the town.

Union gunboats shelled Rodney during the Civil War, and a cannonball is still embedded in the facade of the 1829 **Rodney Presbyterian Church,** the deserted town's most prominent building. Thick grass carpets the brick steps in front of the church, spreading all the way to the front doors. A separate entrance at the side of the building opens to a narrow flight of super-steep stairs leading to the old slave gallery. The ancient town cemetery is hidden behind the church up a steep hill, its overgrown grave sites surrounded by an ornate wrought-iron fence. A second old church, a Masonic lodge, and an old store are the only buildings still standing, and cotton grows in the old riverbed. Formed in 2017, the Rodney History and Preservation Society is raising funds to restore the town to its former glory, but for now, Rodney remins a quiet ghost town.

Getting to Rodney is easy—as long as you don't get lost. Be warned: The route alternates between total gravel and one-step-up-from-gravel asphalt, and will give your shock absorbers a workout they'll never forget. The country roads you'll follow probably have names, but the complete absence of any signage renders them irrelevant.

From the intersection of US 61 South and MS 552, head northwest on 552. At just under 4 miles, you'll see an unmarked asphalt road on your left. Take that left and then travel less than 1 mile to the first right turn. Follow this road 1 mile; then take a right (the asphalt option as opposed to the gravel option) at the fork in the road. This road runs into Rodney about 7 miles and several jarring bumps later. All buildings in Rodney are in disrepair; visitors should explore from the outside. About eight residents still call Rodney home; please be respectful when visiting their community.

When the lonely feel of the ghost town begins to seem a bit unnerving, head back down that bumpy road to US 61 South. When you reach the intersection of US 61 and the ***Natchez Trace Parkway,*** you can take the Trace or continue on US 61 to ***Fayette.*** Either route will eventually lead you to MS 553 and ***Springfield Plantation.***

Springfield boasts a legacy of intrigue and romance few historic homes can rival. In the spring of 1791, Andrew Jackson and Rachel Robards were married in the parlor of this beautiful mansion, touching off a scandal that would haunt the Jacksons for the rest of their lives. At the time of their marriage, both bride and groom mistakenly believed Rachel and her first husband had been granted a divorce. When word of their invalid marriage spread, political opponents began a vicious smear campaign, accusing Jackson of "sleeping under the blanket with another man's wife."

Like many homes with a romantic past, Springfield is rumored to be haunted. The strains of long-ago melodies are said to echo through the home's west wing, where a ballroom once occupied the second floor. Who knows— perhaps the restless spirits of the famous newlyweds still share a wedding-day dance. At the time of this writing, Springfield Plantation was not open for tours. To check on its current status, contact the Port Gibson-Claiborne County Chamber of Commerce at (601) 437-4351.

MS 553 makes a scenic loop west of the Natchez Trace that includes the historic ***Church Hill*** community, home to a number of working plantations, historic homes, and churches, including ***Christ Church***, the oldest Episcopal church in Mississippi. Christ Church sits atop a hill and inspired the community's name. Prior to the Civil War, Church Hill was a community of wealthy planters. Seven of these old plantation homes, all privately owned, line a 12-mile stretch along Highway 553. Over the years, Hollywood has found its way to this sleepy community. The Cedars plantation was once owned by actor George Hamilton, and Wyolah Plantation is the current home of director/producer Tate Taylor.

Directed by Tate Taylor

Movie producer and director and Jackson, Mississippi, native **Tate Taylor** is putting his home state in the spotlight.

Taylor, the director of hit movies like *The Help* and *The Girl on the Train*, always dreamed of living in an antebellum home. "I was the weirdo who asked to go to Colonial Williamsburg for spring break when I was ten," Taylor said in an interview in *Architectural Digest*. Taylor made that dream come true when he purchased and renovated Wyolah, an 1830s Greek Revival mansion on 100 acres in tiny Church Hill, Mississippi. Taylor was soon hosting actors, filmmakers, musicians, and other creative types on the property, moving many of his brainstorming sessions and pre-production meetings from traffic-choked Los Angeles to not-even-one-stoplight Church Hill.

Taylor has also moved the movie making *itself* to Mississippi, opening Crooked Letter Picture Company, a film production company, on the Mississippi River bluff in nearby Natchez. Taylor has filmed multiple movies in Natchez, including *Breaking News in Yuba County*, starring Allison Janney, Mila Kunis, Regina Hall, and Wanda Sykes; *Ma*, starring Academy Award winner Octavia Spencer; and *Get On Up*, starring Chadwick Boseman as James Brown.

Taylor's involvement in the area isn't limited to filmmaking. Taylor is partnering with Nick Wallace, an acclaimed Mississippi chef and winner on The Food Network's *Chopped*, to open eateries in Church Hill and in Natchez. The **Little Easy Café** is a coffee shop in Natchez that doubles as the commissary for film productions. Taylor also has plans to restore **Wagner's Grocery**, an old-fashioned general store in Church Hill.

Taylor's vision is larger than just opening new businesses; his longterm goal is to build a creative economy and foster a creative mindset that will generate new career and educational opportunities in the Natchez area and improve the quality of life in his home state. It seems that while Tate Taylor made it big in Hollywood, Mississippi still plays a starring role in his heart.

For a look at accommodations of a more rustic sort, rejoin the Natchez Trace from MS 553 and head south to the **Mount Locust Inn,** a 1700s version of Howard Johnson's. Restored to its original 1780 appearance (complete with split-rail fences and coonskin caps on the bedposts), Mount Locust offers a glimpse of the "luxury" accommodations of the day. Between 1785 and 1830, more than fifty of these frontier inns or "stands" existed along the Old Natchez Trace. For approximately 25 cents, weary travelers enjoyed a supper of "mush and milk" and the privilege of sleeping in a room packed with saddles, baggage, and other wayfarers. Located approximately a day's walk apart, these establishments offered not only a meal and a place to rest, but a spot

From Slaves to Founders of a Nation

In 1834, **Captain Isaac Ross**, a plantation owner in **Lorman**, freed his slaves and arranged for their passage back to their homeland on the west coast of Africa. There, these freed slaves founded the nation of Liberia.

Years later, their descendants returned to Lorman and placed a commemorative stone at the captain's grave site honoring his kindness and celebrating the magnanimous gesture that led not only to the freeing of their ancestors, but to the founding of their country. Ross's home, known today as Prospect Hill, still stands in Lorman and is now owned by The Archaeological Conservancy.

of civilization in the vast wilderness surrounding the Trace. Mount Locust is the only inn left standing. The former sites of other frontier stands are marked along the parkway. Mount Locust is open daily from 9 a.m. to 4:30 p.m. year-round, except Dec 25.

The next stop on the Trace is even older. Built around 1400 by ancestors of the Creek, Choctaw, and Natchez Indians, **Emerald Mound** is the second-largest Indian mound in the United States. The ceremonial earthen structure covers some eight acres, measures 770 feet by 435 feet at its base, and stands 35 feet high. The Emerald Mound site was a center of Indian civic, ceremonial, and religious rituals from 1300 to 1699.

mississippitrivia

Mount Locust Inn is the scene of a grisly discovery in Mississippi author Nevada Barr's best seller *Hunting Season.*

The Natchez Trace ends at US 61, which runs into the heart of Natchez. But first you'll drive through the old territorial capital of **Washington,** once known as the "Versailles of the Mississippi Territory."

Turn right off US 61 at the sign pointing to historic *Jefferson College.* The first educational institution chartered in the Mississippi Territory, Jefferson College conducted its first classes in 1811. A young Jefferson Davis was a student here, and, according to local lore, naturalist John James Audubon instructed drawing classes on campus, Andrew Jackson was entertained here following the Battle of New Orleans, and former vice president Aaron Burr was arraigned for treason under the campus's giant "Burr Oaks."

The college closed with the outbreak of the Civil War, reopening in 1866 as a preparatory school. Classes were conducted here until the 1960s, when the buildings were restored to their 1800s appearance and the campus became a museum. Historic Jefferson College played West Point in the 1980s miniseries

North and South starring Patrick Swayze and also appeared in *The Horse Sol-diers* starring John Wayne and in Disney's *Huck Finn.* The grounds and build-ings are open by appointment by calling (601) 446-6502 or emailing info@historicjeffersoncollege.com.

Continue on US 61 South to history-rich **Natchez,** the oldest settlement on the Mississippi River. Make your first stop the **Natchez Visitor Center** at the end of Canal Street overlooking the famed Father of Waters. This spacious facility houses the Natchez Convention and Visitors Bureau, the Natchez arm of the National Park Service, and a state-operated Mississippi Welcome Center. The visitor center is home to interesting exhibits, a gift shop, and an excel-lent bookstore devoted to local and regional history, but its strongest asset is a knowledgeable, friendly staff eager to introduce you to the rich heritage of Natchez. The reception center is open Mon through Sat from 8:30 a.m. to 5 p.m., and on Sun from 9 a.m. to 4 p.m. Visit visitnatchez.org.

This corner of southwest Mississippi was the quiet domain of the Natchez Indians until 1716, when French settlers established Fort Rosalie on the bluffs overlooking the Mississippi River. French, British, and Spanish flags each took turns flying over the settlement until 1797, when Andrew Ellicott raised the first American flag over Natchez, signaling the beginning of US governance.

Despite its rich European history, Natchez is best known as a bastion of the antebellum South. Prior to the Civil War, more than half the millionaires in America lived in Natchez, erecting palatial mansions with fortunes built on cotton. Natchez surrendered to Union forces early in the conflict; the city was spared the burning and destruction suffered by much of the South.

All told, Natchez boasts an incredible 500 surviving antebellum structures, including breathtaking homes, ornate churches, and public buildings where history was made.

The grand southern tradition of the pilgrimage was born in Natchez way back in 1932. A late freeze wiped out the blooms scheduled for a weekend gar-den tour, so the members of Natchez's garden clubs opened their antebellum homes for visitors instead. Many of these ladies were hesitant to participate in such a bold venture. Times had been tight in Natchez in the 60 years following the Civil War, they argued. Didn't the homes need remodeling first? Of course, it was the very fact that the homes *hadn't* been changed since the prewar days that made them such an attraction. This impromptu tour was such a fabulous success that in 1932 the ladies scheduled the first *official* Spring Pilgrimage, and the rest is tourism history.

During Spring and Fall Pilgrimages approximately 30 of Natchez's grand old buildings are open for tours. While most Mississippi pilgrimages are held over a week or weekend, the Natchez extravaganza lasts a full month, running

The Ghost of King's Tavern

For a dining experience that's literally out of this world, stop by **King's Tavern** (619 Jefferson St. in Natchez), a steak and seafood house operating in the oldest building in the Natchez Territory. The fare at King's Tavern is quite delicious, but the restaurant's real attraction is Madeline, its resident ghost.

The exact origin of King's Tavern is lost to history, but the building was probably constructed somewhere around 1760. The first mail to the region was carried down the Natchez Trace by Indian runners and left in a small post office on the tavern's first floor. Bullet holes in the heavy doors speak of bandits who once stalked travelers along the Trace, the claw prints of bear and cougar are still visible in the floors, and in the 1930s three skeletons (accompanied by a jeweled dagger) were unearthed in the tavern walls.

A young serving girl named Madeline—rumored to be the mistress of the tavern owner—worked in the midst of all this adventure. Apparently Madeline found King's Tavern so exciting, she just couldn't bear to leave—even 200 years after her death. Restaurant employees and patrons speak of lights switching on and off by themselves, footsteps that ring through the vacant upper floor, and water dripping in certain spots while everything else is dry. Apparently Madeline still tries to keep her customers happy—she operates the old dumbwaiter from time to time.

For hours, call (601) 446-5003 or visit kingstavernnatchez.com. And if you go, ask for a seat at one of Madeline's tables.

from mid-Mar to mid-Apr and again in Oct. No experience on earth is as thoroughly southern. Costumed hostesses recite each magnificent home's history, punctuated by lots of curtseying, plenty of "y'alls," and frequent sips of that quintessential southern cocktail, the mint julep. Visitors marvel at perfectly preserved Aubusson carpets, hand-blocked Zuber and Delicourt wallpaper, marble fireplace mantels, silver-plated doorknobs and bronze chandeliers, priceless paintings and sculptures, and heirloom imported china. Horse-and-carriage rigs clip-clop through downtown, once again the preferred mode of transportation. Magnificent displays of antique roses, camellias, Japanese and saucer magnolias, dogwood trees, jasmine, daffodils, and azaleas remind guests that this spring spectacular began as a garden tour. The festivities aren't limited to the home tours. During the spring pilgrimage, the most popular evening entertainment is the *Historic Natchez Tableaux,* a live performance featuring nearly 300 locals in period dress recounting the area's rich history.

Several of Natchez's mansions are also open during the *Christmas in Natchez* celebration, which features homes decorated in Victorian Yuletide finery, costumed hostesses, and candlelight tours and receptions.

The Roxie Gold Hole

If a visit to Natchez leaves you longing for a mansion of your own, take a side trip 20 miles east of town down US 84 to the *Roxie Gold Hole*, a small pond dug one shovelful at a time by treasure hunters.

According to local legend, a gang of Natchez Trace bandits buried a treasure chest 7 feet wide and 3 feet deep in a sinkhole near Roxie. Treasure hunters dragged shovels around the woods in Roxie for years before finally unearthing a corner of what appeared to be the genuine treasure chest. The problem? All that gold was very heavy. Each time the hunters jarred the chest, it sank a little deeper into the sinkhole. Finally, in 1959, an enterprising group of diggers had the good sense to secure the chest with a thick chain, then brought in heavy equipment to hoist the treasure from its hiding place. Alas, the treasure still slipped away, and eventually people gave up the idea of ever retrieving it.

For pilgrimage dates, details on individual or group tours, reservations for bed-and-breakfast stays, and information and tickets to evening entertainment, call Natchez Pilgrimage Tours at (800) 647-6742 or visit natchezpilgrimage.com.

About fifteen magnificent antebellum homes are open year-round, many of which double as bed-and-breakfasts. Each home has its own tale to tell, which may include unusual architecture, Civil War adventures, or a ghost story. Several of the mansions served as quarters for Union soldiers during the Civil War, and occasionally tales still surface of family treasure hidden behind paintings, buried on the grounds, or dropped down the cistern. Many of the homes have appeared in movies. The tour homes are located all over town, and admission prices and hours vary; stop by Natchez Pilgrimage Tours (located at the corner of Canal and State Streets in the Old Depot Building) for tickets, maps, and up-to-the-minute information before embarking on a tour.

Tour homes of particular interest include *Rosalie,* which served as Union headquarters during the occupation; *Stanton Hall,* where the ghost of Colonel Stanton is said to greet guests with a hearty "Good morning," and his ghostly children scamper the halls, accompanied by their long-dead cocker spaniel; *Linden,* used as the model for Tara's grand entrance in *Gone With the Wind; The Briars,* site of Jefferson Davis and Varina Howell's 1845 wedding ceremony; *The Towers*, which offers a number of themed tours focusing on everything from art to hauntings; and *Magnolia Hall,* which features a pilgrimage costume museum and is rumored to be haunted by a former owner desperate to communicate a message beginning with the letter *M*. The *Natchez National Historical Park* includes *Melrose,* the elegant 1845 urban estate of a wealthy cotton planter. Tours are conducted by docents who love these old houses and know them well. As they recount each home's fascinating story, history long past and people long dead come alive.

Perhaps the most haunting tour home is **Longwood**, the unrealized dream of Dr. Haller Nutt. The largest octagonal house in North America, Longwood was to be the wealthy Louisiana planter's town home—a six-story, 32-room, 30,000-square-foot showplace. No expense was to be spared in the construction, furnishings, or workmanship; Dr. Nutt even arranged for the most skilled northern craftsmen to travel to Natchez to build his splendid palace. By early 1861, the exterior and basement of the home were completed. Then the Civil War swept through the South. The northern carpenters dropped their tools and returned home to join the fight, leaving Longwood unfinished. The war ruined Nutt financially, and he died in 1864, his glorious vision a mere shell. The craftsmen never returned to Longwood, and the mansion came to be known in Natchez as "Nutt's Folly."

Now the property of the Pilgrimage Garden Club of Natchez, Longwood remains exactly as it appeared in 1861; the chisels and hammers are still where the workmen dropped them, and the paintbrushes are still in the original cans. Visitors wander through the oddly shaped, furnished rooms in the basement, then gaze up through level after level of scaffolding surrounding empty space. With such a tragic history, it's no surprise that Dr. Nutt's ghost is still felt around Longwood, perhaps waiting for someone to complete his ill-fated masterpiece. And if a Longwood tour guide should happen to stumble or recite an incorrect statistic during a tour, Dr. Nutt is sure to express his displeasure by making the lights blink.

Prince Among Slaves

Born near Timbuktu in 1762, *Ibrahima* was the son of a powerful African king. For 26 years Ibrahima lived as a prince and celebrated warrior. But in 1788, Ibrahima was defeated in battle and sold to slave traders. He arrived in Natchez on a slave ship and was purchased by planter Thomas Foster.

After nearly 20 years in slavery, Ibrahima was recognized by a visiting doctor, John Cox, who had known Ibrahima's father in Africa. Cox tried to purchase Ibrahima's freedom, but Foster refused to sell his valuable slave. Cox did succeed, however, in making Ibrahima a national celebrity. Under public pressure, Foster finally agreed to free the former prince in the late 1820s. A local newspaper then launched a campaign to return Ibrahima to Africa. Prince Ibrahima sailed as far as the African coast, but died before making the final trip inland to his homeland.

Many of the famous Natchez residents you'll hear about during the home tours are buried in the *Natchez City Cemetery.* Situated on a bluff overlooking the river, the 95-acre cemetery features dozens of beautiful, haunting, and unusual monuments dating to the late 1700s. Inscriptions range from the poignant to the bizarre; countless romantic, tragic, and downright spooky tales lie buried in the old graves. The Natchez City Cemetery comes alive each October during the popular *Angels on the Bluff* event, which features evening tours of the cemetery and living-history performances by descendants of its "residents." Call (601) 446-6345 or (800) 647-6724 for ticket information.

Natchez's rich history includes a strong African-American heritage, showcased in the *Natchez Museum of African-American History and Culture.* The museum houses more than 600 artifacts depicting African-American culture in Mississippi from the 1890s through the 1950s. Located at 301 Main St. in Natchez, the museum is open Mon through Fri from 10 a.m. to 4:30 p.m., and Sat from 10 a.m. to 2 p.m. A historical marker at the intersection of St. Catherine and D'Evereux Streets designates the former site of the *Forks of the Road Slave Market,* one of the two largest slave markets of the antebellum South.

One of the city's most famous African-American sons was William Johnson, "the Barber of Natchez." Born a slave in 1809, Johnson was freed by his owner (who was more than likely also his father) as a young man. He trained as a barber, eventually buying his own barbershop and rising to prominence as a member of the free black aristocracy. Johnson, who himself owned some fifteen slaves, was a successful businessman, popular with both the white and black residents of Natchez. His detailed diary, begun in 1835, represents the most complete account of the daily life of a free African American in the antebellum South.

Johnson was murdered in 1851 over a land dispute. Despite public outcry from both blacks and whites and a trial that required a change of venue, Johnson's white murderer was acquitted. It was against the law for blacks to testify against whites, and all witnesses to the crime were black. The 1841 *William Johnson House* is now a part of the Natchez National Historical Park maintained by the National Park Service.

The rowdy riverboat landing at *Natchez Under-the-Hill* was once the notorious lair of gamblers, thieves, and ladies of the evening, a scandalous embarrassment to the decent citizens of Natchez. Many a boatman of the 1800s trekked up the Old Natchez Trace penniless and exhausted after a visit to the saloons and gambling houses Under-the-Hill, an area dubbed by an evangelist of the day as "the worst Hell hole on earth." Listed on the National Register of Historic Places, the landing is now a respectable, restored area of colorful shops, bars, and restaurants.

The Goat Castle Murder

When eccentric, wealthy recluse *Jennie Merrill* was murdered in her Natchez mansion in 1932, suspicion immediately fell upon her neighbors, the even more eccentric Richard "Dick" Dana and Octavia Dockery.

Dana and Dockery lived next door to Ms. Merrill in Glenwood, a once-opulent mansion fallen into extreme disrepair. Once members of the Natchez aristocracy, Dana and Dockery had suffered a long, slow slide into abject poverty. At the time of the murder, they were barely supporting themselves by raising goats, chickens, cows, and pigs, all of which were allowed to roam freely through the deteriorating mansion. Their behavior was regarded as bizarre by the genteel folk of Natchez long before the time of the murder. Dockery, in fact, had had her own housemate, Dana, declared legally insane.

Bitter blood developed between the neighbors when the goats began wandering onto Ms. Merrill's property, and Ms. Merrill responded by shooting them. When Ms. Merrill's bullet-riddled body was found in a thicket behind her home, the police headed for Glenwood.

The utter squalor confronting them was more bizarre than any could have imagined. The huge, filthy mansion was overrun with livestock, its entire interior covered with dust, fleas, and animal droppings. Wallpaper peeled in sheets from the crumbling walls, framed pictures lay shattered on the floor, and banisters and balustrades hung at crazy angles. Goats had eaten an entire library of leather-bound volumes once perused by Robert E. Lee. The floors were strewn with piles of garbage, and the draperies were chewed as far up as the animals could reach. Dockery had been smoking goat meat in the fireplace in her bedroom; long strips of it were stretched over rusty bedsprings to "cure." The Natchez Democrat dubbed the foul mansion "Goat Castle," adding that the strangest thing about the place was that the goats could stand it.

Within weeks of Dana and Dockery's arrest, a transient confessed to Merrill's murder, and the two were released. They capitalized on their newfound celebrity, opening the squalid Glenwood for public tours. Fifty cents bought visitors a look at the decaying mansion and its famous goats. Dana and Dockery lived in the filthy wreck of a house until their deaths in 1948 and 1949.

Glenwood was razed in 1955, and a new subdivision, with streets named Dana Road and Glenwood Drive, was built on the property. Glenburnie, the scene of the murder, still stands adjacent to the subdivision, and is sometimes open for tours during pilgrimage. Jennie Merrill, Richard Dana, and Octavia Dockery are all buried in the Natchez City Cemetery, where Dockery's tombstone proclaims her the "Mistress of Goat Castle."

The river itself is the backdrop for a popular Natchez festival, the *Natchez Balloon Festival*. This October event features dozens of colorful balloons racing across the Mississippi River (duck when you get to the bridge!). Festivities include arts, crafts, entertainment, and balloon rides for spectators. Expect a champagne dousing after your first flight. For event dates, call the Natchez Convention and Visitors Bureau at (800) 647-6724 or visit visitnatchez.org.

Natchez is home to a number of colorful shopping areas offering one-of-a-kind gifts, specialty foods, local artwork, and too many antiques shops to list. If you're in the market for spirits, Natchez even boasts its own winery. Located just off US 61 at the northern outskirts of Natchez, the **Old South Winery** offers free tours and tastings of its muscadine wine from 10 a.m. to 5 p.m. Mon through Sat. Ole South's most popular selection? A sweet rosé labeled "Miss Scarlett."

Natchez offers several unique options for hungry visitors. Open for lunch year-round and lunch and dinner during the Spring and Fall Pilgrimages, the **Carriage House Restaurant** (401 High St.) behind Stanton Hall serves up traditional southern dishes and is famous for its homemade biscuits. Call (601) 445-5151. **King's Tavern** (619 Jefferson St.) is the place for steaks, seafood, and a good ghost story, and **Monmouth Historic Inn** represents candlelight dining at its absolute finest.

The Natchez experience simply isn't complete without an overnight stay at one of the city's palatial bed-and-breakfast inns. The town is home to more than thirty exceptional bed-and-breakfasts, many of which have been featured on countless television shows and in national travel magazines.

Perhaps the most celebrated of these elegant inns is Monmouth Historic Inn, an 1818 beauty named one of the Top 10 Romantic Places in the US by both *Glamour* magazine and *USA Today*. This breathtaking bed-and-breakfast also earns top honors from *Condé Nast Traveler,* which named Monmouth one of America's Top 25 Small Luxury Hotels and also lists the inn on its Gold List of the World's Best Places to Stay. Monmouth's most famous owner was John Quitman, governor of Mississippi and a US congressman during the 1860s. Today, the 26-acre plantation is owned by Nancy and Warren Reuther.

mississippitrivia

Author and Natchez resident Greg Iles used his hometown as the setting for the bestsellers *The Quiet Game, Sleep No More,* and *Turning Angel.* Iles confesses to using a few of his neighbors as the models for his unforgettable characters.

Marked by enormous azaleas in the spring, caladiums in the summer, brilliant fall foliage, and evergreens twinkling with white lights in the winter, Monmouth is a pleasure in any season. The lushly landscaped grounds are home to thirty luxurious guest cottages and suites, many featuring fireplaces, Jacuzzi tubs, private patios, and spacious sitting rooms. Pea-gravel paths wind through the wooded property, past gazebos and pergolas draped with wisteria, fountains filled with koi, and two scenic ponds populated by what must be very contented ducks.

Cocktails are served each evening in Quitman's Study, or beside the fountain and under the stars in the courtyard. Dinner at Monmouth is a special treat, an affair marked by crystal, candlelight, and five delectable courses. Guests are seated at the General's Table in the mansion's formal dining room or at private tables in the parlor. Your dinner companions may be Natchez locals or travelers from around the world; either way, the setting is elegant and the conversation is sure to be lively. You do not have to be an overnight guest to dine at Monmouth, but seating is limited and reservations are required.

Monmouth is located at 36 Melrose Ave. For more information or dinner or room reservations, call (800) 828-4531 or visit monmouthhistoricinn.com.

Monmouth is just one example of the bed-and-breakfast experience in Natchez. For more information about outstanding bed-and-breakfast inns or reservations in Natchez, call Natchez Pilgrimage Tours at (601) 446-6631 or (800) 647-6742 or visit natchezpilgrimage.com.

If you need a reminder that Mississippi history didn't begin with the antebellum South, stop at the **_Grand Village of the Natchez Indians_** just south of Natchez off US 61 South on the banks of St. Catherine's Creek. The culture of the Natchez Indian tribe reached its peak in the mid-1500s, with the Grand Village serving as the center of activities for the sun worshippers from 1200 to

Little-Known Facts about the Heartland

The world's first human heart and lung transplants were performed in 1964 in Jackson at the University of Mississippi Medical Center.

Myrlie Evers-Williams, widow of assassinated NAACP field secretary Medgar Evers, went on to become the Chairman of the NAACP.

Jackson's Malaco Records is the world's largest gospel music recording label.

Neatniks worldwide owe a debt of gratitude to Harry Cole Sr., of Jackson, the inventor of Pine-Sol.

The Parent-Teacher Association (PTA) was founded in Crystal Springs in 1909.

On May 11, 1887, a most unusual object plummeted from the skies above Bovina during a hailstorm—a 6-inch-by-8-inch gopher turtle, completely encased in ice.

The Easter Flood of 1979 caused more than $200 million in damages in the Jackson area. With the Pearl River 15 feet above flood stage, hundreds of homes were flooded, residents were forced to escape by boat, and much of downtown Jackson was underwater.

1729. The fading journals of French explorers make reference to the ceremonial center at the Grand Village. The Natchez vanished as a nation following a hostile encounter with French settlers at the Grand Village in 1730. The Grand Village site was excavated in 1930, revealing a ceremonial plaza, burial mounds, and rare artifacts now housed in an on-site museum. The Grand Village is open from 9 a.m. to 5 p.m. Mon through Sat, and 1:30 to 5 p.m. on Sun.

The Natchez Trace Parkway

The Lower Natchez Trace is actually the parkway's beginning. The original Natchez Trace was a one-way route that began in Natchez, then ran north to Nashville. In the late 1700s and early 1800s, flatboats floated merchandise downriver to Natchez and New Orleans, but the return trip north was along the Old Natchez Trace. By 1800, as many as 10,000 "Kaintucks"—the local lingo for boatmen from anywhere north of Natchez—annually trekked the Trace, each armed with a rifle and a bottle of whiskey.

The terrain was rough, and a broken leg often spelled death for the lone traveler. Murderous bandits, savage Indians, ferocious wild animals, and other perils encountered along the way earned the Natchez Trace the nickname "Devil's Backbone."

The Lower Natchez Trace runs past a number of historic sites and nature trails, as well as many of the cities and towns listed earlier in this chapter. The nature trail at mile marker 122 in Madison winds through the deep green and heavy silence of the *Cypress Swamp*, where towering trees growing in an old riverbed form a lush canopy overhead. A short, boardwalked path through the swamp is easily explored in half an hour. Just north of Jackson, the Trace hugs the shoreline of the Ross Barnett Reservoir for 8 miles, with a scenic reservoir overlook located at mile marker 105. Beware of vengeful spirits as you explore a section of the *Old Trace* at mile marker 102. The dense wilderness surrounding the narrow trail is the perfect hiding spot for bandits or Indians. This section of the parkway includes a stop at the Bill Waller Mississippi Crafts Center in Ridgeland before coming to a dead end just north of the capital city. To rejoin the Trace, take I-220 to I-20 West, which intersects the parkway south of Jackson.

This final leg of the Trace passes a number of picnic areas and historic sites. If you're traveling in the spring, you'll see a profusion of blooming dogwoods, redbuds, and an occasional patch of daffodils; the Trace's fall foliage display is equally impressive.

Any time of year, you're sure to notice the gray, gossamer substance dripping from the trees along this section of the parkway. That's Spanish moss, a native plant that looks dead, but keeps on growing, even if you move it indoors. Giant oaks laden with the stuff adorn the grounds of many of the area's antebellum homes, adding a gothic touch to the scenery. The farther south you travel, the more moss-draped trees you'll spot.

Forty miles south of Jackson, the **Rocky Springs National Park** offers a campground, picnic tables, and hiking and biking trails, all just a short walk from the forgotten settlement of Rocky Springs. A prosperous community of the 1800s, Rocky Springs was a center of agriculture and commerce, home to several businesses and large homes. The cotton that made the town rich, however, made the soil poor. Gradually the earth became depleted and eroded, and by 1930, Rocky Springs was a ghost town.

A stroll along the boardwalk through the preserved town site begins at a marker reading "the town of rocky springs. population 1860—2,616. population today—0". A church, cemetery, and rusting safe once filled with treasures are all that's left of the once-thriving community. The **Rocky Springs Methodist Church**, built in 1837, still overlooks the old town site and is open to the public. Visitors can also hike along a section of the original Old Trace thick with ferns and bamboo and wade in the shallow waters of Little Sand Creek. A marker at the entrance to the nature trail invites explorers to walk down the shaded trail and leave your prints in the dust, not for others to see, but for the road to remember.

Take a moment to explore a section of sunken trace south of Rocky Springs at mile marker 41. This deeply eroded tunnel through the wilderness is another portion of the original road. A canopy of trees stretches across the dirt bed of the trail—a route perhaps still trekked by the ghosts of earlier adventurers.

ALSO WORTH SEEING

Magnolia Bluffs Casino, Natchez

The Mississippi Children's Museum, Jackson

Treetop Trail at Chautauqua State Park, Crystal Springs
1,500 feet of elevated boardwalk thorugh the treetops

Vicksburg casinos, Vicksburg including Ameristar Casino; H. C. Porter Art Gallery; Lady Luck Casino Vicksburg; Riverwalk Casino & Hotel; Waterview Casino

South of Rocky Springs the Trace parallels US 61 and offers exits to the towns, cities, and attractions described earlier in this chapter, including Port Gibson, Lorman, Fayette, Washington, and, of course, Natchez, where the fabled parkway was born.

Places to Stay in the Heartland

BRANDON

McClain Lodge
314 Clark Creek Rd.
(601) 829-1101
mcclain.ms

BROOKHAVEN

The Inn on Whitworth
210 S. Whitworth Ave.
(601) 340-8807

RAYMOND

Dupree House and Mamie's Cottage
2809 Dupree Rd.
(601) 955-5777

VICKSBURG

Anchuca, Historic Mansion and Inn
1010 First East St.
(601) 661-0111
anchuca.com

Places to Eat in the Heartland

BRANDON

McClain Safari Park and Restaurants
874 Holly Bush Rd.
(601) 829-1101
mcclain.ms
Steakhouse, casual buffet, and tavern

BROOKHAVEN

Dude's Sausage & Biscuits
1248 Hwy 51 NE
(601) 835-1716
Breakfast

CRYSTAL SPRINGS

Dairy Freeze
25076 Hwy 51
(601) 892-1412
Ice cream stand

FLORA

The Gathering Restaurant
106 Livingston Church Rd.
(601) 667-4282
Breakfast, lunch,and dinner in an upscale, yet homey setting with mercantile

JACKSON

Big Apple Inn
509 N. Farish St
(601) 354-4549
Soul food

Cultivation Food Hall
1200 Eastover Dr.
cultivationfoodhall.com
Food hall housing a number of eclectic eateries

Fine & Dandy
100 District Blvd.
(601) 202-5050
eatdandy.com
Gourmet burgers and tater tots, adult milkshakes

Walker's Drive In
3016 N. State St.
(601) 982-2633
walkersdrivein.com
Varied menu; a local favorite

MADISON

Nagoya
111 Colony Crossing Way
(601) 856-5678
nagoya-ms.net
Sushi; try the yum-yum salad

Vasilio's
828 MS 51
(601) 853-0028
vasiliosgrkcuisine.com
Greek, seafood, gyros

MAGEE

The Vault Eatery and Drinkery
101 Main Ave. South
(601) 439-7242
Burgers, steak; located in a
vintage bank vault

NATCHEZ

100 Main Street
100 Main St.
(601) 445-6627
Smoked chicken and
black-bean pizza,
andouille-sausage po'boys,
nachos

Biscuits & Blues
315 Main St.
(601) 446-9922
biscuitsblues.com
Southern cuisine, live blues
music

Magnolia Grill
49 Silver St.
(601) 446-7670
magnoliagrill.com
Seafood, steaks, crawfish;
oldest continuously
operated restaurant at
Natchez Under-the-Hill

Planet Thailand
116 N. Commerce St.
(601) 442-4220
planet116.com
Thai, sushi

RIDGELAND

CAET Seafood
1000 Highland Colony
Pkwy. #9015
(601) 321-9169
caetseafood.com
Upscale food and wine bar

Cock of the Walk
141 Madison Landing Cir.
(601) 856-5500
cockofthewalkrestaurant
.com
Catfish

Ely's Restaurant and Bar
115 W. Jackson St.
(601) 605-6359
Steak, seafood, upscale
atmosphere

Koestler Prime
1000 Highland Colony
Pkwy. #6001
(601) 957-3753
Steak, seafood, upscale
atmosphere

Wasabi Sushi & Grill
1107 Highland Colony
Pkwy. #111
(601) 898-8849
Sushi prepared by a chef
who appeared on *Chopped*

VICKSBURG

Cafe Anchuca
1010 First East St.
(601) 661-0111
anchuca.com
Upscale dining, seafood,
and steaks

Goldie's Trail Bar-B-Que
2430 S. Frontage Rd.
(601) 636-9839
goldiestrailbarbque.com
Barbecue ribs, pork, beef,
chicken, and sausage;
featured in *Southern Living*
magazine and the book
Real BBQ

The Tomato Place
3229 MS 61 South
(601) 661-0040
thetomatoplace.com
Roadside produce stand
and restaurant; specialty
BLTs

Vicksburg's casinos offer
restaurants ranging from
coffee shops to all-you-
can-eat buffets to fine
dining.

Southern Mississippi and the Gulf Coast

Southern Mississippi is a contradictory blend of pioneer spirit and contemporary coastal life, a region where rugged frontier land, thick forests, and tranquil beaches all lie within a couple of hours' drive.

This entire area of Mississippi was hit hard by Hurricane Katrina; some areas of the Coast were simply erased. But Mississippians worked together to rebuild, and the area is now more popular than ever before. Visitors to southern Mississippi can relive the adventures of early explorers, retreat to a quiet artists' colony, and roll the dice in a glitzy casino, all in the same day. This dynamic mix of cultures and lifestyles makes a single trip to southern Mississippi a multifaceted adventure.

The Old Southwest

The southwestern corner of the state is made up of towns and cities still proud of their frontier heritage and, for the most part, still living it today. Much of the area just south of Natchez remains undisturbed and unexplored, peppered with overgrown forts, old-fashioned mercantiles, and sturdy buildings largely unchanged since the first settlers erected them more than a century ago.

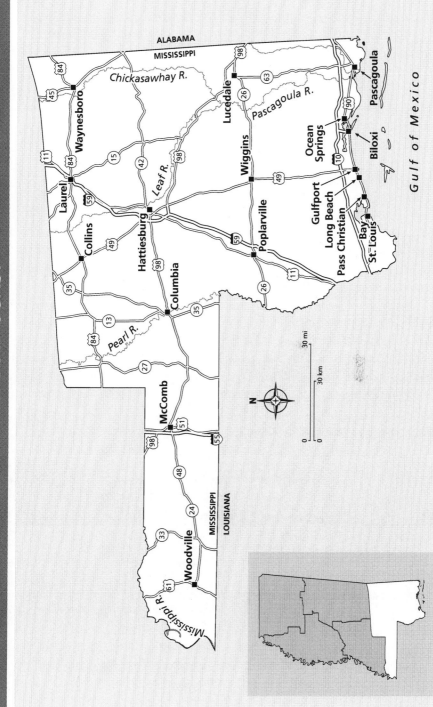

SOUTHERN MISSISSIPPI AND THE GULF COAST

The 35-mile stretch of US 61 South between Natchez and Woodville is sprinkled with antiques shops, junk shops, and trailers housing businesses from dog grooming to palm reading. But don't browse too long—you'll need a day to explore **Woodville,** the charming town Harvard University once described as "best typifying the Old South in appearance, customs, and traditions." That notoriety aside, Woodville remains for the most part an undiscovered treasure. Unlike Natchez, its tourist-oriented neighbor to the north, Woodville actually takes pleasure in remaining off the beaten path. At least for now, visitors can soak up the southern charm without calling for reservations, waiting in line, or catching a shuttle bus.

The town boasts a number of antebellum homes and churches, but Woodville's most famous link to the Old South is **Rosemont,** the childhood home of Jefferson Davis. As you come into town on US 61 South, follow the signs to the 300-acre plantation off MS 24 East where the Confederate States of America's only president spent his boyhood. A sun-dappled gravel road winds through towering trees dripping with Spanish moss, ending at a shaded gazebo where visitors listen to a short recording before touring the main house.

Samuel and Jane Davis moved to this airy planter's cottage with their ten children in 1810. (It's interesting to note that Jefferson, the youngest child, was given the middle name "Finis.") Home to five generations of the Davis family over the next century, Rosemont remains much the same today as it appeared during Davis's childhood. Many of the furnishings and artwork are original Davis family pieces, including Jane Davis's spinning wheel, books inscribed with the family name, chandeliers fueled by whale oil, and champagne glasses once raised in presidential toasts.

AUTHOR'S FAVORITE ATTRACTIONS IN SOUTHERN MISSISSIPPI AND THE GULF COAST

The Beau Rivage Resort Spa, Biloxi

Beauvoir, Biloxi

Clark Creek Natural Area, Pond

The shade of the **Friendship Oak** in July, Long Beach

Mary Mahoney's "Sisters of the Sea" entrée, Biloxi

Hitting blackjack in any casino, Mississippi Beach

Sunset over the water, Mississippi Beach

Everything about downtown **Ocean Springs**

Shopping in **Old Town**, Bay St. Louis

The beaches of **Ship Island**, accessible from Gulfport

A wall in the hallway bears the height charts of several Davis children, and Jefferson Davis's brother-in-law, Isaac Stamps, scratched his name into one of the windows downstairs. Stamps was killed at the Battle of Gettysburg, and Davis's sister traveled all the way to Pennsylvania to bring his body home to Rosemont for burial. Davis issued a presidential pass allowing her to cross enemy lines.

Originally called "Poplar Grove," the plantation was renamed Rosemont in honor of Jane Davis's elaborate flower gardens. Many of the rosebushes still blooming on the grounds today were originally planted by Jefferson Davis's mother in the early 1800s. The property also includes the Davis family cemetery where many members of Jefferson Davis's immediate family, including his mother and Isaac Stamps, are buried. President Davis himself is buried in the old Confederate capital of Richmond, Virginia. Photos displayed at Rosemont capture the throngs of Confederate supporters who attended Davis's funeral in New Orleans in 1889. Some 200,000 mourners came to pay their last respects—the largest funeral attendance in history prior to services for President John F. Kennedy.

The $10 admission includes the house, outbuildings, cemetery, and lavishly landscaped grounds. Rosemont is open Mar 1 to Dec 15, Tues through Sat from 10 a.m. to 4 p.m. At the time of this writing, Rosemont was temporarily closed for repairs. Call (601) 888-6809 for more information and to make sure Rosemont is receiving visitors.

Head back to US 61 and go straight through the four-way stop to downtown Woodville, where you'll find the traditional town square and courthouse. A block south of the courthouse, the **Wilkinson County Museum** features changing exhibits related to local history, including artifacts unearthed during archaeological digs underway at Indian mounds in the area. The museum is housed in a lovely 1838 Greek Revival–style building that originally served as the offices of the West Feliciana Railroad Company. The museum is open from 10 a.m. to noon and 2 to 4 p.m. Mon through Fri, and 10 a.m. to noon on Sat.

Woodville is also home to a number of historic churches just off the town square. There's the 1809 Woodville Baptist Church, the oldest church in Mississippi; the 1823 St. Paul's Episcopal Church, a founding parish of the Episcopal church in Mississippi; and the 1824 Woodville Methodist Church, the oldest Methodist church in Mississippi. Woodville is also home to the state's oldest newspaper and continuously run business, *The Woodville Republican*.

Just around the corner from the museum on First South Street you'll spot the two modest graves that make up the infamous **Oswald Family Cemetery**. It seems that Lee Harvey Oswald had a number of relatives in the Woodville area, and history buffs still come in search of these right-off-the-sidewalk-but-still-hard-to-spot tombs.

TOP ANNUAL EVENTS IN SOUTHERN MISSISSIPPI AND THE GULF COAST

FEBRUARY

Mardi Gras
Mississippi Gulf Coast
(228) 432-8806msgcca.org

MARCH

Hubfest
Hattiesburg
(800) 238-4288
theadp.com/events/hubfest

MAY

Blessing of the Fleet
Biloxi
(228) 435-6339
biloxiblessingofthefleet.com

OCTOBER

Cruisin' the Coast
Mississippi Gulf Coast
(888) 808-1188
cruisinthecoast.com

Sweet Mississippi Tea Festival
Poplarville
(601) 795-0578

NOVEMBER

Peter Anderson Arts and Crafts Festival
(In Marlo's opinion, the best arts festival in Mississippi)
Mississippi Gulf Coast
(228) 875-4424
peterandersonfestival.com

History buffs and outdoor enthusiasts will find a side trip west of Woodville to the microscopic communities of Pond, Pickneyville, and Fort Adams a worthwhile adventure. Head west out of downtown Woodville to MS 24; then follow the Pond-Pickneyville Road 16 miles to the *Pond Store*, an old-fashioned general store in business since 1881. According to local records, the pond for which the store was named was man-made, dug by the county as a watering hole for oxen, horses, and mules used to haul cotton to Fort Adams for shipment aboard steamboats. The mules are long gone, but with hardwood floors, long rows of wooden shelves, and antique display cases, the Pond Store retains its original frontier charm. Proprietors Liz and Norman Chaffin live in back of the store, and for $2.50 they'll give you a look at the traditional lifestyle of the merchant class. The store sells sundries and provides information on the area six days a week from 10 a.m. to 5 p.m. Call (601) 888-4426 to arrange a tour of the proprietors' house.

The Pond Store is located near the entrance to the 1,400-acre *Clark Creek Natural Area*. The terrain at Clark Creek is wild and rugged, made up of steep ravines, water-sculpted rocks, and sheer loess bluffs crisscrossed with hiking trails. The area is home to 14 enchanting waterfalls, the highest of which tumbles some 50 feet down the bluff. This is not the place for a casual stroll.

Reaching the waterfalls requires hiking boots, a healthy water supply, and most of all, stamina. Don't forget to pick up a trail map at the Pond Store—you'll need some help navigating this scenic but remote area. To avoid disappointment, call ahead to the Pond Store to be sure Clark Creek is open. Erosion problems occasionally present a safety hazard and cause the area to close for "repairs."

The Pond-Pickneyville Road continues into equally tiny **Pickneyville**, where you'll find the grave of Oliver Pollack, inventor of the dollar sign, and the **Desert Plantation**, a 1,000-acre plantation and bed-and-breakfast inn. The Desert Plantation is conveniently located 18 miles from both Woodville and St. Francisville, Louisiana, another town famous for its antebellum homes and pilgrimage tours. Call (877) 877-1103 or visit desertplantation.com for rates and reservations.

The neighboring community of **Fort Adams** is a virtual ghost town, home to little more than a handful of hunting and fishing camps. The 1700s fort that gave the town its name has long since been swallowed up by rampant vegetation. Fort Adams was a strategic outpost of the United States prior to the Louisiana Purchase. The fort has strong historical significance, but its most famous resident was fictional. The town was immortalized in Edward Everett Hale's tale *The Man Without a Country* when character Philip Nolan, banished from American soil after denouncing the United States, did time in a Fort Adams prison. Fort Adams is just north of Pond at the end of MS 24, but as one of the town's few residents puts it, "there's nothing much to do once you've gotten here except turn around and go back."

When you're ready to turn back, head east on MS 24, which turns into MS 48 just west of **Liberty** and the **Jerry Clower Museum**. The late Jerry Clower opened this small museum years ago to house an ever-expanding collection of memorabilia accumulated over his decades-long career as America's favorite country comedian. The collection includes the keys to 49 cities, an Indian headdress, numerous stuffed raccoons, and a plaque proclaiming Clower "the World's Nicest Person." Located at 1 Amazing Grace Lane, the museum is open by appointment. Call (601) 249-3453 for directions and to arrange a tour time.

When you've had all the country comedy you can stand, continue on MS 48 East to **McComb**. A bit of musical trivia—the McComb area has been home to a number of renowned musicians, including the legendary Bo Diddley, blues guitarist Vasti Johnson, and R&B singer Brandy Norwood. And while pop superstar Britney Spears actually resided just across the state line in Louisiana, she attended school at McComb's Parklane Academy.

The best time to visit McComb is in late March or early April, during the **Pike County Azalea Festival**. Inspired by Japan's traditional lighting of the cherry blossoms, the first lighted azalea trail was staged in 1953. A drive through McComb provides a look at twinkling, decades-old azaleas of every size, shape, and color. The festival also includes the crowning of the Azalea Queen and a Spring Tour of homes. For dates and a map of the *Azalea Trail*, call the McComb Visitors Bureau at (601) 684-8664 or the Pike County Chamber of Commerce at (601) 684-2291.

Lunch in McComb means a trip to *The Dinner Bell*, a bastion of southern cooking located at 229 Fifth Ave. off US 51 North. Hungry locals and travelers alike have gathered on the front porch of this former private home since 1959 in anticipation of a home-cooked meal and a down-home good time. Diners sit at large, communal tables and take turns spinning a lazy Susan groaning with fried chicken, meatloaf, catfish, mashed potatoes, fresh beans and peas, casseroles of every description, and other hearty southern dishes prepared by cooks who've never heard the words "diet" or "cholesterol." Be sure to sample the house special, fried eggplant prepared with a super-secret recipe. Lunch includes your fill of sweet, sweet tea, fresh-baked biscuits or cornbread, and dessert. The Dinner Bell puts food on the table from 11 a.m. to 2 p.m. Tues through Sun. Spin the lazy Susan as many times as your waistband will allow for a mere $12.99 Tues through Thurs; $14.99 on Fri and Sat; and $15.99 on Sun. Call (601) 684-4883.

Shopping opportunities beckon from just across the street at the *Gulf South Art Gallery*. Showcasing Mississippi artists and craftsmen, the gallery offers paintings, pottery, jewelry, and other collectibles and gifts, including Mississippi's famous McCarty Pottery. The Gulf South Art Gallery is located at 811 Robb St. Call (601) 600-2642.

If you're in the area over the Memorial Day weekend, take a side trip up I-55 North to US 84 East (about 40 miles total from McComb) and spend a day in *Monticello* at the *Atwood Music Festival*. A 30-year tradition, the festival features golf and tennis tournaments, hot-air balloon races, children's activities, and an arts and crafts show; but Atwood's biggest draw is energetic performances by country music's hottest superstars. The festival is held at *Monticello's Atwood Water Park*. For this year's lineup of performers and events, call (601) 587-3007 or visit atwoodmusicfestival.com.

Follow US 98 East into downtown *Columbia*, where the 100-foot-wide Main Street was designed to accommodate horse-and-wagon U-turns. Main Street's *Hill Hardware Company* still stocks plows, horse harnesses, and old-fashioned kitchen implements most modern homemakers would be at a loss to put to use. According to proprietor Leon Bohuslav, "If we don't have it, you probably don't need it." Tradition runs deep at Hill's; Bohuslav is only the third proprietor in the store's one-hundred-year history. Browse the goodies at

Hill Hardware from 7 a.m. until 5 p.m. Mon through Fri, and 7 to 11 a.m. on Sat. Call (610) 736-3417 or visit hillhardware.com.

Main Street is also home to the *Marion County Museum and Archives*. This small, volunteer-run museum displays local artifacts but focuses primarily on Marion County genealogy. The museum also houses a Confederate library—the books written, as one volunteer is quick to point out, "by actual Confederates. Nobody from up North." Call (601) 731-3999.

While exploring Columbia, keep an eye out for descendants of late Mississippi Governor Hugh White's cherished white squirrels. The governor introduced the squirrels to his Columbia estate more than 75 years ago. The frisky alabaster-colored animals have since raised several generations of descendants in the Columbia area, and the city has adopted an ordinance protecting the squirrels.

Early exploration maps of the Columbia area include *Red Bluff*, also known as "Mississippi's Little Grand Canyon." Formed by the natural erosion of the west bank of the Pearl River near Morgan Town, Red Bluff is made up of colorful layers of sand, gravel, soil, and clay plunging 200 feet into a creek that empties into the river. The landscape around Red Bluff changes constantly; the road atop the bluff has been pushed back twice to accommodate the ever-widening canyon. The unusual formation is easily visible from MS 587 about 15 miles northwest of Columbia.

Call ahead for an appointment, then take MS 35 South to *Sandy Hook* and the *John Ford House*. Built in 1809, this sturdy structure served as a frontier inn, fort, and territorial post office. The house has withstood not only the ravages of time but the fury of Hurricanes Camille and Katrina to become the oldest building in the Pearl River Valley. The inn was a center of activity in Mississippi's frontier days. Andrew Jackson slept here en route to the Battle of New Orleans, but he was given the best room in the house only after promising to watch his language. Tours of the home can be arranged through the Marion County Museum by calling (601) 731-3999.

From Columbia, take MS 13 South to I-59 and head straight for the Mississippi Beach, or continue on US 98 East to Hattiesburg and the Piney Woods.

The Piney Woods

The *Piney Woods* begin at the northern tip of the DeSoto National Forest and stretch south to the Gulf Coast, forming a thick green canopy over the cities and towns in their path. Towering loblollies dominate most of this region's landscape, earning the area the nickname "the pine belt."

The largest city in this region, **Hattiesburg**, serves as a cultural dividing line. Towns north of Hattiesburg share the traditional southern personality of Jackson, while communities south of Hattiesburg lean toward the casual indulgence of the Gulf Coast. Life on the boundary line is a pleasant mix of both, with the spirited feel of a college town as an added bonus.

US 98 turns into Hardy Street in Hattiesburg, home of the **University of Southern Mississippi**. The campus is located at the intersection of US 98 and US 49, its main entrance marked by the multicolored, fragrant **All-American Rose Garden**, home to some 750 patented bushes.

Curious George and other beloved characters from childhood are preserved and celebrated in the university's **de Grummond Children's Literature Collection**. Housed in the McCain Library, the museum showcases rare children's books and original manuscripts and illustrations. Exhibits are taken

The Unexpected Philanthropist: Oseola McCarty's Gift

When **Oseola McCarty** died in 1999, she left a legacy of generosity that touched millions. Five years before her death, the 86-year-old laundress with a sixth-grade education donated $150,000 to the University of Southern Mississippi. The gift represented more than half of Ms. McCarty's life savings, earned through 75 years of washing and ironing. The funds were used to establish the Oseola McCarty Scholarship. Through her generous gift, Ms. McCarty provided for others the education she herself had been denied.

Ms. McCarty received countless honors in recognition of her selfless gift, including the Presidential Citizens Medal, the Wallenberg Humanitarian Award, and an honorary doctorate from Harvard University. *The New York Times* described Ms. McCarty as "living proof to impatient young people that dignity and reward in work is what you make of it." *Newsweek* called her "a reminder that even the humblest among us can leave the world a better place for having walked on it."

But fame never changed Ms. McCarty. When asked to comment, Mississippi's most famous benefactress said simply, "I'm just proud I'm leaving something positive in this world. My only regret is that I didn't have more to give." Upon Ms. McCarty's death, Stephanie Bullock, the first recipient of the Oseola McCarty Scholarship, said of her, "She was an inspiration, a blessing, a treasure to the entire earth. Heaven couldn't have gotten a better angel."

Oseola McCarty's humble home has been transformed into a museum honoring her generosity and preserving her legacy. The home was relocated to Hattiesburg's East Sixth Street Museum District, which was already home to the African American Military History Museum. A third museum, the Eureka School Museum focusing on Civil Rights history, is also scheduled to open in the district.

from the University's de Grummond Collection, one of the largest compilations of children's literature in the world. The de Grummond archives include original manuscripts and illustrations by some 1,300 authors and illustrators and more than 180,000 published children's books dating from 1530 to the present. The museum exhibits are open to the public Mon through Fri from 9 a.m. to 4 p.m.; the archives are open by appointment to teachers, librarians, and others with a special interest in children's literature. Call (601) 266-4349 to arrange a visit with some of your oldest and most beloved (albeit fictional) friends or visit: degrummond.org.

From the USM main entrance, pick up US 49 South and head toward the Hattiesburg town limit. Continue on US 49 South about 12 miles past the city limits and follow the signs to the ***Mississippi Armed Forces Museum*** at Camp Shelby. The $4.5 million museum houses artifacts—most donated by Mississippians—representing every branch of the military and every war in which the United States has fought since the War of 1812. Many of the displays go beyond interactive, actually immersing the visitor in "combat." The disturbingly realistic Trench Experience recreates a battlefield trench from World War I, complete with life-size soldiers, earsplitting machine-gun fire, and the acrid scent of smoke and blood. Other exhibits include a signed copy of Hitler's *Mein Kampf,* life-size dioramas, bloodstained maps, thousands of photographs, weapons of every description, and a number of military clocks and watches, all set at just past five o'clock—the hour when officers go off duty.

The Mississippi Armed Forces Museum is open Tues through Sat from 9 a.m. to 4 p.m. Visitors must agree to a security search before proceeding to the museum, which is located in the heart of Camp Shelby. For more information, call (601) 558-2757 or visit armedforcesmuseum.us.

Head back into Hattiesburg on US 49 North, then west on US 98/Hardy Street to Southern Avenue and the ***Hattiesburg Historic Neighborhood District.*** The 115-acre area includes a number of architectural marvels built between 1884 and 1930.

A mix of well-preserved and restored architectural styles including neoclassical revival, Italian Renaissance, and art deco earned downtown Hattiesburg inclusion in the National Register of Historic Places as the ***Hub City Historic District.*** Main, West Pine, Forrest, and Front Streets showcase several public and private buildings reflecting these striking architectural styles. The district is also home to a number of eclectic galleries and eateries offering everything from art to ice cream.

If you're more a flea market hound than a gallery buff, spend your shopping time in Hattiesburg at the ***Calico Mall,*** Mississippi's largest indoor daily flea market, featuring five levels of shops in a 13,000-square-foot area. Browse the glassware, clocks, clothing, furniture, jewelry, linens, and antiques Tues through Sat from 10 a.m. to 5 p.m. Call (601) 582-4351.

Hattiesburg offers a number of diverse dining options, as well as an active nightlife geared toward the college crowd. Excellent choices for discriminating diners include *The Purple Parrot Cafe* and *Crescent City Grill,* both owned by renowned chef, author, and syndicated food columnist Robert St. John. *Mississippi Magazine* has crowned St. John "Mississippi's Best Chef," and a trip to either of his restaurants proves he is deserving of the honor. The Purple Parrot serves elegant southern cuisine ranging from foie gras to grilled tuna to aged beef and offers a five-course chef's tasting menu, all in an upscale ambience. The Crescent City Grill showcases Creole and Cajun dishes, including gumbo, crawfish pie, and fried green tomatoes, in a laid-back setting that's sure to make you feel right at home. The two restaurants share a space at 3810 Hardy St. that's also home to St. John's *Mahogany Bar,* a popular watering hole affectionately known as "the Hog." Call the Purple Parrot at (601) 264-0657, or the Crescent City Grill at (601) 264-0656.

Hattiesburg is the southern end point of the *Longleaf Trace Rails to Trails,* a 39-mile walking, biking, and Rollerblading trail. The Longleaf Trace winds north to south from *Prentiss* to Hattiesburg, following the route of an abandoned Illinois Central Railroad Line. About 80 percent of the 10-foot-wide paved trail runs through dense forestland, yet hikers and bikers are never more than 4 miles from a house or rest stop. A 26-mile equestrian trail runs adjacent to the paved surface. Dogwoods, wildflowers, and tranquil lakes and ponds line the Longleaf Trace, which is generously populated with beavers, otters, deer, raccoons, possums, and other native wildlife.

Future plans for development along the Longleaf Trace include rest stops, horse stables, snack shops, and mileage and historic markers. An official brochure and map of the trail is available by calling (601) 450-5247 or visiting longleaftrace.com.

The trail access and parking lot for the Longleaf Trace in Hattiesburg is located at Jackson Road, just north of West Seventh Street. Adventurers may

Canoe Black Creek

Black Creek, Mississippi's only National Wild and Scenic River, winds through Lamar, Forrest, and Green Counties and flows through the Wilderness Area of DeSoto National Forest. Black Creek attracts canoeists and campers from all over the country. For canoeing and canoe rental information, call (601) 582-8817 or visit blackcreekcanoe.com.

also access the trail at parking areas in the microscopic towns of **Prentiss, Carson, Bassfield, Sumrall,** and **Epley.**

The section of US 49 north of Hattiesburg is punctuated with flea markets, fruit stands, and "outposts" offering canoe trips down **Okatoma Creek.** Billed as Mississippi's only "white water," the Okatoma runs through a series of small waterfalls and rapids as it flows through forests and farmlands. Canoe rentals are about $40 a day and include shuttle service to and from the water. For more information or to book a trip, contact the **Okatoma Outdoor Post** (601-722-4297 or 1-800-OKATOMA; okatoma.com) or **Seminary Canoe Rental** at (601-722-4301 or 866-OKATOMA; seminarycanoerental.com).

Tiny **Seminary** is home to acclaimed potter Claudia Ka Cartee, whose jewel-toned dinnerware and decorative pieces have been shown throughout the South. Claudia's **KA Pottery Studio and Gallery** (506 Shirley Sanford Rd.) is open by appointment, and with a little advance notice, she usually welcomes drop-ins. Call (601) 722-4948 for directions and to arrange a visit or visit kapotterystudio.com. Another popular stop in Seminary is **Shady Acres Village,** an old-timey fruit and vegetable stand located directly on US 49. Shady Acres is the place to find homemade candy, baked goods, and preserves, as well as good old-fashioned hamburgers. For more information visit shadyacresvillage.com.

An interesting dining option awaits down MS 35 South near the Covington County/Jefferson Davis County line. The tiny Prentiss community is home to **Cowboy Jim's Riverside Restaurant,** a colorful seafood and steak house in a remodeled barn. Nestled between the Bouie River and a tranquil lake graced by cypress trees, Cowboy Jim's picturesque setting is as big an attraction as its steaks and seafood. Patrons are welcome to feed the fish in the lake, watch as the restaurant's flocks of ducks waddle up for a cracked-corn treat, or simply relax to the rhythm of the slowly turning waterwheel.

Complimentary fish food and fishing poles are provided for younger diners; the property even includes a "worm farm" for kids who prefer to dig their own bait. Located on MS 35 South in Prentiss, Cowboy Jim's is open Thurs from 4 to 9 p.m., and Fri and Sat from 4 to 10 p.m. Call (601) 765-3125.

From US 49 and Collins, head east on MS 532 to the tiny community of **Hot Coffee.** In the 1800s, weary travelers often parked their horse-drawn carriages at an inn in the area. The innkeeper's wife was known for her home-baked cakes and strong, piping-hot coffee. The inn was referred to as "the Hot Coffee," and eventually, the surrounding area adopted the moniker as well.

An old-fashioned general store in Hot Coffee are worth a quick stop. **McDonald's Store** serves up hand-dipped ice cream, RC Cola, Moon-Pies, hoop cheese by the slice, and plenty of—you guessed it—hot coffee.

McDonald's is open from 8 a.m. to 5:30 p.m. Mon through Thurs, and 8 a.m. to 5 p.m. on Fri and Sun.

Continue east on MS 532 to US 84, then head east 20 miles toward *Laurel*. Along the way you'll pass the Leaf River Church Road turnoff to *Mitchell Farms,* a pick-your-own vegetable farm operated by Dennis and Nelda Mitchell. As many as 400 people a day show up to pick fresh veggies during June and July, harvest peanuts Aug through Dec, and watch Nelda create wood sculptures year-round. Call (601) 765-8609 or visit mitchellfarms.com to find out what's in season.

US 84 leads to the picturesque town of *Laurel*. This sleepy southern hamlet has gained national fame as the setting for HGTV's hit show *Home Town*, which features spouses Ben and Erin Napier helping homebuyers renovate properties in the town. The Napiers also operate a pair of popular shopping stops in Laurel. *The Laurel Mercantile Company* (414 Front St.; 601-682-0936) originally opened its doors in Laurel in 1901, supplying dry goods to the good people of Laurel until the dry goods business dried up and the store eventually closed. In 2016, the Napiers and four of their closest friends bought the mercantile and reopened its doors. Today, the store offers a variety of home décor, apparel, art, and gift items, as well as Ben Napier's exquisite woodworks sold under the brand name Scotsman Woodshop. The Napiers are also the proprietors of the *Scotsman General Store* (1 Spec Wilson Blvd.; 601-340-3991). A throwback to the general stores of old, the Scotsman General Store is a purveyor of clothing, candy, groceries, and more. After a busy morning shopping, step into the Scotsman's walk-in freezer and choose an ice cold soda pop, then settle into a rocking chair and sit a spell. Ben's woodshop is visible from inside the store; you might get a sneak peek at the next handcrafted piece he'll unveil on *Home Town*.

The Laurel Mercantile Co. is located just a half mile from the *Lauren Rogers Museum of Art,* Mississippi's oldest and arguably finest art museum. Permanent collections include eighteenth-century paintings and sculpture, an extensive collection of Georgian silver, eighteenth- and nineteenth-century Japanese Ukiyo-e wood-block prints, and more than 800 baskets from around the world. The museum was founded as a tribute to Lauren Rogers, a 23-year-old newlywed who died in 1922 following an appendectomy. His family chose his unfinished homesite as the location for a library and museum honoring his memory. Located at 565 North 5th Ave., the Lauren Rogers Museum of Art is

mississippitrivia

Lance Bass of the boy band 'N SYNC was born in Laurel and later moved to Clinton.

open Tues through Sat from 10 a.m. to 4:45 p.m., and on Sun from 1 to 4 p.m. Incredibly, there's no admission fee, although donations are suggested. For information about the museum's collections, changing exhibitions, and special

programs and events, call (601) 649-6374 or visit lrma.org.

The museum is located in the heart of Laurel's oak-shaded historic district, which features the largest collection of turn-of-the-twentieth-century homes in the United States; the entire neighborhood is listed on the National Register of Historic Places. **Wisteria** (706 N. Fifth Ave.), one of these lovely homes located just across the street from the Lauren Rogers Museum, offers bed-and-breakfast accommodations. This elegant, lavender-hued house features exquisite handmade window glass and period antiques. Wisteria also offers bed-and-breakfast accommodations. For rates and reservations, call (601) 426-3805 or visit wisteria bedandbreakfast.com.

From the historic district, take Seventh Street east to MS 15 South and **Landrum's Country Homestead and Village.** This detailed re-creation of an 1800s settlement includes a water-powered gristmill, blacksmith shop, pioneer cabin, schoolhouse, general store, Indian village, and more than 35 other painstakingly re-created buildings and displays, all nestled on 10 tranquil, landscaped acres. Members of the Landrum family are on hand to conduct personal tours of the village and talk you into sampling a sugary funnel cake or a slice of fresh bread slathered with freshly churned butter. Take a stroll through the past Mon through Fri from 9 a.m. to 5 p.m., and Sat from 9 a.m. to 2 p.m. Admission is $10 per person for adults and children under 3 are free. Group and package rates are available. Call (601) 649-2546 or visit landrums.com.

Take MS 15 North back to Laurel and pick up I-59 South to the Gulf Coast. Just south of Laurel you'll see the exit to **Ellisville,** once the capital of the **Free State of Jones.**

Confederate deserter Newt Knight shot Major Amos McLemore, a Confederate soldier sent to capture him, in the living room of the **Deason House** in Ellisville. McLemore's blood seeped into the pine floors, staining them so badly the residents finally covered them with new boards. The ghost of the murdered major is still said to roam the halls of Deason House, and the bloodstain occasionally reappears on the floor. Decide for yourself whether Deason House is truly haunted—call (601) 577-1066 to arrange a tour of the murder scene.

Continue on I-59 South past Hattiesburg and through pastoral **Poplarville**, where actor and Mississippi native Gerald McRaney (most recently seen in episodes of Netflix's *Longmire* and NBC's *This is Us*) and his wife, actress

The Free State of Jones

The small farm owners of 1860s Jones County resented the notion of fighting a "Planters' War" and sent a representative to the 1861 Mississippi state assembly to vote against secession from the Union. But once in Jackson, the representative was overwhelmed by the near-hysteria sweeping the capital city and instead cast his lot with the secessionists.

Back home, the good citizens of Jones County burned the representative in effigy, formed an independent government, and actually seceded from the Confederacy. Declaring Ellisville their capital and Confederate deserter Newt Knight their leader, renegades from "the Free State of Jones" raided both Union and Confederate supply bases, supposedly practicing such atrocities that Union POWs quartered in Meridian were given arms to protect themselves.

When the city of Laurel dedicated a monument to the soldiers of the Confederacy decades later, most of the money was provided by a northern-born businessman. The benefactor noted the irony of the occasion, remarking, "You see here a handsome monument, erected with Yankee money to the Confederate dead of the Free State of Jones, which seceded from the Confederacy after the Confederacy seceded from the Union."

Delta Burke (most famous as Suzanne Sugarbaker on the classic comedy series *Designing Women*), own a ranch. When you reach the outskirts of **Picayune**, follow the signs to the **Crosby Arboretum**, home to 100 acres of native plants and trees. Walking trails wind through a savannah filled with carnivorous plants, a wetland thick with cypress trees, and shaded woodlands where azaleas bloom under loblolly pines. The arboretum's **Pinecote Pavilion** is the first building in Mississippi to win the American Institute of Architecture's Honor Award for Design Excellence. Get back to nature at the Crosby Arboretum Wed through Sun from 9 a.m. to 5 p.m. Admission is $5 for adults, $4 for seniors and military, and $2 for children under 12. The Arboretum also hosts a full calendar of lectures, tours, identification classes, plant sales, and workshops covering everything from pine-needle basket weaving to bird-watching to gardening. For a schedule of events and programs, call (601) 799-2311 or visit crosbyarboretum.msstate.edu.

Before you leave Picayune for the Mississippi Beach, stop by **Paul's Pastry Shop** (1 Sycamore Rd.), one of the nation's largest shippers of king cakes. These cream-cheese and fruit-filled pastries topped with green, gold, and purple frosting are a staple of Mardi Gras celebrations in New Orleans and throughout the South. Each cake is baked with a tiny plastic baby inside; whoever bites the baby has to host the next party, or at least buy the next king cake. Call (601) 798-7457, or to place an order after you've returned home, call (800) 669-5180 or visit paulspastry.com.

The Mississippi Beach

From Waveland to Ocean Springs, a chain of resorts, casinos, artists' colonies, and fishing villages is linked by 26 miles of sugar-white sand, the longest man-made beach in the world.

On Monday, Aug 29, 2005, Hurricane Katrina slammed into this lovely section of the Mississippi Gulf Coast, leaving a wake of indescribable destruction and loss. At its time the greatest natural disaster in American history, Katrina virtually erased the coastal villages of Waveland, Bay St. Louis, and Pass Christian and destroyed much of the cities of Gulfport and Biloxi. Massive casino barges broke free of their moorings and floated inland, crushing hotels and businesses in their paths. Grand waterfront homes melted into the 30-foot storm surge. Centuries-old buildings and beloved coastal landmarks vanished, gone in the blink of Katrina's giant eye.

But from Waveland to Ocean Springs, the Mississippi Gulf Coast bounced back. Residents rebuilt their homes and their lives, resorts reopened bigger and better than before, and visitors once again discover plenty to see and do along the Coast.

Take I-59 South from Picayune to MS 43 South, which intersects with US 90 at the beach. Your first glimpse of the beach comes at the sleepy little fishing village of **Waveland**. Waveland was once a haven for pirates, and much of the local lore revolves around notorious swashbucklers complete with parrots, wooden legs, and buried treasure.

It's little wonder that a favorite pastime on the Gulf Coast is cruising oak-studded US 90, the scenic route that parallels the beach. From Waveland, follow US 90 East, nicknamed "The Hospitality Highway," into **Bay St. Louis**. Take a right off US 90 at the Hollywood Casino sign; then take a right onto Main Street and into the heart of Bay St. Louis's **Old Town**. Prior to Hurricane Katrina, Old Town was home to more than forty unique galleries, boutiques, and restaurants that earned Bay St. Louis a listing in the book *The 100 Best Small Art Towns in America*. Katrina devastated the area, but the artists of Bay St. Louis made a strong comeback, and Old Town has resumed its tradition of live entertainment and extended hours the second Saturday of every month.

From Old Town, drive (or if the weather's pleasant, stroll) down Beach Boulevard a few blocks east and take a right down Union Street to the **Historic L&N Depot District**. Built in 1928, the old depot at 1928 Depot Way houses the Hancock County Visitors Center and the **Mardi Gras Museum**, a display of elaborate costumes from Coastal Mardi Gras krewes.

The depot's second floor is home to the **Alice Moseley Folk Art & Antique Museum**. Mrs. Moseley was in her 60s when she began painting folksy, down-home scenes recalled from her childhood. She gave her colorful paintings of life in the South equally colorful titles, including *Living High, Low, and Middle on the Hog*, *Three Sheets to the Wind*, and *Coons in Heaven Better Hide Tonight*. People began purchasing her work, and soon the retired schoolteacher was pursuing painting as a successful second career. Mrs. Moseley came to Bay St. Louis in 1988 for an art show and never left. She made her home and studio in a bright blue house in the Depot District and welcomed visitors for many years. When I was lucky enough to meet Mrs. Moseley in her 80s, she shared with me her now well-known philosophy on what kept her hard at work. "I wake up and read the obituaries and if my name is not in them, I get up and get dressed. It's nice to be so busy at my age, but what I wouldn't give to be seventy again!" One of Mrs. Moseley's most popular works is a self-portrait of the artist dancing in front of her house, clad in her trademark red beret and patchwork vest. The piece is titled "The House is Blue, but the Old Lady Ain't." A few years after Mrs. Moseley's passing at the age of 94, her son, Tim, opened the museum to preserve and share her work. The Alice Moseley Folk Art & Antique Museum is open Tues through Sat 10 a.m. to 4 p.m. In keeping with Mrs. Moseley's generous spirit, admission is free.

Bay St. Louis's restaurants are as varied as its shops and galleries. Back in Old Town, you can savor the fresh seafood and learn how the po'boy got its name at **Trapani's Eatery** (116 North Beach Blvd.; 228-467-8570) or dine in the charm of **The Sycamore House** (210 Main St.). Call (228) 469-0107 or visit thesycamorehouse.com. The preferred attire at all Bay St. Louis restaurants is "coast casual."

As you drive in and around Bay St. Louis, keep an eye out for the **Angel Trees**. Chainsaw artist Dayle K. Lewis of Indiana transformed live oak trees damaged by Hurricane Katrina into Angel Trees, inspirational wood sculptures that remind visitors of the hope and resilience that rebuilt the Mississippi Coast.

Before leaving Bay St. Louis, pause for a moment of quiet contemplation at the **Lordes Grotto** on the grounds of **St. Augustine's Seminary**. This inspirational structure was designed and built in 1944 by Thaddeaus Boucree, an artistically gifted African-American bricklayer. Boucree used debris from a hurricane as his raw material. The words "watch" and "pray" hang over the arched entrance to the gray stone grotto. Inside, the filtered sunlight illuminates scenes of Jesus in prison prior to the Crucifixion; the Last Supper; and the Resurrection. The exit is adorned with the words "peace be to you". The seminary and

Praline Alley

The stretch of US 90 between Bay St. Louis, Mississippi, and New Orleans, Louisiana, is marked by countless roadside stands, souvenir shops, and country cafes all hawking one thing—pralines.

Sinfully caloric and sweet enough to make your teeth ache, the *praline* (repeat after me, "praw-lean") is a staple in every Southern cook's repertoire and a mandatory treat when visiting Mississippi. Whether your personal preference is gooey, crunchy, or somewhere in between, Mississippi has a praline that's just right for you—that perfect mating of sugar and nuts that will have you buying (and devouring) them by the bagful.

Of course, the best pralines are homemade. So after you've sampled a few of the Mississippi-made variety, test the recipe below in your own kitchen.

Mississippi Pralines

2 cups sugar
1 cup buttermilk
½ teaspoon baking soda
2 tablespoons Karo syrup
2 tablespoons butter or margarine
2½ cups pecans (repeat after me, "puh-cahns")

Cream sugar, milk, soda, and Karo. Boil five minutes, stirring often. Add butter and pecans. Stir for five minutes. Remove from heat. Cool one minute. Beat until creamy and then drop by the teaspoon onto wax paper. Let sit for five minutes before serving. Enjoy in moderation.

grotto are located at 199 Seminary Dr. just off US 90 in Bay St. Louis. For more information, call (228) 467-6414.

It's a short drive over the Bay St. Louis bridge to neighboring **Pass Christian.** (Don't give yourself away as a tourist—it's pronounced "Kris-chee-ann" or simply referred to as "the Pass.")

From Pass Christian, US 90 continues east into **Long Beach,** another coastal community marked by blue sky, warm breezes, and sun-spangled waters. The beaches here are uncrowded and quiet, dotted with fishing piers stretching far into the Mississippi Sound. Take the exit to the University of Southern Mississippi–Gulf Coast, then drive straight ahead on campus to Hardy Hall and the **Friendship Oak.** According to legend, those who step into the shadow of this 500-year-old live oak tree must "remain friends through all their lifetime, no matter where fate may take them." At 50-feet tall with a 151-foot spread of foliage, the tree casts an enormous shadow indeed. The average length of the Friendship Oak's enormous limbs—which are supported by heavy cables and rest on blocks—is 66 feet from the trunk. A platform nestled high in its branches is a popular spot not only for photos, but also for wedding ceremonies. If estimates of its age are accurate, the Friendship Oak was a sapling when Christopher Columbus set sail for the New World. The Friendship Oak is the most famous of the many live oak trees found along the coast. Many of the trees bear names indicating age and wisdom ("Councilor" and "Patriarch," to name a couple) and are registered with the Live Oak Society. Visit usm.edu/university/friendship-oak.php.

As US 90 crosses into *Gulfport,* the quiet artists' colonies and rustic fishing piers are replaced by the glitz and glitter of floating casinos and the hustle and bustle of the *Port of Gulfport.* (A navigational note: The section of US 90 that runs through Gulfport and neighboring Biloxi is also referred to as Beach Boulevard.)

Gulfport is home to a number of well-marked, modern beach pleasures, including Jet Ski rentals, pleasure-boat rides, and sailing and deep-sea-fishing charters. Gulfport also offers excursions to *West Ship Island* 12 miles off the Mississippi mainland. The Mississippi Sound meets the Gulf of Mexico at Ship Island, one of four natural barrier islands that are part of the *Gulf Islands National Seashore.* Clear waters and constant surf make Ship Island the most popular spot for sunbathing and beachcombing on the coast; in fact *USA Today* named the beach at Ship Island one of the top ten in the United States. Snacks, beverages, and chair and umbrella rentals are available, and lifeguards may be on duty in season. The boardwalk leading to the gulf side of the island is about one-third of a mile, so travel lightly. A word of warning—take plenty of sunscreen.

Ship Island is also home to *Fort Massachusetts.* Under construction from 1859 to 1866, the Fort saw limited action during the Civil War. Ship Island, however, was the site of a Confederate POW camp. The island even housed one female prisoner, a New Orleans housewife charged with laughing at a Union officer's funeral procession and teaching her children to spit on Union officers. Guided tours of the fort are available daily Mar through Oct, and history buffs can explore the structure anytime on their own.

Excursion boats bound for Ship Island leave the Gulfport Yacht Harbor on US 90 daily March through October. Call (228) 864-1014 or (866) 466-7386 for the day's schedule. Visit msshipisland.com for more information. Round-trip excursions are $30 for adults and $20 for children ages 3 to 10. The hour-long ride to the island is an adventure in itself—playful dolphins usually accompany the ferry to its destination.

You'll hardly notice you've left Gulfport and crossed into *Biloxi,* your next stop on US 90. Once a quiet community frequented by families in search of

The Hurricane Katrina Memorial

The *Hurricane Katrina Memorial* stands watch over Biloxi's Town Green off US 90, a stone monument honoring the Gulf Coast victims of America's greatest natural disaster. Dedicated on February 15, 2006, by the crew of ABC's *Extreme Makeover*, the memorial stands 12 feet tall, approximately the same height reached by the water at the Town Green during Katrina's storm surge.

a budget beach vacation (and hung with the unfortunate nickname "Redneck Riviera"), Biloxi is now a hopping resort town offering year-round golf, deep-sea-fishing boat charters, and 24-hour casino gaming.

Of course, not everything in Biloxi revolves around a slot machine. Just as you come into town from Gulfport, you'll spot a sign directing you to ***Beauvoir,*** the last home of Confederate president Jefferson Davis. Davis purchased this seaside estate from a family friend in 1879 for $5,500. Once you step onto the quiet grounds, it's easy to understand why the former president chose to spend the last years of his life writing his memoirs and enjoying the peace and solitude of the coast.

Davis was revered by southern patriots, and in the years following the war, Beauvoir ("beautiful view") hosted a constant parade of veterans and well-wishers—so many visitors, in fact, that neighbors had to lend the Davis family enough food to entertain them. Following Davis's death in 1889, his widow, Varina, rejected an offer of $100,000 for Beauvoir, instead selling the property to the Mississippi Division of the Sons of Confederate Veterans for $10,000 with the stipulation that Beauvoir be used as a home for Confederate veterans and their families. More than 2,000 residents signed the roster of the Beauvoir Confederate Soldiers' Home, including several former slaves who fought for

Jayne Mansfield's Last Performance

Hollywood bombshell *Jayne Mansfield* gave her final performance at Biloxi's Gus Stevens Supper Club on June 28, 1967. Patrons from a four-state area flocked to Biloxi to see Mansfield's show, never imagining it would be her last.

In the early hours of June 29, Mansfield was killed on US 90 when the car she was riding in slammed into an 18-wheeler. Rumors that Mansfield was decapitated in the wreck persist to this day. A witness to the accident reported seeing a "flying head," which was actually Mansfield's blond wig placed upon a hat form.

the Confederacy. In 1941, the main house was opened as a shrine honoring Jefferson Davis. In 1957, the last two war widows were moved to a nursing home, and Beauvoir, its outbuildings, and grounds became a museum. The estate is still owned and managed by the Mississippi Division, United Sons of Confederate Veterans, who operate the attraction under the name "Beauvoir, the Jefferson Davis Home and Presidential Library."

Beauvoir is open for tours from 9 a.m. to 5 p.m. daily. Information about reenactments and other events is available at visitbeauvoir.org.

Continue east on US 90 to the ***Ohr-O'Keefe Museum of Art*** (386 Beach Blvd.), which is housed in a striking, 25,000-square-foot facility designed by renowned architect Frank Gehry. George E. Ohr was a colorful Biloxi folk artist of the 1890s whose eccentric behavior and 2-foot-long mustache earned him the nickname "the Mad Potter of Biloxi." Ohr supported his wife and ten children through sales from his small shop, aptly named the "Pot-Ohr-E." His contemporaries described Ohr as "one fork short of a place setting," a reputation he cultivated in order to draw attention to his art. Photos of Ohr would seem to indicate that his talent for facial contortions was on par with his gift for throwing pots.

Ohr was frustrated by critics who didn't appreciate his "mud babies," and at one time even buried a cache of pots in hopes a more "enlightened" generation would unearth them. That future generation has arrived. In 1968, a respected art and antiques dealer purchased pieces of Ohr's pottery and offered it for sale in New York, turning the art world on its collective ear. Ohr came to be known as the "father of American pottery," recognized for his innovative sculptural vessels with unusually thin pinched, crimped, and fluted walls. Dismissed by his contemporaries, Ohr is now celebrated as a genius; his pots have sold for as much as $100,000. The Ohr–O'Keefe Museum houses a permanent collection of 250 of the Mad Potter's original works, the largest public collection of Ohr pottery in the world.

Continuing along US 90, you'll spot the 65-foot ***Biloxi Lighthouse,*** the only lighthouse in the United States beaming from smack in the middle of a four-lane highway. The 65-foot structure has guided seafarers and fishermen home since 1848. Visit biloxi.ms.us/visitor-info/museums/lighthouse/ for more information on tours and admission prices.

For your own up-close-and-personal look at the Gulf Coast seafood industry, head to sea on the ***Biloxi Shrimping Trip.*** You'll sail into coastal waters on a real shrimping expedition with an experienced crew, who'll identify specimens caught during the voyage. The Biloxi Shrimping Trip leaves from the Biloxi Small Craft Harbor. For sail days and times, rates, and reservations, call (228) 392-8645 or visit biloxishrimpingtrip.com.

There's no better place to sample some of that fresh seafood than ***Mary Mahoney's Old French House,*** the Coast's legendary courtyard restaurant. In the days following Hurricane Katrina, one of the most inspirational sights in Biloxi was a simple message spray-painted on the restaurant's exterior wall: "We Will Be Back." A few months later, residents and visitors alike were thrilled to see the words "Will Be" replaced by the word "Are."

The building, former slave quarters, and oak-shaded courtyard that make up the Mary Mahoney complex remain much the same as when they were originally constructed in 1737; the towering ***Patriarch Oak*** in the courtyard is estimated at more than 2,000 years-old. And if the ambience isn't enough to inspire a visit, the seafood and steaks at Mary Mahoney's are nothing short of delicious. Ms. Mahoney once catered a party for President Ronald Reagan on the White House lawn; an autographed photo of Mary with the president still hangs in the restaurant. In 1985 the city of Biloxi even hosted a "Mary Mahoney Day" in honor of its most famous restaurateur. The restaurant complex includes several dining rooms in the main house and a lounge in the old slave quarters. You'll find Mary Mahoney's at 110 Rue Magnolia in the heart of Biloxi. The restaurant is open Mon through Sat from 11 a.m. until 9 p.m. Call (228) 374-0163 or visit marymahoneys.com.

Across from Mary Mahoney's you'll spot the ***Magnolia Hotel,*** a fashionable coastal retreat built in 1847 for a cost of $2,500. The oldest hotel on the Gulf Coast no longer rents rooms, but does house the ***Mardi Gras Museum,*** a collection of colorful costumes and memorabilia donated by royalty of the coast's Mardi Gras krewes. You can see the krewes in action each February or March, when Mardi Gras parades roll through Biloxi and other coastal communities. Mardi Gras on the Gulf Coast is equally colorful but a little more family-oriented (read "tame") than the same celebration in neighboring New Orleans. For dates and parade routes, contact the Gulf Coast Carnival Association at (228) 432-8806.

mississippitrivia

Mary Mahoney's Old French House restaurant is featured in John Grisham's bestsellers *The Runaway Jury* and *The Partner.*

For an adventure so far off the beaten path you almost have to swim there, book an excursion with ***North Star Sailing Charters***. You and up to five friends can sail to remote Horn Island aboard a 31-foot Polaris sailboat, enjoying an afternoon of dolphin watching, swimming, snorkeling, and island exploration, followed by a gourmet dinner under the stars. For more information or to book a charter, call (228) 617-8057 or visit northstarsailingcharters .com.

Follow US 90 east over the bridge and into lovely **Ocean Springs,** a tranquil artists' colony so peaceful and so serene it's as if the action-packed resorts just three miles to the west don't even exist.

Take a right off US 90 (known within the Ocean Springs city limits as Bienville Boulevard) onto Washington Avenue, and you'll find yourself in Ocean Springs's charming business district. Washington Avenue crosses Robinson Avenue and Government Street, then runs 4 more blocks before dead-ending at the beach. While the Ocean Springs beachfront was destroyed by Katrina, this charming area of galleries, shops, art studios, and restaurants was miraculously spared. As one shop owner said, "We didn't even have a limb down."

A co-op gallery operated by the Ocean Springs Art Association, **The Art House** features hand-painted rugs, sculpture, pottery, paintings, and weavings by thirty working artists, with two artists in residence every day. A tour of The Art House doesn't stop indoors; the outdoor sculpture garden features whimsical statues made entirely of found objects. Located at 921 Cash Alley, The Art House is open Mon through Sat from 10 a.m. to 4:30 p.m. Call (228) 875-9285.

If all that shopping and strolling leaves you hungry, you're still in the right place. Downtown Ocean Springs is home to several eateries and snack shops every bit as eclectic and charming as its boutiques and galleries. **Martha's Tea Room** (2113 Government St.) offers sandwiches, salads, and homemade desserts in a cozy atmosphere. Call (228) 872-2554. The **Tatonut Shop** (1114 Government St.) is the state's sole purveyor of doughnuts made from potatoes. Call (228) 872-2076. Sinful treats are also available at the **Candy Cottage** (702 Washington Ave.), where the pralines are made fresh in the front window. Call (228) 875-8268.

You'll appreciate Ocean Springs's artistic legacy even more after a visit to the **Walter Anderson Museum of Art** (510 Washington Ave.). Creative types have been drawn to Ocean Springs for centuries, but the town's most famous son was eccentric painter Walter Inglis Anderson (1903–1965). Anderson was known for his vivid paintings and block prints depicting the rich plant and animal life of the Gulf Coast, its marshes, and wetlands.

The artist spent much of the last eighteen years of his life on Horn Island, one of a group of barrier islands that now make up the Gulf Islands National Seashore. Anderson would row the 12 miles from the mainland to the island in a small skiff, carrying minimal necessities and his art supplies. He lived on the uninhabited island for weeks at a time, working in the open and sleeping under his boat in blistering summers, freezing winters, and through hurricanes. Anderson painted and drew a multitude of the island flora and fauna species, crawling through wild thickets on hands and knees and lying submerged in lagoons to more fully "realize" his subjects.

Little-Known Facts about Southern Mississippi and the Gulf Coast

The world's first can of condensed milk was produced in Liberty, Mississippi, by inventor Gail Borden.

A plane carrying the rock group Lynyrd Skynyrd crashed just south of McComb on October 20, 1977, killing six people.

Columbia's Walter Payton was the first football player ever featured on a Wheaties cereal box.

Hattiesburg's Camp Shelby is the largest National Guard training facility in the United States.

Leontyne Price of Laurel was the first African American to achieve international stardom in the world of opera, performing with the New York Metropolitan Opera.

Before monster storm Katrina in 2005, the Mississippi Coast weathered major hurricanes in 1893, 1901, 1915, 1947, and 1969.

Astronaut Fred Haise of Biloxi was aboard the ill-fated flight to the moon immortalized in director Ron Howard's *Apollo 13*. Haise was played by actor Bill Paxton.

Confederate president Jefferson Davis was restored to US citizenship in 1978—during the presidency of Jimmy Carter.

Barq's Root Beer was invented in 1898 by Edward Barq of Biloxi.

New Orleans may have made it famous, but Mardi Gras was first celebrated in the New World in Mississippi. The original "Fat Tuesday" was observed in 1699 by explorer Pierre Le Moyne d'Iberville and his crew at Fort Maurepas in Ocean Springs.

The rarest of North American cranes, the Mississippi sandhill crane, lives in a protected area in the grassy savannahs of Jackson County. The county's annual Crane Festival attracts naturalists from around the country.

In the early 1950s, Anderson began retreating for weeks at a time to a tiny cottage in Ocean Springs to work in solitude. When his family opened the cottage after his death in 1965, they discovered brilliant murals painted on every inch of the walls and ceiling. The entire "little room" mural, which depicts a coastal day from sunrise to sunset crowned with a brilliant zinnia on the ceiling, has been moved to the museum. Hundreds of Anderson's watercolors, drawings, oils, block prints, ceramics, and carvings are all represented in the museum's permanent collection. *The Islander,* an award-winning film shown in the museum theater, reveals more about Anderson's unusual life and timeless art.

The museum adjoins the ***Ocean Springs Community Center,*** the interior walls of which Anderson adorned with brilliant murals. Anderson worked on the spectacular 3,000-square-foot murals from 1951 to 1952, charging the community $1 for his efforts. The murals are appraised today at more than $1 million. Look for the slightly darker blue jay in the upper left corner as you face the stage. It was painted by Anderson's wife, Sissy.

The Walter Anderson Museum of Art is open Mon through Sat from 10 a.m. to 5 p.m. The museum stages changing exhibits, many featuring the work of other significant artists, and offers a full calendar of workshops, lectures, and special events. For more information call (228) 872-3164 or visit walteranderson museum.org.

If you'd like to take a piece of Anderson's genius home, choose a print from the museum gift shop or **Realizations: The Walter Anderson Shop** (1000B Washington Ave.), which also carries clothing featuring Anderson's work.

Walter Anderson is the most famous member of an entire family of gifted artists. Walter's talented brother Peter established **Shearwater Pottery** in 1928.

mississippitrivia

Artist Walter Anderson's son, John, was the first park ranger assigned to the Gulf Islands National Seashore. This national park includes Horn Island, Walter Anderson's greatest source of inspiration.

Shearwater is still a family affair, now run by Peter's son, James. The twenty-four-acre Shearwater artists' colony, studio, and showroom were destroyed by Hurricane Katrina, but the family has rebuilt and reopened in the colony's original location. The Shearwater Pottery collection includes dinnerware, vases, and sculpture. Pieces and table settings can be custom ordered, but don't expect to receive your shipment in the usual five to seven business days. Each piece is an individual work of art, and Shearwater Pottery doesn't do rush orders. Follow Washington Avenue past the Ocean Springs harbor and across the bridge to the Shearwater complex at 102 Shearwater Dr. Before heading out, call (228) 875-7320 for current workshop and gallery hours.

Ocean Springs honors Shearwater's founder the first weekend of November during the spectacular **Peter Anderson Arts and Crafts Festival.** Fine artists display and sell paintings, pottery, woodcrafts, jewelry, and furniture in downtown Ocean Springs. For more information call the Ocean Springs Chamber of Commerce at (228) 875-4424.

The work of yet another talented Anderson descendant graces the wall at Washington Avenue and Bowen Avenue in downtown Ocean Springs. Christopher Inglis Stebly, Walter Anderson's grandson, was commissioned to paint a mural commemorating Ocean Springs's 300th anniversary. Titled **Ocean**

Springs: Past, Present, and Future, the 80-foot mural is a bright, joyous tribute to life in this vibrant coastal city.

Founded in 1699, Ocean Springs is one of the oldest cities in the United States. Three centuries ago, Pierre Le Moyne d'Iberville stepped ashore at Ocean Springs and claimed the area for France. The annual **Landing of d'Iberville** celebrates this momentous event with a spring historical ball and pageant and a full-scale reenactment of the landing at a replica of the French **Fort Maurepas** located on the beach at the foot of Jackson Avenue (1 block west of Washington Avenue).

Active visitors can bike their way through Ocean Springs along the **Live Oaks Bicycle Route.** This 15½-mile route departs from the Old L&N Train Depot, winds through the streets of downtown, and leads to the Davis Bayou Area of Gulf Islands National Seashore before returning to the depot. Bikers

The Heat Is On

Mississippi is hot.

Oh, forecasters may try to soften the blow with euphemisms like "sultry," "balmy," or the highly understated "very warm," but take my word for it, the best description for Mississippi in the summertime is "sweltering."

Temperatures reach the upper nineties before noon. The sun is relentless, the breeze . . . nonexistent. And the humidity? You almost need scuba gear just to breathe.

When we describe summer conditions in Mississippi to our friends "up North," they invariably ask (with a look of horror), "How on earth can you live there?"

So, how do Mississippians cope with a summer heat index that seems perpetually stuck at 110? Well, from June through September we pretty much stay indoors and give thanks for air-conditioning and iced tea.

But when October rolls around, we breathe a sigh of relief and celebrate the crisp days and brilliant colors of fall. Come January, we marvel at the plight of northerners up to their eyeballs in snow and wonder if we'll really need to take a jacket with us on our daily stroll. And in early March, when most of the country is still looking forward to another six weeks of snow and ice and slush, we see the first of our spring flowers in bloom.

Truth is, while we may complain about it, Mississippians have long since made peace with the heat. It's a small inconvenience that's simply part of life here in the Deep South—a life most of us would never trade for an existence in a winter wonderland.

Let a little heat and humidity run us die-hard southerners out?

When Mississippi freezes over.

can pick up a map of the route at the Ocean Springs Chamber of Commerce (1000 Washington Ave.) or simply follow the green-and-white designated bike route signs located on the right side of the city streets.

Ocean Springs is home to a number of restaurants welcoming hungry travelers, most specializing in—you guessed it—fresh seafood. Enjoy lunch or dinner with a view at **Anthony's Steak and Seafood Restaurant,** an elegant eatery nestled among 400-year-old oaks overlooking Fort Bayou. The upscale menu includes steak, seafood, and veal. Anthony's serves dinner Tues through Sat and kicks off the week with a Sun champagne brunch—the corks start popping at 11 a.m. Anthony's is located at 1217 Washington Ave. north of US 90. Call (228) 872-4564.

Another local favorite is **Patrick's,** housed in the hard-to-miss bright-fuchsia cottage on US 90 (2105 School St.). When the Ocean Springs restaurant where she worked changed hands, cook Jocelyn Mayfield decided to take her recipes and strike out on her own. She transformed her in-laws' small house into a restaurant, painted it pink, and opened her doors to diners hungry for her sophisticated approach to seafood, beef, and chicken. Patrick's is open for dinner 5:30 to 9:30 p.m. Wed through Sat. Call (228) 875-1925.

Other excellent dining choices include **Aunt Jenny's Catfish Restaurant** (1217 N. Washington Ave.; 228-875-9201), a down-home, friendly eatery where the catfish, fried chicken, and shrimp are served with a bayou view, and **Phoenicia Gourmet Restaurant** (1223 Government St.; 228-875-0603), the place to go for an authentic Greek or Lebanese lunch or dinner.

Continue on US 90 East to the well-marked entrance to the Mississippi headquarters of the **Gulf Islands National Seashore.** The national seashore extends some 150 miles from Mississippi to Florida. The Mississippi portion of this national park begins at **Davis Bayou** on the mainland, then stretches into the Mississippi Sound to include the Barrier Islands of West Ship, East Ship, Horn, and Petit Bois. West Ship and East Ship Islands were originally one; Hurricane Camille split the island in two in 1969. Horn Island—a favorite inspiration of artist Walter Anderson—and Petit Bois Island have been designated wilderness areas by the US Congress. Protected from development and human interference, these islands provide habitats for uncommon species of birds, animals, and marine and plant life.

The headquarters at Davis Bayou includes miles of secluded marshlands brimming with wildlife, a campground, picnic shelters, nature trails, and boat launches. Misty mornings are prime time for bird-watchers, photographers, and fishermen. The marsh provides a home for creatures representing every level of the food chain. From industrious fiddler crabs to stately great blue herons to inquisitive alligators, you're sure to spot something scurrying, splashing, or flying in every corner of the bayou at every hour of the day. The Davis Bayou visitor center houses exhibits describing the flora and fauna of the mainland marshes and the islands.

There's no beach at Davis Bayou, but excursion boats departing from Gulfport transport visitors to the swimming and recreational beaches at West Ship Island daily during spring, summer, and fall. Information about charter boats licensed to ferry adventurous explorers and campers to the wilderness islands is available at the visitor center and at the Ocean Springs Chamber of Commerce.

Ocean Springs is home to several tranquil bed-and-breakfast inns that provide a welcome break from the road. The *Inn at Ocean Springs* offers two luxurious guest suites in the heart of downtown Ocean Springs (228-875-4496; oceanspringsinn.com). *The Eaves* (228-875-8173; theeaves.org) and *Oak Shade* (228-324-6686 or 888-875-4711) are also excellent choices.

Leave Ocean Springs on US 90 East and drive through the quiet community of *Gautier* (Go-shay). When you spot the giant shipyards lining the beach, you'll know you've arrived in *Pascagoula*. Continuing on US 90 East, you'll cross the *Pascagoula River,* also known as the "Singing River." The river has apparently been musically inclined for centuries; French explorers d'Iberville referenced the "Singing River" in journal entries dated 1699.

One of the most historically significant landmarks in Pascagoula is *Scranton's Restaurant and Catering.* Operating in Pascagoula's original 1924 fire station/city hall/city jail, the restaurant is also a mini-museum, displaying

The Legend of the Singing River

Legend has it that centuries ago, a young princess of the Biloxi Indian tribe was betrothed to a hot-tempered Biloxi warrior. The princess, however, fell in love with a young chieftain of the peaceful Pascagoula tribe, and the two ran away together.

The spurned Biloxi warrior then led his braves in an attack on the Pascagoula. Rather than face death or slavery at the hands of the enemy, the entire Pascagoula tribe linked hands and walked into the Pascagoula River, singing a traditional tribal death chant as they surrendered their souls to the waters.

How much of the legend is true will forever remain a mystery, but whether the source is Indian ghosts or scientific phenomena, the Pascagoula River does sing. The music has been likened to everything from buzzing bees to the strains of a harp, and it usually reaches its highest volume on late summer and early autumn evenings. In fact, the river's song has been so loud, it has actually stopped traffic on the bridge.

Is it a trick of the sand and silt, or the last sad song of a people long extinct? Spend a summer evening listening to the concert firsthand, and then decide for yourself.

memorabilia and photos from Pascagoula's history. The fire engine lounge still features the original fire door, lifted when the trucks raced out to battle fiery disasters. Scranton's is open Mon through Fri from 11 a.m. to 9:30 p.m. But be warned before you go—the restaurant has been struck by lightning not once, but twice. Scranton's is located in the downtown plaza near the old depot. Call (228) 762-1900 for reservations.

Continuing east on US 90 you'll reach the MS 63 junction. Take MS 63 North to Lucedale, or continue a few miles farther on US 90 to the **Gulf Coast Gator Ranch.** The self-proclaimed "fastest, most furious, fun-filled extravaganza in Mississippi," the Gator Ranch offers airboat tours of a marshland area populated by alligators, beavers, and other creatures that call the swamp home. The tall marsh grasses provide camouflage for hundreds of the scaly gators—keep your fingers out of the water! Airboat tours and a stroll through the gator farm are $30 for adults, $15 for children, and free for kids three and under. A gift shop sells gator skulls, teeth, rubber impostors, and other gator memorabilia. Call (228) 475-6026 or (866) 954-2867. Stop by for a tour 8 a.m. to 6 p.m. (summer), and 8 a.m. to 4 p.m. (winter). For more information visit airboatswamptoursofmississippi.com.

Fruitland Park

The small community of Fruitland Park had its origins in a plan to attract prosperous Yankee farmers to the South.

In 1914, F. B. Mills, owner of a vegetable seed business in New York state, bought 20,000 acres in south Mississippi to develop as a planned community he christened "Fruitland Park." Mills distributed brochures to northern farmers describing a rich, fertile land with a pleasant climate, and a variety of "orchard home packages." For a mere $1,250, the Mills Company would build you a fine "Mississippi Style Orchard Cottage," complete with six spacious rooms and indoor plumbing.

Frostbite-weary farmers poured in from Ohio, Wisconsin, Michigan, and Minnesota, dreaming of a new life in the blessed warmth of the South. Alas, a series of disasters befell Mills's little utopia. A hailstorm wiped out the watermelons and a hard freeze zapped nearly 300 acres of figs. The northern transplants had expected winter to last only a week or two, and were shocked to discover that 30 degrees in Mississippi wasn't any warmer than 30 degrees above the Mason-Dixon line. Residents soon became discouraged and left. His dream failed, Mills sold Fruitland Park in 1917.

One of the few remaining buildings from the original Fruitland Park is the 1914 **New York Hotel**, which is listed on the National Register of Historic Places. The hotel's register lists some of the disappointed farmers who failed to tame a land designed by Mother Nature to grow pine trees.

ALSO WORTH SEEING

Fallen Oak Golf Course, Biloxi

Hard Rock Casino, Biloxi

Hattiesburg Zoo, Hattiesburg

Hollywood Casino, Bay St. Louis

INFINITY Science Center and the NASA Stennis Visitors Center, Pearlington

IP Casino, Biloxi

The Lucky Rabbit, Hattiesburg
Two-story vintage and pop culture shop open only the first Thurs thorugh Sun of each month; featured on HGTV's *Home Town*

Lynn Meadows Discovery Center, Gulfport
Children's museum

Mississippi Aquarium, Gulfport

The Teddy Bear House Museum, Picayune

Places to Eat in Southern Mississippi and the Gulf Coast

BILOXI

The White Pillars
1696 Beach Blvd.
(228) 207-0885
Seafood; upscale, historic atmosphere

GULFPORT

The Blow Fly Inn
1201 Washington Ave.
(228) 265-8225
blowflygulfport.com
Steaks and seafood, served with a plastic blowfly garnish

HATTIESBURG

Birdhouse Café
6763 Hwy 98
(601) 606-7203
Unique menu items created by Food Network Chef Katie Dixon

Ed's Burger Joint
3800 Hardy St.
(601) 602-2601
Specialty burgers and shakes; named Best Burger in Mississippi by Trip Advisor

Keg & Barrel Brewpub
1315 Hardy St.
(601) 582-7148
6 Marketplace Dr.
(601) 402-7320
60 beers on draught, plus full menu including fish and chips, shrimp and grits, chicken and waffles, and burgers

KILN

Front Street Bar
206 Front St.
(601) 255-4260
Creative nouveau cuisine

Lazy Magnolia Brewery and Taproom
7030 Roscoe Turner Rd.
(228) 467-2727
lazymagnolia.com
Mississippi's oldest craft brewery; over a dozen beers, plus pizza, pretzels, and tasty munchies; brewery tours

Leatha's Bar-B-Que
6374 US 98
(601) 271-6003
World-famous mouth-watering, finger-licking ribs

Sakura Japanese
6194 US 49
(601) 545-9393
Sushi

OCEAN SPRINGS

The Shed BBQ & Blues Joint
7501 MS 57
(228) 875-9590
theshedbbq.com
Barbecue

Index